The Multinationals and East–West Relations

By the same author

THE ECONOMICS AND POLITICS OF EAST–WEST TRADE

THE ECONOMICS OF SOCIALISM

TOWARDS MULTILATERAL PAYMENTS IN COMECON FOREIGN TRADE

SOCIALIST ECONOMIC DEVELOPMENT AND REFORMS

PROSPECTS FOR THE EXPORT OF AUSTRALIAN FARM PRODUCTS

PROFIT, RISK AND INCENTIVES UNDER SOCIALIST ECONOMIC PLANNING

TECHNOLOGY IN COMECON

The Multinationals and East–West Relations

Towards Transideological Collaboration

J. WILCZYNSKI

Routledge
Taylor & Francis Group
LONDON AND NEW YORK

First published 1976 by Westview Press

Published 2018 by Routledge
52 Vanderbilt Avenue, New York, NY 10017
2 Park Square, Milton Park, Abingdon, Oxon OX14 4RN

Routledge is an imprint of the Taylor & Francis Group, an informa business

Library of Congress Cataloging in Publication Data

Wilczynski, Jozef, 1922–
The multinationals and East–West relations.

Includes indexes.
1. International business enterprises.
2. International economic relations. 3. Government business enterprises—Communist countries.
I. Title.
HD2755.5.W54 338.8'8 76-2080
ISBN 0-89158-540-0

ISBN 13: 978-0-367-02142-9 (hbk)

ISBN 13: 978-0-367-17129-2 (pbk)

Contents

List of Tables

Preface

WHEN in the future historians examine the second half of the twentieth century, they will no doubt identify the accelerated internationalization of production as a landmark comparable with the Industrial Revolution. In this process multinational enterprises have been leading actors in the past twenty-five years and are certain to continue to be so in the next quarter-century. In 1975 the sales of the Western multinational corporations represented one-fifth of the Gross National Product of all capitalist countries. If their growth is maintained at the same rate as over the period 1950-75, by the end of the century this share will be nearly one-half and the whole capitalist economy may very well be dominated by some 200 giant corporations of which three-quarters may be American-based.

Although much has been written about the might, benefits and evils of multinational corporations in the capitalist world, little attention has been given to their relations with Socialist countries, the countries which after all constitute over one-third of the world's population and industrial output. One would not expect much affinity between the large bourgeois corporations and the Communist regimes, and indeed for a long time the relations between them were marked by mutual antagonism in words and deeds.

One of the most paradoxical developments in international relations in recent times is that these two natural adversaries have embarked on far-reaching collaboration. The turning point came roughly in the early 1960s. Trade in machinery, equipment and even complete industrial plants, licences, production and marketing co-operation and joint ventures have become objects of mutual interest. Some of the deals recently concluded run into thousands of millions of dollars and cover periods up to the end of this century.

It is not generally realized that Socialist countries now also have multinationals. These enterprises operate not only in a number of

Socialist countries but also in the West – with subsidiaries mushrooming in the best bourgeois tradition. This development is not merely a question of curiosity. Socialist multinationals are already producing an impact in Western countries and are likely to become a factor to reckon with in capitalist markets in the future.

The operations of the Western and Socialist multinationals across what was once known as the Iron, or Strategic, Curtain are introducing a new dimension in East–West relations. The economic and technological links being developed may very well prove to be a more solid and lasting basis for co-operation between Western and Socialist countries than other attempts made in the past. These developments involving capitalist and Socialist partners are ushering in a new age – the era of 'transideological collaboration'. The internationalization of production is becoming truly worldwide, irrespective of the basic differences between the two social systems.

Much of the research for this book was carried out at the University of Pittsburgh as Visiting Professor in 1974 at the invitation of the Russian and East European Studies Program. It is my pleasure to thank Professor Janet G. Chapman, Director of the Program, for facilitating my work in several ways. I am also indebted to Professor Carl H. McMillan, Institute of Soviet and East European Studies, Carleton University, Ottawa, who provided several valuable sources and comments, particularly when he was working at the Wiener Institut für Internationale Wirtschaftsvergleiche during 1974/1975. I also wish to express my gratitude to Mrs Joy Kemp, Secretary of the Department of Economics, for her most competent secretarial assistance and typing.

University of Pittsburgh and University of New South Wales at Duntroon

JOZEF WILCZYNSKI

1 The Traditional Mutual Prejudice

A. THE MULTINATIONAL CORPORATIONS' POSTURE AND GRIEVANCES

ONE would hardly expect the multinational corporations[1] to entertain much goodwill and trust towards communism in general and the Socialist countries[2] in particular. Communism, after all, basically stands for almost everything that the corporations dread – state intervention, nationalization, workers' control, left-wing militancy and subversion. Although the corporations have wielded a good deal of power in the capitalist world, they have often proved powerless when confronted with the Socialist countries. Moreover many multinationals fell victim to Socialist policies and practices and the history of these grievances goes back to the Bolshevik Revolution in 1917.

The Communist takeover in all these countries was soon followed

[1] The multinational corporation is defined broadly in this book, meaning a large firm with branches, subsidiaries or associates in more than one (capitalist) country and whose degree of foreign operations can be measured by the proportion of the foreign content of its total assets, employment, production or sales. The description 'multinational' – rather than 'international' or 'transnational' – is used here as it is well established and it is irrelevant in this study whether a corporation is home-oriented or not. A multinational corporation consists of the *parent company* and *affiliates*. An affiliate may be either a *subsidiary*, in which the parent company owns 50 per cent or more of the share capital, or an *associate* when (in general) the parent company holds 15-50 per cent of the stock. A *wholly-owned subsidiary* is a distinct legal entity whilst a *branch* (or *division*) is also wholly owned but has no separate status. Affiliates may have sub-subsidiaries or sub-associates and so on in different combinations.

[2] The following 14 countries, which are ruled by Communist Parties: Albania, Bulgaria, the People's Republic of China, Cuba, Czechoslovakia, the (East) German Democratic Republic, Hungary, the Democratic People's Republic of (North) Korea, Mongolia, Poland, Romania, the Union of the Soviet Socialist Republics, the Democratic Republic of (North) Vietnam and Yugoslavia. For the purposes of this study, these countries constitute the 'East'. In accordance with the Marxian distinction between the 'lower phase of communism' (also called 'socialism') and the 'higher phase' ('full communism' or simply 'communism'), at this stage of development all these countries describe themselves as 'Socialist' (not 'Communist') and this description is used in this book.

by the expropriation of foreign companies without, or with only nominal, compensation. Here are a few examples of cases involving substantial amounts and firms which the reader will encounter in the course of this study:[3]

British Petroleum (UK)	– in Romania
Chase Manhattan Bank (US)	– in China
Creusot-Loire (Fr)	– in Czechoslovakia
Deutsche Bank (FRG)	– in Bulgaria, Czechoslovakia, Hungary, Romania
Dresdner Bank (FRG)	– in Poland
Du Pont (US)	– in Cuba
International Harvester (US)	– in the GDR, USSR
International Telephone and Telegraph (US)	– in Cuba
Nestlé (Swi)	– in Cuba
Royal Dutch-Shell (Ne-UK)	– in Cuba, Romania
Schneider (Fr)	– in Czechoslovakia
Schöller-Bleckmann (Au)	– in Romania
Singer (US)	– in Poland, the USSR
Standard Oil of N.J. (US)	– in Cuba, Romania
Westinghouse Electric (US)	– in the USSR

There are obvious problems in calculating the total value of the expropriated assets in the 14 countries, but a rough estimate suggests a figure in the order of tens of billions of dollars. Thus the value of the investments by Singer (including a manufacturing plant and 1,000 outlets for the distribution and servicing of its sewing machines) in Czarist Russia was $100m. at 1914 prices.[4]

[3] The abbreviations for Western and Socialist countries used in this book are:

Au = Austria	GDR = (East) German DR	Po = Poland
Be = Belgium	Hu = Hungary	Ro = Romania
Bu = Bulgaria	It = Italy	Sp = Spain
Ca = Canada	Ja = Japan	Swe = Sweden
Ch = PR of China	Mo = Mongolia	Swi = Switzerland
Cu = Cuba	Ne = Netherlands	UK = United Kingdom
Cz = Czechoslovakia	NK = DPR of (North) Korea	US = United States
De = Denmark	No = Norway	USSR = Union of the Soviet Socialist Republics
Fi = Finland	NV = DR of (North) Vietnam	Yu = Yugoslavia
Fr = France		
FRG = FR of (West) Germany		

[4] J. Ramsey, 'In East–West Trade, Co-operation Is In', *Fortune*, 11/1973, p. 179.

Another form of 'exploitation' by Socialist countries was the poaching of technology, of which the largest Western firms were naturally the main victims. The copying of Western products, in spite of patent protection, and engagement in industrial espionage have a long and exciting history, and in many cases they were facilitated by left-wing elements in the West. Thus before the Second World War the Soviets obtained technology from Krupp for certain machines, from Siemens – for microphones and teletype machinery, and during the war from General Motors – for diesel engines of landing craft. Similarly, after the war they pirated designs for communication equipment from AEG Telefunken (FRG) and for aircraft (Douglas DC-3) from McDonnell Douglas (US) and they contrived to rifle the secrets of chemical processes from Farbwerke Höchst (FRG), computer technology from International Business Machines (US) and engineering and metallurgical inventions from Siemens (FRG); they also tried to obtain the electronic secrets of Westinghouse Electric (US) but failed.[5] East Germans (in the early 1960s) pilfered closely-guarded photographic processes from Kodak in Britain.[6] The high rates of growth of industrial production scored by Socialist countries in the 1950s have been attributed by some Western observers largely to this unscrupulous plunder of Western technology.[7]

Another charge levelled against Socialist countries was that of indiscriminate dumping in capitalist markets. The Socialist price-undercutting, up to 75 per cent below the prevailing levels, was most acute during 1958-62. The goods dumped at one stage or another included: aluminium – by the USSR; chemicals – by China, Czechoslovakia, the German DR, Hungary, the DPR of Korea, Poland, Romania, the USSR and Yugoslavia; glassware and pottery – by China, Czechoslovakia, the German DR and Poland; industrial

[5] D. J. Dallin, *Soviet Espionage*, New Haven, Yale U.P., 1955, pp. 105-7, 369, 432, 452; *Canberra Times*, 1/11/1974, p. 7 and 17/1/1975, p. 4.

[6] P. Hamilton, *Espionage and Subversion in an Industrial Society*, London, Hutchinson, 1967, pp. 53-6.

[7] According to a United Nations source, the average annual rate of growth of industrial production in Eastern Europe and the USSR over the period 1950-60 was 11.4, compared with 4.0 in the West (2.4 in the United Kingdom, 2.6 in the USA, 3.9 in Sweden, 5.3 in France, 7.8 in Italy and 9.4 in the FR of Germany). *Yearbook of National Accounts Statistics 1968*, New York, United Nations, 1969, vol. II, pp. 106-11.

machinery, machine tools and vehicles – by Czechoslovakia, the German DR, Hungary, Poland, the USSR and Yugoslavia; photographic equipment – by China, the German DR and the USSR; sewing machines – by China and Czechoslovakia and, above all, textiles – by practically all Socialist countries.

Again, amongst the main sufferers were large traditional Western suppliers dependent on world markets, such as Agfa-Gevaert (FRG-Be), Alcan Aluminium (Ca), Borg-Warner (US), Corning Glass Works (US), Du Pont (US), Imperial Chemical Industries (UK), Pilkington (UK), Singer (US) and even such low-cost producers as Mitsubishi (Ja) and Mitsui (Ja). Socialist dumping was often interpreted as a carefully engineered sinister conspiracy calculated to cause market disruption and cripple private enterprise – large international firms in particular. The latter were most active in pressurizing distributors to boycott Socialist goods and governments to strengthen anti-dumping legislation and enforcement.[8]

But the most sensational case of Socialist dumping was represented by the Soviet 'oil export offensive' during 1958-64. Oil and oil products were unloaded by Soyuznefteexport, the Soviet foreign trade enterprise with the exclusive right of exporting and importing oil and products, in large quantities in Western Europe, Asia, Africa and Latin America at price discounts typically in the range of 5-30 per cent (and even more). The Soviets embarked upon their drive at the time when Western oil companies were already suffering from excess capacity and over-production, made worse by the Saharan developments. The USSR as well as Czechoslovakia and Romania were also providing technical and financial aid to many less developed countries for the exploration, extraction and processing of their own oil (especially if undertaken by the State) in defiance of Western firms.[9]

All this provoked the unprecedented wrath of the Western oil companies, such as British Petroleum (UK), Gulf Oil (US), Mobil Oil (US), Royal Dutch-Shell (Ne-UK), Tenneco (US) and Texaco

[8] For further details, see *The Communist World as a Customer and Competitor*, New York, Business International, June 1959, esp. p. 18; J. Wilczynski, *The Economics and Politics of East–West Trade*, London, Macmillan, 1969, pp. 146-90.

[9] For further details, see R. E. Ebel, *Communist Trade in Oil and Gas*, New York, Praeger, 1970.

(US). Testifying before the US Congress in October 1962, the spokesman for the Standard Oil Co. of New Jersey (now Exxon), the world's largest oil company (owned mostly by the Rockefellers), pointed out:

> Soviet oil is the most important element in the Soviet politico-economic offensive in the free world.... It is a weapon with which they hope to destroy the private oil industry.[10]

The oil companies took various measures, individually and collectively, to counter this embarrassing raider encroaching on markets which they considered to be their royal preserve. In 1960 Standard Oil of N.J. issued an instruction to all its subsidiaries around the world to boycott shipowners and brokers engaging in business with any Socialist country, in particular transporting Soviet oil. Other private oil companies – aware of their superior bargaining power (being very important customers in world shipping) – apparently applied this measure, too, which came to be known as the 'Esso clause'.[11]

They also exerted pressure on NATO and US diplomatic channels to stem the flood of Soviet oil, and furthermore to embargo Western exports of large-diameter pipes to the USSR which was building oil pipelines from Siberia to Central Europe. The first approach to this effect was made by Gulf Oil and the Standard Oil Co. of N.J. in November 1960. Although little success was achieved in restricting Western imports of Soviet oil, a ban was imposed by NATO in November 1962 on the export of the pipes to the USSR.[12]

Other examples of the anti-Communist posture nourished by multinational corporations in the past, particularly before the early 1960s, may be briefly noted. With some exceptions, they supported the Western strategic embargo which developed into a formidable system of controls after 1947. The embargo applied not only to arms but also to certain instruments, machinery, equipment and licences

[10] S. F. Clabaugh and R. V. Allen, *East–West Trade: Its Strategic Implications*, Washington, Center for Strategic Studies, 1964, pp. 62-3.

[11] G. Adler-Karlsson, *Western Economic Warfare 1947-1967*, Stockholm, Almqvist & Wicksell, 1968, pp. 129-30, 137.

[12] Ibid., p. 130; US Senate, Committee on the Judiciary, *Problems Raised by the Soviet Oil Offensive*, Washington, GPO, 1962, esp. p. 13.

embodying advanced technology – of which the corporations were the main source. Their attitude was conditioned not only by patriotism and hostility towards communism in general, but also by a selfish desire to preserve their technological superiority over any potential Socialist competition. Amongst the most zealous advocates of the 'strategic curtain' were many American corporations, some of which for many years pressed for further restrictions. In a statement to the US Secretary of Commerce in August 1958, on the American export of manufactures to the USSR, the President of the Manufacturing Chemists Association declared:

> We enable her [the USSR] to continue to devote all her energies to a military program aimed at this country. The wholesale transfer of technical know-how might have a disastrous effect on our economy in the years ahead. It would afford the Russian Government a very effective way of undermining our profit economy, in breaking the price and bargaining structure with regard to industrial products in this country and in other countries outside the Iron Curtain.... No American corporation or company or group of companies could possibly compete with Russia in such a situation.[13]

According to a Soviet oil expert, the zeal with which the American oil companies exploited oil in the Middle East was prompted by their determination to drain all oil deposits before they fell into Communist hands.[14]

B. THE MARXIST THEORY OF INTERNATIONAL MONOPOLIES

Although the founders of Marxist ideology did not specifically deal with multinational corporations they had a good deal to say about monopolies and their foreign operations. The central thesis in the writings of Marx and Engels was that capitalism necessarily leads to exploitation – domestically of one class (the proletariat) by another (the bourgeoisie) and internationally of one nation (the less developed) by another (the more developed). In both these processes

[13] US Congress, Senate, Committee on Foreign Relations, *East–West Trade*, Washington, GPO, 1965, Pt II, p. 209.

[14] B. Rachkov, ('Oil Without Illusions'), *Izvestiya*, Moscow, 24/5/1966, p. 2.

monopolies played a prominent part. Their inroads into foreign markets were basically prompted on the one hand by their insatiable greed and on the other by the 'falling rate of profit' at home, one of the Marxian laws applicable to higher stages of capitalist development.[15]

However neither Marx nor Engels had anticipated the extent, intensity and intricacies of the internationalization of capital and monopolies. A much stronger and better substantiated attack was made by later Marxist thinkers, especially Rosa Luxemburg, N. Bukharin, K. Kautsky and V. I. Lenin, and to this pleiade K. Nkrumah must also be added. Rosa Luxemburg highlighted the role of military production and the exploitation of undeveloped and defenceless colonies as the new source of monopoly profits propping up an ailing and doomed capitalism. In her book published in 1913 she stated:

> Militarism fulfils a quite definite function in the history of capital, accompanying as it does every historical phase of accumulation.... the taxes extorted from the workers afford capital a new opportunity for accumulation when they are used for armament manufacture.[16]

In the same book she reasoned that:

> The external market is the non-capitalist social environment which absorbs the products of capitalism and supplies producer goods and labour power for capitalist production.... Internal capitalist trade can at best realize only certain quantities of value contained in the social product.... That part of the surplus value, however, which is earmarked for capitalization must be realized elsewhere.[17]

Bukharin advanced similar arguments (first in 1915)[18] as did Kautsky (some ten years earlier). The latter in fact went further in one important respect by putting forward a concept of 'ultra-imperi-

[15] K. Marx, *Capital*, New York, International Publishers, 1967, vol. 1, pp. 751 *et seq.*; vol. 2, pp. 251, 468, 470; vol. 3, pp. 150-51, 196, 224, 238, 240, 306, 438, 582-3. K. Marx, *The Poverty of Philosophy*, Chicago, Charles Kerr, 1884, p. 152. K. Marx and F. Engels, *The Manifesto of the Communist Party*, Moscow, Progress Publishers, 1952, pp. 42-52, 70-71.

[16] Rosa Luxemburg, *The Accumulation of Capital*, London, Routledge & Kegan Paul, 1951, pp. 454, 464.

[17] Ibid., p. 366.

[18] See Rosa Luxemburg and N. Bukharin, *Imperialism and the Accumulation of Capital*, ed. by K. J. Tarbuck, Harmondsworth, Penguin, 1972.

alism'. He envisaged a collusive exploitation of the world by a united international syndicate replacing the rivalry of the national banking and financial monopolies.[19]

But the most trenchant condemnation of the role played by international monopolies in the historical evolution of capitalism was delivered by Lenin, mostly in his best known pamphlet, *Imperialism. The Highest Stage of Capitalism* (written in 1916). Partly utilizing the ideas and facts put forward by such Marxist writers as J. A. Hobson (*Imperialism*, London, 1902) and R. Hilferding (*Finanzkapital*, Vienna, 1910), Lenin argued that imperialism is a logical and ultimate stage of capitalism, and international monopolies constitute the spearhead in this development. He explained:

> Imperialism is capitalism at that stage of development at which the dominance of monopolies and finance is established; in which the export of capital has acquired pronounced importance, in which the division of the world among the international trusts has begun.[20]

In a caustic vein, he further went on:

> Monopolies, oligarchy, the striving for domination and not for freedom, the exploitation of an increasing number of small or weak nations by a handful of the richest or most powerful nations – all these have given birth to those distinctive characteristics of imperialism which compel us to define it as parasitic or decaying capitalism.[21]

He charged large companies with 'balance-sheet jugglery' facilitated 'by setting up "daughter companies" or by annexing them ... for various purposes – legal and illegal'.[22] He also saw international monopolies as wreckers of the solidarity of the working class, thereby blocking the road to world revolution:

> The receipt of high monopoly profits by the capitalists ... makes it economically possible for them to bribe certain sections of the workers ... and win them to the side of the bourgeoisie.[23]

[19] In *Neue Zeit* (New Times), 11/9/1914, p. 921 and 30/4/1915, p. 144, (quoted from V. I. Lenin, *Collected Works*, Moscow, Progress Publishers, 1964, vol. 22, p. 271).

[20] V. I. Lenin, *Collected Works*, Moscow, Progress Publishers, 1964, vol. 22, pp. 266-7.

[21] Ibid., p. 300.

[22] Ibid., pp. 229-30.

[23] Ibid., p. 301.

Lenin further insisted that 'monopoly capitalism' necessarily degenerates into 'state monopoly capitalism'. He believed that the political interest and role of the large capitalist firms converged with those of the nation state, so that monopoly capital absorbs the state power, turning it into a convenient instrument for nefarious schemings. The greed and rivalry amongst the international monopolies in league with their imperialist nation-states inevitably leads to wars and not to harmonious co-operation as Kautsky had maintained. He described Kautsky's 'peaceful ultra-imperialism' as a 'reactionary silly little fable'.[24] Lenin's explanation of the real cause of the First World War was 'to decide whether the British or German group of financial plunderers is to receive the most booty'.[25]

Lenin also conceded that under state monopoly capitalism, state-owned corporations may emerge either through nationalization or the establishment of new enterprises or agencies. But neither he nor his faithful supporters of 'revolutionary socialism' regarded it as a welcome development. They viewed it as a betrayal of Marxism – a compromising form of opportunism and revisionism designed to bolster up a decaying capitalism and thus postpone the Socialist revolution. Instead, they insisted that the changeover from capitalism to socialism must be achieved not through a gradual opportunistic process but in a violent revolutionary way amounting to the destruction of the old system.

In his caustic indictment of international monopolies Lenin was quite specific. Amongst the villains he proscribed were the following well-known multinationals which will loom prominently later in this book: Banque de Paris et des Pays Bas (Fr), Crédit Lyonnais (Fr), Deutsche Bank (Germany), General Electric (US), Krupp (Germany), Morgan (US), Schneider (Fr), Shell (UK), Siemens (Germany), and Standard Oil (US).[26]

The disintegration of the colonial empires since the Second World War has not led to the Marxist rehabilitation of multinational corporations but has been followed by a new wave of denunciation – in the form of charges of neo-colonialism. These charges were best formulated by K. Nkrumah, a left-wing leader of Ghana (deposed

[24] Ibid., pp. 267-73, esp. p. 273.

[25] Ibid., p. 191.

[26] Ibid., pp. 211, 214, 219-22, 228, 230, 244, 247-50, 292. For country abbreviations, see footnote 3, p. 2.

in 1967), in his book published in the mid-1960s.[27] Nkrumah, who has been described as a 'black Lenin', meant his book to be a continuation of Lenin's analysis. Although he hardly introduced anything original beyond the arguments advanced long before by writers in the Socialist countries, his contribution has added the weight of authenticity and first-hand evidence to the controversy. The essence of his case is that in spite of a *de jure* political emancipation, the former colonies are still *de facto* economic dependencies of the leading capitalist powers. The key role in this enslavement is played by large international mining, manufacturing and service companies and banks, as well as by various state instrumentalities of the Western countries administering the so-called foreign aid. He amplified Lenin's list of 'multinational plunderers' by adding such names as Alcan Aluminium (Ca), Armco Steel (US), Bank of America (US), Bank of Tokyo (Ja), Barclays Bank (UK), BASF (FRG), Bayer (FRG), British Steel (UK), British Petroleum (UK), De Beers (South Africa), Farbwerke Höchst (FRG), Fiat (It), General Motors (US), Hawker-Siddeley (UK), ICI (UK), Monsanto (US), Philips (Ne), Solvay (Be), Sumitomo (Ja), A. Thyssen (FRG), Unilever (Ne-UK), US Steel, and Volkswagen (FRG).[28] According to Nkrumah, between 1950 and 1959 the American companies alone invested $4,500m. in less-developed countries but the *net* profits extracted from these countries amounted to three times as much – $8,300m. plus millions of dollars in trading profits, interest on loans, freight charges and other pickings.[29]

C. DIATRIBES IN THE SOCIALIST COUNTRIES

The ideological attitudes to multinational corporations in the Socialist countries have, of course, been conditioned by the writings of the traditional Marxist thinkers. This has been reflected in frequent official pronouncements as well as non-official polemics ever since the establishment of the first Socialist state in 1917, and they

[27] K. Nkrumah, *Neo-Colonialism. The Last Stage of Imperialism*, London – Ibadan – Nairobi, Heinemann, 1965.

[28] Ibid., pp. 44, 45, 52, 61-3, 67, 79, 81, 92, 94, 98, 100, 101, 208, 213, 223, 231.

[29] Ibid., p. 58.

were particularly strong before the mid-1960s. At the 22nd Congress of the Communist Party of the Soviet Union in 1961, N. Khrushchev told the delegates (including guests from all over the world):

> Giant monopolies controlling the bulk of social production dominate the life of the nation. A handful of millionaires and multimillionaires wield arbitrary power over the entire wealth of the capitalist world and make the life of entire nations mere small change in their selfish deals.[30]

The official reaction to the formation of state enterprises and the growing state intervention in Western countries was made quite clear at the same Congress:

> World wars, economic crises, militarism and political upheavals have accelerated the development of monopoly capitalism into state-monopoly capitalism.... State-monopoly capitalism combines the strength of the monopolies and that of the state into a single mechanism whose purpose is to enrich the monopolies, suppress the working-class movement and the national-liberation struggle, save the capitalist system, and launch aggressive wars. The right-wing socialists and revisionists are making out state-monopoly capitalism to be almost socialism. The facts give the lie to this contention.... Far from altering the position of the principal classes in the system, it widens the rift between labour and capital, between the majority of the nation and the monopolies.[31]

In the international arena, the Socialist countries have traditionally advocated strict controls over the practices of multinational corporations and international cartels. They endeavoured to embody such provisions in the Charter of the UN International Trade Organization, proposed at the Havana Conference in 1947. But the Charter has never been ratified by the leading capitalist countries. 'The opponent-in-chief to the ratification of the Havana Charter', according to a Soviet source, 'was the USA which, in opposition to the creation of the ITO contrived to establish GATT as the latter provided better scope for the American monopolies to force tariff cuts from their trade partners.'[32] The proposal for

[30] *The Road to Communism*, Documents of the 22nd Congress of the CPSU, Moscow, FLPH, 1961, p. 471.

[31] Ibid.

[32] *Ekonomicheskaya gazeta* (Economic Gazette), Moscow, 29/2/1964, p. 31.

the creation of ITO (to replace GATT) was taken up again by the Socialist countries in 1956, and then in 1964 (at the UN Conference on Trade and Development in Geneva) but without success.[33]

A good deal of attention has been given in Socialist polemics to the 'unscrupulous' growth of the Western multinationals since the Second World War. It has been pointed out that the concentration of capital has been accelerating through mergers and takeovers and their profits have been growing twice as fast as of other firms.[34] At the same time 'the giant monopolies have a whole bag of tricks that help them conceal a large part of their profits and avoid tax'.[35] The corporations' liquid assets add up to $268,000m., which is twice the amount of the foreign exchange reserves held by all the Western central banks put together. This represents a menace to international monetary stability.[36]

It has been further argued that the capitalist world is in fact controlled by some 60 largest multinational corporations, which are richer than the states in which they operate. The corporations' presidents exercise more power than the heads of the governments in capitalist countries and no one is able to control them.[37] The multinationals have not only been labelled as the 'citadels of capitalism' but have also been accused of the ruthless exploitation of natural resources, environmental pollution, the pre-emptive buying out of patents with no intention of utilizing them, a stubborn opposition to disarmament, the division of the world market into their exclusive spheres of exploitation and of attempts at draining the Socialist countries of trained brain power.[38] In the less developed

[33] For details, see Yu. Ogarev, ('Soviet Arguments in Favour of Establishing an International Trade Organization'), *Mirovaya ekonomika i mezhdunarodnye otnosheniya* (World Economy and International Relations), Moscow, 2/1964, pp. 60-73.

[34] Ewa Michalska, ('Multinational Corporations and Economic Growth'), *Gospodarka planowa* (Planned Economy), Warsaw, 5/1973, p. 347.

[35] *International Affairs*, Moscow, 4/1974, p. 99.

[36] Ibid.

[37] *Życie gospodarcze* (Economic Life), Warsaw, 23/6/1974, p. 12.

[38] T. Emelyanov, 'Environment and Monopolies', *New Times*, Moscow, no. 17, April 1973, pp. 25-7; T. Grabowski and S. Lysko, *Ekonomia polityczna kapitalizmu* (Political Economy of Capitalism), Warsaw, PWE, 1973, pp. 200, 361 *et seq.*; N. A. Tsagolov (ed.), *Kurs politicheskoi ekonomii* (Textbook of Political Economy), Moscow, IEL, 1963, vol. I, pp. 530-608 *passim*; L. Urban, *Kapitalismus a obzbrojeni* (Capitalism and Disarmament), Prague, NPL, 1964, pp. 13 *et seq.*

countries the corporations have been accused of being the main obstacle to economic emancipation and of 'technological imperialism'.[39] In the future the corporations are seen as a continuing reactionary force impeding social progress. According to a Polish economist:

> ... the growth of the multinational corporations will lead to further exacerbation of contradictions in the development of capitalist countries and to the annihilation of the 'welfare state' so laboriously erected in the postwar period to moderate such contradictions.[40]

Some of the most acrimonious denunciations have been directed against the Western oil companies. In an article written in English for the benefit of readers in the capitalist world, the well-known Soviet oil expert, B. Rachkov, declared:

> Since the middle of the 1950s the world has repeatedly found itself faced with the threat of world war, arising directly or indirectly from the machinations of powerful imperialist oil concerns. ... there is hardly a group of monopolies that has displayed as much destructive energy, craft, intrigue and special inclination to international piracy as the oil business in its efforts to secure control both of domestic political relations in various countries and of the principal factors of world politics.[41]

It was also claimed that the death in an air 'accident' in 1962 of E. Mattei, President of Ente Nazionale Idrocarburi (the Italian state-owned petrochemical enterprise) had been engineered by American oil companies (under Mattei's leadership, in spite of several warnings, ENI absorbed large quantities of oil from the USSR during the Soviet export drive in the late 1950s and early 1960s).[42] The Rockefellers were labelled as the traditional instiga-

[39] e.g. see M. Volkov, 'Economic Independence and Neocolonialism', *Intern. Affairs*, M., 7/1974, pp. 39, 40: 'Multinational corporations now represent the most powerful force for undermining and obstructing the economic independence of developing countries. ... "Third World" countries pay the monopolies tribute for their technological backwardness ranging from 2 to 4 per cent of their national income, or from $6,000m. to $12,000m. annually.'

[40] Ewa Michalska, op. cit., p. 353.

[41] B. Rachkov, 'Oil, Trade and Politics', *Intern. Affairs*, M., 4/1966, pp. 14, 20.

[42] B. Janiszewski, ('Oil Monopolies – Today and Tomorrow'), *Nowe drogi* (New Paths), Warsaw, 4/1974, p. 128.

tors of oil cartel arrangements, and British Petroleum as the promoter of cartel swindles in the United Kingdom; the civil war in Nigeria was interpreted as an attempt by oil companies to separate the Biafran oilfields from the Federation.[43] Oil companies were also blamed for the recent energy crisis and vicious price rigging, and the whole affair was described as the 'theft of the century'.[44]

D. ATTACKS BY WESTERN RADICAL ELEMENTS

A good deal of bitter attack against multinational corporations has also come from Western militant trade unions, Communist parties, the New Left and other left-wing groups and individuals. The abuses attributed to them by some trade unions include the downward pressure on wages by the threat or actual transfer of plants to countries with low labour costs and weak trade unions,[45] the breaking of strikes by drawing on stockpiles in, or switching production to, another country, the indiscriminate takeover of weaker firms leading to the dismissal of workers and the feverish proliferation of subsidiaries abroad – thereby also reducing employment opportunities at home.[46] The corporations have also been blamed for the international spread of inflation and for the undermining of state policies with regard to credit, regional development, monopolies and international cartels and the protection of domestic

[43] Ibid., p. 131.

[44] A Soviet economist made the following assessment in the leading organ of the CPSU: 'The 1973-74 energy crisis was brought about by the policies of the multinational oil corporations in the Middle East and it exemplifies speculative price fixing. The corporations manipulated the crisis and scored the "theft of the century" – the steep price increases swelled their profits on the average by 100 per cent.' I. Ivanov, ('The Economic Expansion of International Corporations'), *Kommunist*, Moscow, 12/1974, p. 77.

[45] This was confirmed in an enquiry carried out by the International Labour Office in 1973: 'The activities of multinational corporations had led to a depression of wages and the governments' search for foreign capital had led to restrictive labour legislation.' *Multinational Enterprises and Social Policy*, Geneva, ILO, 1973, p. 144.

[46] Thus in the USA, where there has been considerable unemployment (averaging nearly 5 per cent over the past decade), the foreign operations of the American companies have reduced domestic employment – according to a Polish source – by 1.3m. *Bank i kredyt* (Bank and Credit), Warsaw, 5/1973, p. 206.

industries – all to the workers' disadvantage.[47]

Many trade union leaders have been alarmed at the growing spread and power of the multinationals. The increasing number of options at the disposal of the corporations is upsetting the precarious balance between employers and trade unions. At the Ninth World Congress of the International Confederation of Free Trade Unions, held in Brussels in July 1969, it was felt that:

> multinational corporations may undermine established industrial relations systems, restrict the right of the workers to organize in defence of their interests, limit their right to enter into co-ordinated collective bargaining ... and exploit international labour cost differentials in order to increase profits.[48]

ment in reactionary, right-wing schemings. Gus Hall, the General The resolution passed at the same Congress calls for 'international solidarity of the workers and co-ordination of trade union effort to take up the multinational challenge'.[49] A similar resolution was adopted by the International Metalworkers' Federation at its 22nd Congress in Lausanne in October 1971.[50]

Another charge levelled against the multinationals is that of their complicity in the 'military-industrial complexes' and their involve-Secretary of the Communist Party of the USA, recently pointed out:

> The military-industrial complex is a new and higher level of the process of militarization. ... The self interests of the monopoly corporations and the military staff merge in war goods production. It provides an opportunity for huge profits and easy payoffs. The secret agreements are turned into cash when members of the military brass take early retirement and step into executive titles in the big corporations. The payoff is in the form of big salaries and stock dividends.[51]

[47] For details, see J. Gennard, *Multinational Corporations and British Labour*, London, British-North American Committee, 1972; H. Günter (ed.), *Transnational Industrial Relations*, London, Macmillan, 1972; G. Paquet (ed.), *The Multinational Firm and the Nation State*, Don Mills, Ont., Collier-Macmillan, 1972. Also see two books written by the Secretary-General of the International Federation of Chemical and General Workers Union: C. Levinson, *Capital, Inflation and the Multinationals*, New York, Macmillan, 1972; C. Levinson, *International Trade Unionism*, London, George Allen & Unwin, 1972.

[48] Quoted from *Multinational Enterprises and Social Policy*, p. 84.

[49] Ibid.

[50] Ibid., p. 87.

[51] Gus Hall, *Imperialism Today*, New York, International Publishers, 1972, p. 102.

A West German Communist leader warned: 'Keeping international tension, the war psychosis and bellicose anti-communism is a must for the military–industrial complex.'[52]

Such attacks in the West have been widely publicized in the Socialist countries and given support in one way or another in the interest of the 'class-war'. In a recent issue of the theoretical organ of the CPSU,[53] two West German Communist Party leaders were praised for the publication of a militant book against West German monopolies.[54]

On many occasions, especially coinciding with bitter industrial disputes, radical groups in the Western countries have demanded the nationalization of such multinational corporations as British Leyland (UK), Fiat (It), Krupp (FRG), Philips (Ne), Saint-Gobain (Fr), and Volvo (Swe), as had already been done with Alfa Romeo (It), British Steel (UK), Renault (Fr), Salzgitter (FRG), Statsföretag (Swe), VÖEST-Alpine (Au) and many others. It may be observed here that although the Communist Parties in the Socialist countries are sceptical and even contemptuous of what they regard as 'state-monopoly capitalism', the Western left-wing groups place great hopes in state enterprises. At the International Conference on State-Monopoly Capitalism, held in Paris in May 1966 under the auspices of the French Communist Party, there was a general agreement amongst Western delegates with the proposition put forward by the French Communist Paul Boccara:

> The working-class movement acting through the state can wrest power from the monopoly oligarchies by embarking on a profound democratization of economic life. ... Under these conditions the democratic revolutionary movement can lead to the isolation and gradual liquidation of monopolies.[55]

[52] K. Engelhardt, 'Strategy of the War Monopolies', *World Marxist Review*, Toronto, 7/1970, p. 72. Also see a book by another West German Communist, F. Schmid, *Der Militär-Industrie-Komplex* (The Military-Industrial Complex), Frankfurt/M, Verlag Marxistische Blätter, 1972.

[53] N. Izvolenskaya, ('The Struggle of the West German Working Class against Monopoly Power'), *Kommunist*, Moscow, 4/1974, pp. 122-4.

[54] W. Gerns and R. Steigerwald, *Probleme der Strategie des Antimonopolistischen Kampfes* (Problems of the Strategy of the Anti-monopolist Struggle), Frankfurt/M, Marxistische Blätter, 1973.

[55] Quoted from *Nowe drogi*, 10/1966, p. 94.

In fact, in most leading Western countries the extent of the state sector is surprisingly large, especially in certain key industries.[56]

[56] Thus according to Socialist sources, the proportion of industrial output produced by state enterprises exceeds 5 per cent in Britain, 18 per cent in Sweden (co-operative enterprises included) and 25 per cent in France. The percentage of share capital owned by the state in the FR of Germany is 18 and of total investment contributed by state enterprises in Italy is 38. In the FR of Germany state enterprises produce about 70 per cent of aluminium, 40 per cent of iron ore, 33 per cent of ships and 25 per cent of black coal, and in Italy one (the largest) state enterprise alone, IRI (Istituto per la Ricostruzione Industriale), contributes 77 per cent of iron and steel, 25 per cent of the engineering output and 25 per cent of electricity. Even in the USA, now about 20 per cent (compared with 7 per cent in 1900) of the nation's capital is owned by the state. Based on: T. Grabowski and S. Łysko, op. cit., pp. 355-7; *Ekonomika i organizacja pracy* (Economics and Organization of Labour), Warsaw, 3/1974, p. 138; *Foreign Trade*, Moscow, 2/1972, p. 18.

2 The Expedient Turn to Collaboration

A. THE AMAZING REVERSAL OF ATTITUDES

IN history there is, of course, nothing permanent. Yesterday's enemies may become today's allies. The development of relations between Western multinational corporations and the Communist regimes since the Second World War bears witness to this rule. The strange marriage of convenience between these natural antagonists evident since the early 1960s – against a previous background of mutual fear, contempt and incompatibility – must be regarded as one of the most paradoxical cases of bilateral *volte-face* in recent history. Recriminations of the type considered in the preceding chapter, although by no means openly repudiated, appear to have been conveniently forgotten in favour of collaboration to mutual advantage.

It may be noted here that commercial dealings between the two sides went on before the early 1960s, too, but the developments since that time and especially since the early 1970s represent qualitative leaps. Many multinational corporations have become the most persistent advocates of the relaxation of the strategic embargo. Indeed not a few of them, disappointed with lagging official moves, used their own ingenuity to circumvent the controls in one way or another. Thus to beat the stricter US version of the embargo, the American corporations engaged in so-called back-door trade with the Socialist bloc, using their 1,000 or so subsidiaries in Western Europe and Japan for the purpose.[1] Some of them, like many Western European and Japanese companies became adepts in find-

[1] R. S. Kretschmar, Jr, and R. Foor, *The Potential for Joint Ventures in Eastern Europe*, New York, Praeger, 1972, p. 58.

ing loopholes, pulling strings, forging documents, etc., to pull off lucrative deals.[2]

After the Chinese Government in 1960 introduced the rule of trading only with 'friendly' Japanese firms, many large companies, noted for their anti-communist sentiments, soon set up dummy subsidiaries to pass for 'friendly' firms, and business went on more or less as usual. When this rule was further strengthened by the declaration of the 'Four Principles of Chou En-lai' in 1970,[3] most of the Japanese multinationals yielded to these conditions and further strove to mend their ways and image to qualify for acceptability.[4]

Many Western corporations have established special departments to handle business with Socialist countries. For example Rank Xerox (UK), which is only one of the 'lesser' multinationals, has set up such a department and its original staff of three has soon grown to more than 100 – and a separate building is to be constructed for it.[5] International Business Machines (US) has recently established a new sales division (IBM Trade Development) in Paris to cover the Soviet market.

But the initiative in embarking on far-reaching East–West business co-operation has essentially come from the Communist regimes. Most of the Socialist countries have agreed to pay at least some compensation for the nationalized assets of the Western firms (ex-enemy countries, i.e. Germany, Italy and Japan excepted). They have also become more cautious in their export drives to avoid accusations of dumping and market disruption. In particular, by the mid-1960s the Soviets had discontinued their undercutting of oil prices, raising them to the levels maintained by Western oil companies, and even supported collusive agreements to restrict supplies.

[2] See, e.g., J. B. Hutton, *The Traitor Trade*, London, Spearman, 1963; G. Adler-Karlsson, *Western Economic Warfare 1947-1967*, Stockholm, Almqvist & Wicksell, 1968, Part III.

[3] Conditions applicable to Japanese firms wishing to trade with China: (1) No moral or material aid to Taiwan for military purposes. (2) No heavy investment in Taiwan and South Korea. (3) No supply of arms to the USA in Indochina. (4) No significant involvement with American companies.

[4] Amongst the leading companies which conformed were: C. Itoh & Co., Marubeni-Ida, Mitsubishi, Mitsui & Co., Nissan Motor, Tokyo Shibaura Electric, and Toyota Motors.

[5] *Pravda*, Moscow, 14/9/1974, p. 4. For country abbreviations, see footnote 3, p. 2.

Largely as a consequence of the Sino-Soviet conflict, China has been increasingly turning to the Western multinationals for trade. Although in the past several large Japanese corporations – such as Caterpillar-Mitsubishi, Hitachi, Izusu Motor, Sony, Sumitomo, Teijin, Tokyo Shibaura Electric and Toyota Motors – were blacklisted and boycotted as not 'friendly' or violating the 'Four Principles',[6] recently they have been embraced by the Chinese as reliable and indispensable trade partners. In effect, Chou En-lai's 'Four Principles' were thrown overboard in early 1973. China has also been looking further afield – to Western Europe and even (since 1972) to the USA. Thus instead of patronizing such Soviet foreign trade enterprises as Avtoexport (vehicles), Mashinoexport (machinery), Promsyreimport (iron and steel), Stankoimport (metal-working machinery), Tekhnoexport (industrial plants) and Tyazhpromexport (mining and oil development) as she had been before 1960, she has turned to Citroën (Fr), General Motors (US), Hawker-Siddeley (UK), Krupp (FRG), Mannesman (FRG), Monsanto (US), Occidental Petroleum (US), Olivetti (It), Verenigde Machinenfabrieken (Ne), Volvo (Swe) and other Western 'super-monopolies' (for further details of China's trade reorientation, see Ch. 3A, pp. 49-50).

The Iron and Bamboo, as well as the Strategic, Curtains have developed serious cracks through which travel in both directions has become easier, particularly for negotiating business deals. In January 1971 the élite of the West German industrial firms was invited by Mr A. Kosygin to inspect the riches and development of Siberia. Later over a glass of vodka in the Kremlin he declared: 'Gentlemen, you have seen the great possibilities. Please help yourselves.'[7] Since the early 1960s the managers of most larger multinational corporations have made their pilgrimage to Socialist countries as members of official or semi-official trade missions, or negotiators of agreements or large contracts – and have been received with great

[6] Caterpillar-Mitsubishi is jointly owned by Caterpillar Tractor (US) and Mitsubishi Heavy Industries (Ja), Izusu Motors is partly owned by General Motors (US, 34 per cent of the share capital), and Tokyo Shibaura Electric – by General Electric (US, 12 per cent), whilst Hitachi and Toyota Motors have industrial plants in Taiwan and Sony one in South Korea.

[7] *Canberra Times*, 12/8/1971, p. 22.

courtesy and pomp by the Party, government and industrial leaders.[8]

Amongst these visitors was Mr David Rockefeller, the Chairman of the Board of the Chase Manhattan Bank (with 56 affiliates in 44 foreign countries) who went to Moscow in May 1972 at the invitation of the Soviet Government. It may be of interest to mention here that it was his grandfather, John D. Rockefeller, who made a large fortune in oil and banking and became the world's first billionaire (in 1901). Mr David Rockefeller went to open an office of his bank in the very heart of the Communist anthill – at No. 1 Karl Marx Square in Moscow, to be exact. He was also fêted by such personages as Mr A. Kosygin (Prime Minister), Mr N. Baibakov (Chairman of the State Planning Commission, *Gosplan*), Mr V. Garbuzov (Finance Minister) and Mr M. Kuzmin (Deputy Minister for Foreign Trade), and many a vodka was drunk to the success of this strange partnership. One wonders if either the capitalist guest or his Communist hosts called to mind what Lenin had to say about the Rockefellers' international spider's web and schemings.[9] If they did – well, perhaps each of them thought that after all *pecunia non*

[8] Thus over the period 1972-4 alone the chairmen or presidents of the following well-known multinationals visited one or more Socialist countries: Air France (Fr) – China; Alfa Romeo (It) – USSR; Bank of America (US) – USSR; Bank of Tokyo (Ja) – China; Boeing (US) – Romania; Chase Manhattan Bank (US) – China, Poland, USSR; Clark Equipment (US) – Poland; Ente Nazionale Idrocarburi (It) – GDR; Fiat (It) – Poland, Romania; First National Bank of Chicago (US) – Poland; First National City Bank of New York (US) – USSR; Fuji Bank (Ja) – China; Gutehoffnungshütte (FRG) – China, USSR; Hitachi (Ja) – China; International Business Machines (US) – USSR; International Paper (US) – USSR; International Systems & Controls (US) – Bulgaria; Ishikawajima-Harima Heavy Industries (Ja) – Poland; Kobe Bank (Ja) – China; Krupp (FRG) – China, USSR; Manufacturers Hanover Trust (US) – China; Mitsubishi Chemical Industries (Ja) – Czechoslovakia; Montedison (It) – USSR; Occidental Petroleum (US) – USSR; Pan American Airways (US) – China; Pechiney-Ugine-Kuhlmann (Fr) – USSR; Pepsi-Co. (US) – USSR; Rhône-Poulenc (Fr) – Poland; Rockwell International (US) – USSR; Salzgitter (FGR) – USSR; Sanwa Bank (Ja) – China; Siemens (FRG) – USSR; Sperry Rand (US) – USSR; Sumitomo Bank (Ja) – China; Thomson-CSF (Fr) – Poland; Tokai Bank (Ja) – China; Tokyo Shibaura Electric (Ja) – USSR; and Westinghouse Electric (US) – China. (For the extent of the multinational affiliations of these entities, see the Complete List and Index, pp. 197-232, and of their dealings with Socialist countries, Tables 2, 3, 4 and 13, pp. 36-47 and 122-5.)

[9] V. I. Lenin, *Collected Works*, Moscow, Progress Publishers, 1964, vol. 22, pp. 219, 248-50.

olet. That, at least, is what Vespasian, the Roman Emperor, had had to say some two thousand years earlier.

There are now 19 Western multinational banks and some 50 industrial and commercial multinational companies with offices in Moscow with the blessing of the Soviet government. Taking all the Socialist countries as a whole, more than 150 Western multinationals have established representative offices or agencies there, and some of them in more than one centre. Thus the Banque National de Paris (Fr) has such representations in Moscow and Warsaw, the First City National Bank (US) – in Budapest and Moscow, Ataka & Co. – in East Berlin, Moscow and Sofia, Bayer (FRG), – in Bucharest, Sofia and Warsaw, Brown, Boveri (Swi) – in Bucharest and Sofia, Ciba-Geigy (Swi) – in Bucharest, Budapest, Sofia and Warsaw, Creusot-Loire (Fr) – in Moscow and Warsaw, Daimler-Benz (FRG) – in Sofia and Warsaw, Farbwerke Höchst (FRG) – in Moscow, Sofia and Warsaw, Imperial Chemical Industries (UK) – in Bucharest, Budapest and Warsaw, Nissho-Iwai (Ja) – in Bucharest, East Berlin and Warsaw, Sandvik (Swe) – in East Berlin and Warsaw, Sandoz (Swi) – in Bucharest, Budapest, Sofia and Warsaw, Shell (UK) – in Bucharest, Budapest and Sofia and Volvo (Swe) – in Bucharest and Sofia.[10]

Even China appears to be departing from her previous closed-door attitude, judging by her authorization given in 1972 to C. Itoh & Co. (Ja) and Arthur Andersen (US) for permanent representations in Peking. Those Western companies which have not been able to establish permanent offices in the Socialist countries have set up bridgeheads in such convenient locations as Vienna, Hong Kong or Tokyo. It is estimated that about 300 Western multinational companies have done this in Vienna; of these some 200 are American, for whose benefit in 1973 the US Embassy established an East–West Trade Center.

Multinational corporations have become eager participants in East–West conferences and seminars on commercial, industrial, scientific and technical co-operation. During 1972-4 the writer could

[10] For country abbreviations, see footnote 3, p. 2, and for the extent of the multinational affiliations of the firms shown, see the Complete List and Index, pp. 197-232, (and for further details of the larger parent companies, Tables 2, 3 and 4, pp. 36-47).

identify at least 50 important meetings of this nature held in Socialist and Western countries. At the Round Table Conference arranged by Business International in East Berlin in February 1973, 70 top-ranking executives of 50 multinational corporations attended, together with the President, Minister of Foreign Trade, Chairman of the State Planning Commission, Minister for Science and Technology and other dignitaries of the German DR.[11]

The corporations have also become dominant participants in the trade fairs and exhibitions now regularly held in Socialist countries in such well established centres as Belgrade, Bratislava, Brno, Bucharest, Budapest, Canton, Leipzig, Leningrad, Moscow, Peking, Plovdiv, Poznan, Prague, Tientsin, Warsaw and Zagreb. In the Leipzig Spring Fair of 1973 over 2,000 multinational firms took part. Some of the most enthusiastic exhibiting in the last few years has been witnessed in China, with official invitations extended to Japanese, Western European and American corporations, with a most remarkable response. It is rather strange that in Peking such events are held in the Exhibition Centre built by the USSR in the palmier days of the Sino–Soviet comradeship – and it was hardly meant to host such 'international plunderers' as Borg-Warner (US), Citroën (Fr), Fiat (It), General Electric (UK), Hawker-Siddeley (UK), Krupp (FRG), Mitsubishi (Ja), and Radio Corporation of America (US).[12]

B. FRAMEWORK COLLABORATION AGREEMENTS

Collaboration between the multinational corporations and the Socialist countries has been greatly facilitated by improving East–West relations and the consequent official and semi-official agreements providing a favourable background for the development of direct ties at the operational level. The Soviet declaration of the policy of Peaceful Coexistence in 1956 and the signing of the Anti-Test Ban Treaty (between the USA and the USSR) in 1963 marked important steps towards the East–West detente, and the reciprocal visits by (the then) President Nixon and the Party Secretary L.

[11] *Eastern Europe Report*, 8/2/1974, p. 34.

[12] For further paradoxical cases of collaboration between Western multinationals and Socialist countries, see Ch. 10A, pp. 176-86.

Brezhnev, and of President Nixon to China, during 1972-3 virtually put an end to the Cold War. In 1972 the USA extended diplomatic recognition to China and in 1974 to the German DR, and several important Western trading nations (such as Australia, the FR of Germany, Italy and Japan) established diplomatic missions in Peking.

Practically all Western countries have concluded inter-governmental agreements on economic, industrial, scientific and technical co-operation with at least some Socialist countries. These agreements usually cover 5-10 years and provide a general basis for collaboration in specific directions. In recent years agreements of this nature have been signed between such relevant countries as:

Austria – with Bulgaria, Czechoslovakia, Hungary, Poland, Romania, the USSR and Yugoslavia.
Belgium – with Bulgaria, Czechoslovakia, the German DR, Hungary, Poland, Romania and the USSR.
Canada – with the USSR and Yugoslavia.
Denmark – with Bulgaria, Czechoslovakia, the German DR, Hungary, Poland, Romania and the USSR.
Finland – with Bulgaria, the German DR, Hungary, Poland, Romania and the USSR.
France – with Bulgaria, Cuba, Czechoslovakia, the German DR, Hungary, Poland, Romania, the USSR and Yugoslavia.
FR of Germany – with Bulgaria, Czechoslovakia, the German DR, Hungary, Poland, Romania, the USSR and Yugoslavia.
Italy – with Bulgaria, China, Czechoslovakia, the German DR, Hungary, Poland, Romania, the USSR and Yugoslavia.
Japan – with Bulgaria, Czechoslovakia, the German DR, Hungary, Poland, Romania, the USSR and Yugoslavia.
Netherlands – with Bulgaria, Czechoslovakia, the German DR, Hungary, Poland, Romania and the USSR.
Norway – with Bulgaria, Hungary, Poland, Romania and the USSR.
Sweden – with Bulgaria, Czechoslovakia, the German DR, Hungary, Poland, Romania, the USSR and Yugoslavia.
Switzerland – with Albania, Bulgaria, Hungary, Poland and the USSR.
United Kingdom – with Bulgaria, Czechoslovakia, the German DR, Hungary, Poland, Romania, the USSR and Yugoslavia.
United States – with Poland, Romania, the USSR and Yugoslavia.

To guide the co-operation policies along mutually desired lines, in many cases 'joint commissions' have been established headed by a minister on each side, as exemplified by the Austrian–Hungarian, British–Czechoslovak, Franco–Polish, Italian–Romanian and Japanese–Soviet intergovernmental commissions. Such commissions often include working parties in specific fields, in which Western commercial and industrial interests and their Socialist counterparts are represented.

In some cases, semi-official bodies may perform these functions. Thus in 1974 the US–Soviet Trade and Economic Council was created which on the American side is overwhelmingly dominated by multinational corporations.[13] A similar body was established in 1973 to promote American trade with China, viz. the National Council for US–China Trade, in which one-half of the membership is represented by major multinationals.

Some multinational corporations have in fact gone further and have individually concluded co-operation agreements with Socialist countries at the ministerial level – either with the state instrumentality for science and technology or/and the relevant ministry. This co-operation usually involves periodical meetings to exchange information and experience, and in most cases there is jointly conducted or co-ordinated research and development (R & D) in directions of mutual interest. For example, the USSR has entered into such agreements with more than 150 Western firms, of which some 100 are large and medium multinational corporations (and of which at least 35 are American). The most important agreements – extending over long periods (mostly five years, but in some cases 10 or more years) and covering wider scope – are those which have been concluded by the State Committee for Science and Technology. A list showing the 60 best known multinationals is given in Table 1.

Thus the agreement signed by the Verenigde Machinenfabrieken of the Netherlands in 1973 provides for close working ties in the development of the production technology for turbine blades, rotary screen printing machines, perforated and galvano-plastic screens,

[13] Its Board of Directors includes the Presidents or Chairmen of the following corporations: American Express, Armco Steel, Bank of America, Caterpillar Tractor, Chase Manhattan Bank, Combustion Engineering, Du Pont, General Electric, General Motors, IBM, Kaiser Industries, Minnesota Mining and Manufacturing, Occidental Petroleum, Pepsi-Co., Pullman, Rockwell International, Singer, Textron and Xerox. Mr D. M. Kendall (Chairman of Pepsi-Co.) was appointed as the first Co-Chairman.

sterilized milk and milk products and modern spray drying systems for the production of dry milk and derivatives. A possibility of entering into joint production with a view to marketing in third countries is also envisaged. In the implementation of the agreement, International Telegraph & Telephone has co-operated in putting a satellite communication link between Washington and Moscow into operation (in 1974) utilizing the American *Intelsat* and the Soviet *Molnaya* communication satellites. Most of the corporations listed in Table 1 as well as some 100 other multinational companies have entered into similar agreements with authorities in other Socialist countries at ministerial or industrial branch association levels.

TABLE 1 LONG-TERM CO-OPERATION AGREEMENTS CONCLUDED BY SELECTED MULTINATIONAL CORPORATIONS WITH THE STATE COMMITTEE FOR SCIENCE AND TECHNOLOGY OF THE USSR

Multinational Corporation (and its Parent Country in brackets*)	Field of Co-operation
AEG Telefunken (FRG)	Communications, data processing, energy
Agfa-Gevaert (FRG-Ne)	Photochemistry
AKZO (Ne)	Chemicals, textiles
American Can (US)	Packaging and containers
Armco Steel (US)	Metallurgical and chemical equipment
BASF (FRG)	Plastics, pigments, liquid fuels
Bayer (FRG)	Pigments, plastics, rubber
Beecham Group (UK)	Antibiotics
Bendix (US)	Electronic and scientific instruments
Boeing (US)	Civil aviation
R. Bosch (FRG)	Automotive engineering
Brown & Root (US)	Gas and oil transport engineering
Burroughs (US)	Computer technology and applications
Ciba-Geigy (Swi)	Pharmaceuticals, plastics
Coca-Cola (US)	Food processing, water purification
Control Data (US)	Computer plants and networks
Daimler-Benz (FRG)	Motor vehicles, pollution
Dresser Industries (US)	Oil and gas extraction
ENI (It)	Petrochemicals, textiles
Farbwerke Höchst (FRG)	Pharmaceuticals, other chemicals
Fiat (It)	Motor vehicles, machine-building
G. Fischer (FRG)	Metal casting, engineering
Food Machinery Corporation (US)	Food processing and packaging machinery
General Dynamics (US)	Aircraft, shipbuilding, communications
General Electric (US)	Electrical and electronic engineering

Multinational Corporation (and its Parent Country in brackets*)	Field of Co-operation
Henkel (FRG)	Detergents, other chemicals
Hewlett-Packard (US)	Electronics, measurement instruments
ICI (UK)	Pharmaceuticals, other chemicals
Industrial Nucleonics (US)	Automatic production control
International Paper (US)	Timber exploitation
ITT (US)	Telecommunications, electronics
Joy Manufacturing (US)	Heavy machinery
Kaiser Industries (US)	Aluminium, iron and steel, cement
Kraftwerk Union (FRG)	Automic power engineering
F. Krupp (FRG)	Metallurgical processes
Linde (FRG)	Cryogenics, sewage, gas refining
Mannesmann (FRG)	Large-diameter pipes, machinery
Matsushita Electric Industrial (Ja)	Electrical and electronic engineering
Mitsubishi (Ja)	Machinery and industrial equipment
Monsanto (US)	Rubber, new chemicals and processes
Montedison (It)	Synthetic fibres and engineering
P. Morris (US)	Tobacco, packaging, chemicals
Nippon Electric (Ja)	Communications, electronics
Rank Xerox	Copying, duplicating machines
Reichhold Chemicals (US)	Chemical products and processes
Renault (Fr)	Motor vehicles, machine tools
Schering (West Berlin-FRG)	Chemicals
Schöller-Bleckmann (Au)	High-alloy, high-speed steels
Siemens (FRG)	Electronic equipment, metallurgy
Singer (US)	Textile machinery, measurement equipment
Sperry-Rand (US)	Computers, measurement and control systems
Sumitomo (Ja)	Metallurgy, industrial engineering
Tokyo Shibaura Electric (Ja)	Electrical and medical equipment
Union Chimique Belge (Be)	Chemical process and engineering
Universal Oil Products (US)	Petrochemicals, plastics
Verenigde Machinenfabrieken (Ne)	Turbines and industrial machinery
VÖEST-Alpine (Au)	Special steels and metallurgy
Volvo (Swe)	Motor vehicle engineering
O. Wolff (FRG)	Rolling mills
Zanussi (It)	Electrical household goods

* For country abbreviations, see footnote 3, Ch. 1, p. 2. The extent of foreign affiliations of the firms listed is shown in the Complete List and Index, pp. 197-232 and further details of the larger entities – in Tables 2, 3 and 4, pp. 36-47.

Sources. Based on daily and periodical literature published in the USSR and Western countries.

To facilitate further East–West commercial collaboration, industrial and trading interests on each side have formed 'joint chambers of commerce' such as the American–Yugoslav, Belgian–Polish, British–Czechoslovak, British–Soviet, Finnish–Polish, Franco–Czechoslovak, Franco–Soviet, West German–Czechoslovak, Italian–Soviet, Swedish–Polish and Swiss–Czechoslovak. But there are other organizations active in this field, too. In Britain there is the East European Trade Council, the '48 Group' (to promote trade with China) and the Korean–British Trade Council (to foster trade with North Korea), in Italy – the Association for Economic Relations with Comecon, and in Japan – the Japan–China Technical Interchange Committee and the Chinese and Asian Trade Structure Centre.

In all these organizations multinational corporations have come to play a dominant role. Thus the Chinese and Asian Trade Structure Centre established in 1971 includes amongst its members: the Fuji Bank, C. Itoh & Co., Marubeni-Ida, Mitsui, Nissho-Iwai, the Sanwa Bank, Showa Denko and Sumitomo.

C. MOTIVES

We shall now examine the driving forces on each side behind this remarkable reversal of previous convictions and practices. Because the initiative in this newly discovered community of interests has essentially come from the Socialist countries, we shall bring out the motives on the Eastern side first. The most pervading consideration and crucial to all other motives is *technology*. The Socialist countries have been well aware of the 'technological gap' separating them from the most advanced capitalist nations. Here is some evidence afforded by Western and Socialist sources.

In 1962 the lag in civilian technology in different branches of the Soviet economy behind the USA ranged from 5 to 40 years, and the lag was in fact greater in 1962 than in 1940.[14] In Poland in 1958, according to an investigation carried out by the State

[14] M. Boretsky, 'Comparative Progress in Technology, Productivity and Economic Efficiency: USSR versus USA', in US Congress, Joint Economic Committee, *New Directions in the Soviet Economy*, Washington, GPO, 1966, Part II-A, pp. 149-59.

Council, the following proportions of production technologies were obsolete, compared with average world standards: 25 per cent in machine-building, 30 per cent in the chemical industry and 75 per cent in the textile industry.[15] In Hungary in the early 1960s, 86 per cent of the products of the machine-building industry was classed by a state testing authority as obsolete.[16] But even in Czechoslovakia and the German DR – technologically the most mature Socialist countries – the situation was disquietening. In the early 1960s, 64 per cent of the industrial output in Czechoslovakia was officially rated as not measuring up to world standards,[17] and in the German DR the share of new products in industrial output was less than 5 per cent, compared with 15 per cent in the FR of Germany.[18] There was a prevalent conviction amongst specialists in the USSR that in the mid-1960s about one-quarter of Soviet imports of equipment for chemical and oil refining industries from other Comecon countries was below world quality standards.[19]

The technological lag was due not only to the Socialist concentration on basic industrialization and the quantitative growth of production in the past but also because, as a Polish economist conceded, 'the Socialist economy was not able to develop effective methods for the stimulation of technological progress and a fuller utilization of technology in the interest of a more dynamic economic growth'.[20] Up to the early 1960s the Socialist countries based their developmental strategy predominantly on the so-called 'extensive factors', i.e. on the physical extension of the resources employed. This policy produced very good results as long as there were idle reserves of labour, capital and land to draw upon. But by 1960 these reserves, especially in the more developed European Socialist

[15] *Gospodarka planowa* (Planned Economy), Warsaw, 12/1972, p. 721.

[16] *Voprosy ekonomiki* (Problems of Economics), Moscow, 9/1967, p. 128.

[17] *Mirovaya ekonomika i mezhdunarodnye otnosheniya* (World Economy and International Relations), Moscow, 2/1966, p. 29.

[18] *Gospodarka planowa*, 10/1969, p. 38.

[19] Yu. F. Kormnov, *Mezhdunarodnaya spetsializatsiya proizvodstva* (International Specialization of Production), Moscow, Ekonomika, 1968, p. 50. Comecon at that time included Bulgaria, Czechoslovakia, the German DR, Hungary, Mongolia, Poland, Romania, in addition to the USSR.

[20] J. Meisner, *Kapitalizm a socjalizm: Współzawodniczące systemy ekonomiczne* (Capitalism and Socialism: The Rival Economic Systems), Warsaw, PWE, 1973, p. 129.

countries began to dry up and waste and stagnation followed.[21]

Confronted with these setbacks, the Socialist leaders decided to turn to productivity increases as the source of growth of national income in their desperate effort to sustain rapid economic development. In this new strategy technological progress has thus assumed new and in fact critical importance. Now, multinational corporations provide the most obvious reservoir of Western technology and short-cut ways for bridging the embarrassing 'gap'. The corporations have been recognized as technological leaders and the most dynamic element in the industrial growth of the most advanced capitalist countries – since the early 1950s the corporations' output has been expanding at an average annual rate of 10-11 per cent whilst the Gross National Product in the capitalist world has been growing at 5 per cent p.a.[22] In a new appraisal of the multinationals a Polish economist concluded:

> Multinational corporations above all provide the main channel for the transfer of technology ... they modernize the structure of industry ..., which in a sense leads to the internationalization of technical progress and the division of labour.[23]

The second, closely related, consideration is that the corporations represent a source of *know-how* which, although less recognizable than embodied technology and licences, is nevertheless most valuable to ensure maximum efficiency benefits. Through closer co-operation, advanced Western managerial expertise applicable to large enterprises (and these are typical in Socialist countries) can be assimilated in the interest of a more effective reorganization and rationalization of production. For this assimilation close personal contacts in the form of visits by top executives in both directions, the exchange of specialists, training schemes and production and marketing are often desirable or necessary.

[21] Thus, whilst over the period 1950-55 the average annual rate of growth (of national income at constant prices) in Comecon reached 11 per cent, during 1961-3 the rate slumped to about 4 per cent (Czechoslovakia having recorded a negative rate in 1963, viz. −2.2 per cent). Based on: *Rozwój gospodarczy krajów RWPG 1950-1968* (Economic Development of the Comecon Countries 1950-1968), Warsaw, GUS, 1969, pp. 16-43; *Statistická Ročenka 1967* (Statistical Yearbook 1967), SNTL, 1967, pp. 132, 136.

[22] Ewa Michalska ('Multinational Corporations and Economic Growth'), *Gospodarka planowa*, 5/1973, p. 347.

[23] Ibid., p. 350.

The third attraction is *diversification and flexibility*. As the corporations are large firms with wide foreign affiliations, they command varied production capacities, and are used to operating under different institutional conditions. They are also more inclined and able to adapt their strategies to rapidly changing circumstances. Consequently, they are most suitable partners for large package deals involving complex deliveries and technologies.

Fourth, the Western multinationals provide a great potential as a *market* for Socialist exports. Being large, diversified and multinational, the corporations have a great need for varied inputs, and further they command extensive marketing networks. The Socialist countries have traditionally had great difficulties in marketing their products in the capitalist world owing to their poor marketing techniques, their inadequately developed distribution and servicing channels and to various forms of discrimination at both official and unofficial levels. In particular in many cases they have been confronted with severe global competition and hostility from the well-entrenched multinationals. Now, the latter provide the possibility of alleviating this predicament. They can directly provide a large market for minerals, agricultural raw materials, components and sub-assemblies. Moreover, through their international marketing networks, they can facilitate or directly undertake the marketing of Socialist products as a result of 'counter-purchases',[24] production co-operation and the joint construction of projects. This has become of special importance in the case of manufacturers – with the growing need for large-scale production and consequently larger and larger markets.

Fifth, the corporations can ease the Socialist *foreign exchange* problem. These countries have always suffered from acute shortages of foreign exchange, particularly of Western hard currencies. On the one hand, the multinationals' counter-purchases, and their deliveries of equipment, licences and then components under production co-operation and joint-venture arrangements, minimize the Socialist countries' direct foreign exchange expenditure. On the other, sales to the multinationals can provide extra earnings of foreign exchange.

The sixth advantage of dealing with the corporations is the possi-

[24] The acceptance of Socialist goods by the corporation in part-payment for sales to the Socialist buyer. For further details, see Ch. 7A, pp. 116-17.

bility of obtaining substantial long-term *credits*. They naturally have large financial resources, and furthermore they have a good deal of influence with banks and finance companies (mainly through affiliate relations). They themselves often provide supplier credits or, especially in the case of larger deals, they can exercise strong pressure on banks to extend loans to the Socialist countries, on favourable terms at that, in order to promote their own sales.

Finally, the Socialist countries prefer to deal with *large and well-known firms*. Only such firms are in a position to meet large and complex orders, have a capacity for long-term co-operation and are unlikely to go bankrupt. These are important considerations for the Socialist state which usually places large orders (on behalf of the whole country) and attaches great importance to continuous and stable economic development. It is also more convenient administratively for Socialist negotiators to deal with firms large enough to arrange their own sub-contracting efficiently and to reduce the number of parties to the contract to a minimum. In fact, in several respects multinational corporations are not unlike the Socialist states – they have to 'think big', they engage in long-term planning and have a hierarchical technocratic outlook (see Ch. 10A, pp. 176-7). In a recent appraisal, a Socialist economist pointed out:

> Small Western firms, petty-minded and suspicious as they are, are more difficult to negotiate with.... On the other hand, larger companies, especially those with multinational affiliations, are more experienced in international dealings, and as they operate in several fields their approach to industrial co-operation is more positive.[25]

It may be remarked here that for a long time in the past the big ambition of the Socialist countries was to become self-sufficient and independent of the capitalist world. It is rather ironical that the continued rapid economic development in these countries has in fact been making them more dependent on the advanced capitalist nations and on Western big business in particular.

Multinational corporations are well aware of the technological, commercial and financial attractions they hold for the Socialist countries. But in contrast to their previous attitude (largely influenced by the strategic embargo), they are less perturbed by the

[25] W. Mostowicz, ('Problem of Prices in Co-operation Agreements'), *Rynki zagraniczne* (Foreign Markets), Warsaw. 15/12/1973, p. 4.

benefits accruing to their Socialist partners and are increasingly preoccupied with their own gains. And the opportunities offering are most impressive and varied, as befits large and diversified companies, which we shall now examine in turn.

(a) Large Deals. Business deals offered by the Socialist countries are usually large because orders for a particular broad class of imports are normally placed by one large foreign trade enterprise on behalf of the whole country, and not by individual smaller firms as is typical in the capitalist world. As they attach the utmost importance to rapid and continuous development – industrialization in particular – these countries provide large and growing opportunities for the export of capital and technology, which the corporations are well equipped to supply. Even China, which for a long time in the past endeavoured to keep aloof from Western big business, has recently displayed growing interest in large deals with the multinationals. An American specialist on China described her as a 'mini-market with maxi-potential'.[26] Individual contracts signed with the Socialist countries typically run into millions of dollars, and not a few of those recently concluded have exceeded $100m. each. In fact some deals negotiated in recent years have involved billions of dollars each (see Ch. 3B-C, pp. 56-8 and Ch. 5C, pp. 90-6). As multinational corporations – being large entities with production plants all over the capitalist world – often suffer from excess capacity and operate on decreasing costs, the windfall Socialist contracts are the more welcome.

(b) Access to the Large and Growing Socialist Market. Economic collaboration with one Socialist country may open avenues to markets in other Socialist countries. This is the case with a member country of Comecon,[27] particularly when industrial co-operation and joint ventures are involved – as the Socialist partner often facilitates or directly undertakes the marketing of the products concerned.

(c) Indirect Access to Markets in Some Developing Countries.

[26] J. A. Ramsey, 'The People's Republic of China: A Mini-Market with Maxi-Potential', *Columbia Journal of World Business*, Sep–Oct 1972, pp. 7-14.

[27] Also known as CMEA, CEMA or CEA (being abbreviations for the 'Council for Mutual Economic Assistance'), established in 1949 and amounting to the 'Socialist Common Market'. Its full members now include Bulgaria, Cuba, Czechoslovakia, the German DR, Hungary, Mongolia, Poland, Romania and the USSR. In addition Yugoslavia was admitted to associate membership in 1964 (and in 1973 Finland was accorded a kind of co-operating status).

Many multinational corporations encounter a good deal of hostility in less-developed countries where sentiments against ex-colonial powers, the USA and neo-colonialism are strong and further nourished by nationalist as well as left-wing groups. Not burdened with historical liabilities and at the same time anxious to captivate the 'uncommitted nations of the Third World', the Communist regimes have established good relations with most developing nations. They have also, *inter alia*, concluded bilateral trade and payment agreements with them. Under these accords, imports from the Socialist countries do not necessarily have to be paid for in convertible foreign exchange. Consequently, the developing nations are in many cases more inclined to obtain their imports from these countries, rather than from the Western multinationals which as a rule conduct their business in hard currencies. Production co-operation and joint ventures with the Socialist partners provide the route to this extra market.

(d) Escape from Anti-Monopoly Charges. As the corporations are usually very large firms and they often hold exclusive patents for the production of some of the most profitable articles, they are frequent targets for anti-monopoly action. In particular establishing new subsidiaries or taking over existing firms in the parent or host capitalist countries is liable to provoke such action. However, the corporations may still maximize their profits and overcome this danger by expanding their production capacity in collaboration with Socialist partners in the form of industrial co-operation or joint ventures.

(e) Economic Integration and Currency Realignments. The development of economic groupings in the capitalist world has increased competition and has made entry for outsiders more difficult. This problem has been further compounded by recent currency revaluations in such trade-oriented countries as Austria, Belgium, the FR of Germany, Japan, Sweden and Switzerland, making imports more competitive and exports more arduous to market in capitalist countries.

(f) Convenient Sources of Imports. So far we have emphasized the export side. But it must be realized that as the multinationals maintain extensive networks of production plants, they have large and varied needs for raw materials and semi-finished products. In

their global calculations they recognize that some of their plants may be more conveniently supplied with materials from the Socialist countries. Owing to lower labour costs (than in the West), many manufactured inputs can also be obtained more economically. The diversification of the sources of imports may also be deemed desirable. The best example of this thinking is provided by the American and Japanese multinationals' involvement in oil and gas developmental projects in the USSR and China after having learnt a lesson from the 1973-4 Arab oil embargo.

(g) Socialist Technology. Although on the whole multinational corporations command higher levels of technology, they are finding to their surprise that in some fields of metallurgy, power generation, high-voltage long-distance transmission of electricity, communication equipment, low-temperature engineering, lasers, atomic energy, high-speed aviation and space exploration the (European) Socialist countries are ahead of the West. These countries have developed a broad and powerful R & D base, and scientific and technical co-operation with them is no longer a question of Western charity but a matter of mutual benefit. The import of certain industrial items and licences has become a commercial proposition for some corporations.

(h) Business Reputation. Western manufacturers, traders and bankers all agree that the Socialist countries have proved to be most reputable business partners, having established a payment record unparalleled by capitalist firms. Although negotiations may be long and arduous, once the contract is concluded the Socialist partner adheres to it to the letter. The American 'Business International', based in Geneva, had this to say to its clients recently:

> When East Europeans sign a contract, they live up to it 100%. Their record is impeccable. ... the profit margins of many companies from dealing with Eastern Europe are higher than in most Western markets.[28]

D. THE OVERALL EXTENT OF DEALINGS

Of the approximate total number of 3,000 Western-based multinational corporations of any importance, about one-third has had

[28] *Eastern Europe Report*, 16/11/1973, p. 336.

TABLE 2 THE LARGEST INDUSTRIAL MULTINATIONAL DEALINGS WITH

Name (and Parent Country in brackets*)	Industry	Sales in 1973† $m.
AEG Telefunken (FRG)	Electrical goods, electronics	4,187
AKZO (Ne)	Synthetic fibres, chemicals	3,385
American Can (US)	Engineering, containers	2,182
Armco Steel (US)	Metallurgy	2,390
BASF (FRG)	Chemicals, pigments	5,384
Bayer (FRG)	Chemicals, pharmaceuticals	4,654
R. Bosch (FRG)	Electrical equipment, electronics	2,440
British Leyland Motor (UK)	Motor vehicles	3,827
British Petroleum (UK)	Petroleum products	7,726
Brown, Boveri (Swi)	Engineering	2,290
Caterpillar Tractor (US)	Construction machinery	3,182
Ciba-Geigy (Swi)	Chemicals	2,585
Cie Générale d'Electricité (Fr)	Electrical equipment	2,897
Citröen (Fr)	Motor vehicles	2,561
Continental Can (US)	Packaging, containers	2,540
Courtaulds (UK)	Chemicals, textiles	2,312
Daimler Benz (FRG)	Motor vehicles	5,551
Dow Chemical (US)	Chemicals	3,068
Du Pont (US)	Chemicals	5,276
Dunlop-Pirelli Union (UK-It)	Rubber products, cables	3,275
Estel-Hoesch (Ne-FRG)	Metallurgy	2,804
Exxon (US)	Petrochemicals	25,724
Farbwerke Höchst (FRG)	Chemicals	5,591
Ford Motor (US)	Means of transport	23,015
General Electric (UK)	Electrical equipment	2,765
General Electric (US)	Electrical engineering	11,575
General Motors (US)	Means of transport	35,798
Guest, Keen & Nettlefolds (UK)	Building and industrial equipment	2,008
Gulf Oil (US)	Petrochemicals	8,417
Gutehoffnungshütte (FRG)	Engineering, non-ferrous metals	2,926
Honeywell (US)	Electronics, computers	2,391
IBM (US)	Computers, office equipment	10,993
ICI (UK)	Chemicals	5,309
International Harvester (US)	Agricultural and constr. machinery	4,193
C. Itoh & Co. (Ja)**	Trading, metals, cables	..
ITT (US)	Telecommunication equipment	10,183
F. Krupp (FRG)	Metallurgy, engineering	2,905
Lockheed Aircraft (US)	Aircraft	2,757
Mannesmann (FRG)	Pipes, machinery, chemicals	3,456
Marubeni-Ida (Ja)**	Trading, chemicals, food	..

CORPORATIONS SIGNIFICANTLY INVOLVED IN COMMERCIAL
SOCIALIST COUNTRIES

Assets in 1973† $m.	Foreign Affiliations in Capitalist World§	Foreign Content in %≠	Socialist Partner Countries‡
2,725	19 (34)	30 *S*	Ch, Cz, **GDR**, Hu, Po, Ro, **USSR**, **Yu**
3,240	21 (85)	84 *S*	GDR, Po, **USSR**
1,544	22 (50)	..	**Bu**, Ch, **Ro**, **USSR**
2,259	22 (36)	11 *E*	**USSR**, Yu
4,841	24 (48)	47 *S*	Ch, **GDR**, **Hu**, Po, **Ro**, **USSR**, Yu
5,020	28 (57)	55 *S*	Bu, **Cz**, **GDR**, Po, **Ro**, **USSR**, **Yu**
1,546	30 (43)	39 *S*	**GDR**, Hu, Po, **USSR**, Yu
2,403	30 (160)	14 *S*	Bu, Cu, Cz, GDR, **Po**, Yu
10,414	50 (182)	88 *S*	Bu, GDR, **Hu**, Po, Ro, **USSR**
2,537	18 (26)	76 *S*	Bu, **Ch**, Cz, Hu, **Po**, **Ro**, **USSR**, **Yu**
2,233	15 (16)	53 *S*	Ch, Po, **USSR**, Yu
3,759	46 (91)	98 *S*	**Bu**, Ch, GDR, **Hu**, **Po**, **Ro**, USSR, **Yu**
3,793	21 (54)	20 *S*	Cz, Hu, **Po**, Ro, USSR, Yu
389	15 (43)	33 *S*	**Ch**, Cu, Hu, **Po**, **Yu**
1,753	12 (16)	..	Ch, Po, **USSR**
2,336	33 (223)	22 *S*	Cz, Po, Ro, **USSR**
2,161	16 (25)	45 *S*	Bu, GDR, Hu, Po, **USSR**, **Yu**
3,896	29 (56)	40 *S*	**GDR**, Hu, Ro, **Yu**
4,832	21 (32)	18 *S*	GDR, Hu, Po, **USSR**
3,164	33 (105)	52 *S*	Bu, Ch, GDR, **Po**, **Ro**, **USSR**, **Yu**
3,373	17 (42)	25 *S*	Cz, **Ro**, **USSR**
25,079	23 (89)	50 *S*	Bu
5,979	46 (139)	42 *S*	Bu, Ch, Cz, **GDR**, Hu, **Po**, **Ro**, **USSR**, **Yu**
12,954	30 (57)	26 *S*	**Cu**, Ch, Cz, Hu, Yu
3,164	39 (256)	25 *S*	Ch, Cz, Hu, Ro, **USSR**
8,324	36 (71)	16 *S*	Cz, Hu, **Ro**, **USSR**, Yu
20,297	26 (42)	19 *S*	Ch, Hu, **USSR**, **Yu**
1,692	30 (129)	16 *S*	Bu, Cz, GDR, **Po**, Ro, **USSR**
10,074	31 (97)	45 *S*	Ro, USSR
2,535	24 (45)	38 *S*	**Ch**, **GDR**, Hu, **Ro**, **USSR**, Yu
2,583	29 (88)	35 *S*	Ch, GDR, Hu, **Po**, USSR, Yu
12,298	15 (22)	39 *S*	Bu, Ch, **Cz**, **GDR**, Hu, Po, **Ro**, **USSR**, **Yu**
6,442	48 (224)	35 *S*	Bu, Ch, Cz, GDR, Hu, **Po**, **Ro**, **USSR**, Yu
2,813	27 (33)	25 *S*	Hu, **Po**, Ro, **USSR**
..	11 (13)	40 *S*	**Ch**, Cz, GDR, Hu, **Po**, **Ro**, **USSR**
10,133	57 (217)	42 *S*	Bu, **Ch**, Cz, Hu, **Po**, Ro, **USSR**, **Yu**
2,018	17 (33)	23 *S*	Bu, Ch, **GDR**, **Hu**, **Po**, **Ro**, **USSR**
1,855	12 (17)	3 *S*	USSR, Yu
1,981	16 (43)	41 *S*	**Ch**, Cz, **GDR**, NK, Po, **Ro**, **USSR**
..	15 (23)	40 *S*	**Ch**, Cz, GDR, Hu, **Po**, **Ro**, **USSR**

TABLE 2 THE LARGEST INDUSTRIAL MULTINATIONAL DEALINGS WITH

Name (and Parent Country in brackets*)	Industry	Sales in 1973† $m.
Matsushita Electric Industrial (Ja)	Electrical and electronic equipment	4,409
Minnesota Mining & Manuf. (US)	Metallurgy, engineering	2,546
Mitsubishi (Ja)**	Trading, engineering	..
Mitsui & Co. (Ja)**	Trading, chemicals, engineering	..
Mobil Oil (US)	Petrochemicals	11,390
Monsanto (US)	Chemicals	2,648
Montedison (It)	Chemicals	4,452
Nestlé (Swi)	Food products	5,205
Nissho-Iwai (Ja)**	Trading, chemicals	..
Occidental Petroleum (US)	Petrochemicals	3,178
Pechiney-Ugine-Kuhlmann (Fr)	Metallurgy, chemicals	3,612
Philips (Ne)	Electronic and electrical equipment	8,108
RCA (US)	Telecommunication equipment	4,247
Rhône-Poulenc (Fr)	Chemicals	3,300
Rockwell International (US)	Engineering, apparatus	3,179
Royal Dutch-Shell (Ne-UK)	Petrochemicals	18,672
Saint Gobain (Fr)	Building materials, packaging	3,547
Siemens (FRG)	Electrical and electronic equipment	5,523
Singer (US)	Sewing machines, apparatus	2,528
Sperry Rand (US)	Computers, communication equipment	2,229
Tenneco (US)	Petrochemicals, gas	3,910
Thomson-Brandt (Fr)	Electronics, computers	2,016
A. Thyssen-Hütte (FRG)	Iron and steel	4,243
Unilever (Ne-UK)	Food, detergents	11,010
Union Carbide (US)	Mining, chemicals	3,939
United States Steel (US)	Metals, mining	6,952
Volkswagenwerk (FRG)	Motor vehicles	6,412
Volvo (Swe)	Motor vehicles, machinery	2,064
Westinghouse Electric (US)	Electronics, engineering	5,702
Xerox (US)	Office equipment	2,390

* For country abbreviations, see footnote 3, Ch. 1, p. 2.

† The data are taken from *Fortune* (May and August, 1974) and may in some cases apply to 1972 or (in the case of sales) to a financial year partly covering the latter months of 1972 or early months of 1974. For qualifications to the figures as given, see *Fortune* quoted in the *Sources* on the next page.

§ The number of foreign countries is followed (in brackets) by the number of foreign affiliates – branches, subsidiaries and associates, including sub-affiliates.

≠ These figures must be treated as approximate, applying to the late 1960s or early 1970s; A = of Assets, E = of Employment, F = of the total number of Affiliates, S = of Sales.

CORPORATIONS SIGNIFICANTLY INVOLVED IN COMMERCIAL SOCIALIST COUNTRIES—*continued*

Assets in 1973† $m.	Foreign Affiliations in Capitalist World§	Foreign Content in %≠	Socialist Partner Countries‡
3,935	18 (23)	23 *S*	Ch, GDR, **USSR**
2,281	39 (63)	36 *S*	Hu, USSR
..	34 (75)	41 *S*	Bu, **Ch**, Cz, GDR, Hu, **Po**, **Ro**, **USSR**
..	24 (40)	43 *S*	Bu, **Ch**, **Cz**, GDR, **Po**, **Ro**, **USSR**, Yu
10,690	67 (92)	45 S	Ch, Hu, Po, Ro, USSR
2,545	39 (93)	24 *S*	Ch, GDR, **Po**, **USSR**
5,727	34 (67)	37 *S*	**Bu, Cz, GDR, Hu, Po, Ro, USSR, Yu**
3,829	25 (101)	98 *S*	Hu
..	11 (14)	48 *S*	**Ch**, Cz, **GDR**, **Po**, Ro, **Yu**
2,871	25 (62)	46 *S*	Bu, Po, Ro, **USSR**
4,541	15 (27)	12 *S*	**USSR**, **Yu**
8,557	34 (128)	73 *E*	Cu, Cz, Hu, Po, Ro, USSR, Yu
3,301	43 (133)	..	**Ch**, USSR, Yu
4,210	30 (96)	47 *S*	**Ch**, Po, **USSR**
2,014	15 (27)	..	Ch, Po, **USSR**
22,797	93 (329)	80 *S*	**Bu**, Cz, GDR, **Hu**, Po, **Ro**, **USSR**
3,995	15 (55)	20 *S*	Bu, Po, Ro, **USSR**, **Yu**
6,184	19 (32)	40 *S*	Bu, Ch, **Cz**, **GDR**, **Hu**, **Po**, **Ro**, **USSR**, **Yu**
1,897	31 (114)	37 *S*	Hu, **Po**, Ro, **USSR**, Yu
1,841	26 (114)	35 *S*	Hu, Po, **USSR**, Yu
5,427	24 (82)	..	**USSR**
2,021	28 (94)	25 *S*	Hu, Po, Ro, USSR
3,570	22 (56)	20 *S*	Cz, Po, **USSR**, **Yu**
5,676	55 (171)	80 *S*	Cz, Hu, Po, **Ro**, Yu
4,162	40 (115)	30 *S*	Cz, Po, **USSR**
6,919	19 (32)	..	Ch, USSR, Yu
4,793	15 (36)	70 *S*	Hu, Ro, **Yu**
1,924	23 (75)	70 *S*	Bu, Ch, **GDR**, **Hu**, NK, **Po**, **USSR**, Yu
4,408	19 (50)	..	Ch, **Hu**, **Po**, **Yu**
3,103	22 (36)	30 *S*	USSR

‡ These entries should be regarded as minimal, as unreported or unnoticed dealings are not included. Bold type indicates a substantial scale of dealings in terms of value or extent. For country abbreviations, see footnote 3, Ch. 1, p. 2.

** Although essentially a trading firm, it plays an important part in industry. See the text, p. 41.

.. = not available.

Sources. Based on *Fortune*, 5/1974, pp. 232-51 and 8/1974, pp. 176-81; *Japan Company Directory 1973*, Tokyo. The Oriental Economist, 1973; *Who Owns Whom: Australasia and the Far East 1973*, *Who Owns Whom 1973/74: Continental Edition*, *Who Owns Whom: North America 1973*, *Who Owns Whom 1974; U.K. Edition* – all published in London by Roskill; daily and periodical literature published in Socialist and Western countries.

dealings of one sort or another with the Socialist countries since the early 1960s. Of greatest interest to us in this study are those which operate in the industrial field. The number of Western privately-owned[29] industrial corporations of large and medium size, i.e. those with affiliates in five or more foreign countries and whose sales in 1973 exceeded $500m., was 500. Of this total, at least 140 have had significant commercial dealings with one or more Socialist countries – and over one-third of them, with five or more of these countries – in recent years.

The spheres of business in which the corporations have been engaging include one or more of the following: the export or import of goods, the sale or purchase of licences, industrial co-operation and joint ventures. The relevant particulars concerning the 140 private, and in addition 10 state-owned, multinationals are presented in Tables 2, 3 and 4, pp. 36-47. In each case the details include the parent country, industry, sales, assets, the extent of foreign affiliations and operations and the Socialist partner countries.

Table 2 shows the data for the 70 largest private multinationals. They are those whose sales in 1973 exceeded $2,000m. and which have affiliates in more than 10 foreign capitalist countries. These corporations are economic giants by any standards. The sales of General Motors alone exceed the Gross National Product of each of the following Socialist countries: Yugoslavia, Bulgaria, Hungary, DR of Vietnam, DPR of Korea, Cuba, Albania or Mongolia. The tanker fleet of Exxon is some 50 per cent larger than that of the USSR, and the latter is now the largest oil producing country in the world! The proceeds from the sales of the 10 largest of these corporations (General Motors, Exxon, Ford Motor, General Electric of the USA, Mobil Oil, IBM, ITT, Gulf Oil, Royal Dutch-Shell and Unilever), amounting to over $165,000m. in 1973, would be enough to give the 58m. members of the Communist Parties in all the 14 Socialist countries a six-month holiday at the American standard of living.

There is another group of privately-owned multinational corporations which are 'lesser giants', designated for our purposes as

[29] i.e. as distinct from state-owned or controlled. Although some of them may be partly owned by the state (or other public authority), control essentially rests with private shareholders.

'medium', viz. those with sales in 1973 of at least $500m. and with affiliates in at least five foreign capitalist countries *and either* whose sales were below $2,000m. *or* which had affiliates in less than 11 countries, *or* both. The selected number of these corporations having significant business relations with the Socialist countries is also 70 and their relevant particulars are set out in Table 3.

With regard to Tables 2 and 3 a brief note is warranted on the Japanese corporations. Although in Japan there are many very large industrial companies, few of them have a large number of affiliates located in foreign countries. At the same time there are several large and powerful trading houses with extensive foreign affiliations. These trading houses have close ties with manufacturing companies and banks, and in some cases they themselves engage in industrial activities. They have proved most imaginative and persevering in their export drives not only in capitalist but also Socialist countries, utilizing their domestic and foreign affiliates to great effect. Their trade offensive in the USSR and Eastern Europe has reached a new unprecedented pitch since the inauguration of container transport across the USSR (mainly using the Trans-Siberian Railway) made possible by a Japanese–Soviet agreement of 1968.

As has been shown in the preceding chapter (p. 9), Communist regimes do not basically regard the formation of state enterprises in industrialized capitalist countries as a welcome development, but rather as evidence of decay, social opportunism and a betrayal of the world revolution. Such enterprises are still viewed essentially as tools in the hands of the bourgeois state to serve the interests of private monopolies. If this conviction is still genuinely held, then there must be an airtight separation of business practice from ideology on this front too, as in the case of the private corporations. Table 4, showing the 10 largest state-owned multinational enterprises, supports this contention. The extent of dealings with British Steel, Ente Nazionale Idrocarburi, Renault and VÖEST-Alpine is particularly noteworthy.

The 150 privately- and state-owned firms operating in the industrial sphere represent a powerful establishment in terms of technology, production capacity and wealth. They include most of the best known technological leaders in their respective fields in the capitalist world and they constitute an impressive reservoir of

TABLE 3 MEDIUM INDUSTRIAL MULTINATIONAL
COMMERCIAL DEALINGS WITH

Name (and Parent Country in brackets*)	Industry	Sales in 1973† $m.
Agfa-Gevaert (FRG-Ne)	Photographic equipment	831
Alcan Aluminium (Ca)	Aluminium	1,872
Alfa Laval (Swe)	Engineering	564
Allis-Chalmers (US)	Engineering	1,166
ASEA (Swe)	Electrical equipment	1,206
Ataka & Co. (Ja)**	Trading, foods	..
Beecham Group (UK)	Pharmaceuticals, foods	818
Boeing (US)	Aircraft and equipment	3,335
Borg-Warner (US)	Engineering	1,547
Burroughs (US)	Office machines, computers	1,264
Clark Equipment (US)	Construction equipment	1,128
Coca-Cola (US)	Beverages, foods	2,145
Cockerill (Be)	Metallurgy, engineering	1,233
Combustion Engineering (US)	Industrial equipment	1,273
Control Data (US)	Computers	936
Corning Glass Works (US)	Glassware, ceramics	946
Creusot-Loire (Fr)	Metallurgy, engineering	1,096
Deutsche Babcock & Wilcox (FRG)	Metals, machinery	766
Dresser Industries (US)	Petrochemicals	1,025
L. M. Ericsson (Swe)	Telecommunications equipment	1,197
Fiat (It)	Motor vehicles	4,075
FMC (US)	Machinery, chemicals	1,719
General Dynamics (US)	Engineering, chemicals	1,642
General Tire & Rubber (US)	Rubber products, equipment	1,380
Gillette (US)	Steel, engineering	1,064
Gränges (Swe)	Mining, metals	917
Hawker-Siddeley Group (UK)	Aircraft, missiles, machinery	1,358
Henkel (FRG)	Chemicals, cosmetics	1,586
Hewlett-Packard (US)	Electronic measuring instruments	661
Hitachi (Ja)	Construction equipment	5,972
Honda Motor (Ja)	Motor cycles, vehicles	1,340
Illinois Central Industries (US)	Transport equipment	1,172
Ingersoll-Rand (US)	Engineering	1,039
Kaiser Industries (US)	Metallurgy, engineering	..
Kanebo (Ja)	Textiles, pharmaceuticals	1,529

CORPORATIONS SIGNIFICANTLY INVOLVED IN SOCIALIST COUNTRIES

Assets in 1973† $m.	Foreign Affiliations in Capitalist World§	Foreign Content in %≠	Socialist Partner Countries‡
588	26 (44)	..	Cz, **Hu**, Po, USSR
2,449	30 (126)	42 *A*	Ch, Cu
536	27 (65)	65 *F*	Cz, **GDR**, Hu, **NK**, Po, Ro, **USSR**
916	9 (14)	..	**USSR**
1,568	32 (70)	55 *F*	Ch, Cz, **Po**, Ro, **USSR**, Yu
..	7 (7)	35 *S*	Bu, **GDR**, Ro, **USSR**
790	31 (78)	50 *F*	Hu, **USSR**
1,683	5 (6)	..	Ch, Ro, **USSR**, **Yu**
1,171	21 (64)	..	Ch, Po, USSR
1,696	19 (28)	43 *A*	USSR
798	15 (51)	30 *S*	Hu, **Po**, USSR
1,394	9 (115)	30 *S*	**Bu**, Cz, **Hu**, Po, **USSR**, Yu
1,260	12 (46)	..	Po, USSR
816	13 (21)	..	**USSR**, **Yu**
1,779	24 (75)	..	Bu, Ch, Cz, GDR, Po, **Ro**, **USSR**, Yu
863	21 (30)	..	Hu, Yu
1,604	5 (8)	7 *F*	GDR, **Po**, Ro, **USSR**, Yu
950	7 (32)	47 *F*	Bu, **Cz**, GDR, NK, Ro, **USSR**, Yu
806	34 (76)	40 *A*	Hu, **USSR**
1,919	35 (85)	79 *F*	**Hu**, **Po**, USSR, Yu
3,174	8 (11)	25 *S*	Ch, Cu, **Hu**, **Po**, **Ro**, **USSR**, **Yu**
1,380	18 (48)	10 *S*	Po, **USSR**
954	16 (30)	..	**USSR**
1,234	19 (35)	..	**Ro**, **USSR**
810	31 (46)	40 *A*	Cz, Yu
1,146	16 (48)	45 *A*	Po, **USSR**, Yu
1,091	22 (105)	35 *S*	**Ch**, Cz, Po, Ro
654	27 (44)	30 *S*	Po, Ro, **USSR**, **Yu**
580	25 (28)	..	Cz, **USSR**
7,309	5 (6)	40 *S*	Bu, **Ch**, Hu, Po, USSR
1,180	8 (9)	54 *S*	Ch, Cz, USSR, **Yu**
1,737	15 (27)	..	**USSR**
1,008	27 (48)	33 *S*	Ro, **USSR**, Yu
..	8 (18)	..	Bu, **USSR**
1,456	8 (12)	..	USSR

TABLE 3 MEDIUM INDUSTRIAL MULTINATIONAL COMMERCIAL DEALINGS WITH

Name (and Parent Country in brackets*)	Industry	Sales in 1973† $m.
Kanematsu Gosho (Ja)**	Trading, chemicals	..
Klöckner-Humboldt-Deutz (FRG)	Heavy motor vehicles	1,205
J. Lucas (UK)	Vehicle, aircraft equipment	977
Massey-Ferguson (Ca)	Farm, building machinery	1,506
Metallgesellschaft (FRG)	Metals, engineering, chemicals	1,747
NCR (US)	Office equipment, computers	1,816
Nippon Electric (Ja)	Telecommunications equipment	1,556
Nissan Motor (Ja)	Motor vehicles	4,883
Olivetti (It)	Office equipment, electronics	1,096
Pepsi-Co (US)	Beverages	1,698
Pilkington Brothers (UK)	Glass and products	548
Plessey (UK)	Communication equipment	793
PPG Industries (US)	Chemicals, engineering	1,513
Pullman (US)	Industrial equipment	1,002
Rank Organization (UK)	Audio-visual products	631
Rheinstahl (FRG)	Metallurgy, engineering	1,648
Saab-Scania (Swe)	Means of transport	1,243
Sandoz (Swi)	Pharmaceuticals, pigments	1,146
Sandvik (Swe)	Carbide, special steels, engineering	549
Schering (FRG)	Chemicals	563
Schneider (Fr)	Steel, engineering	722
Solvay (Be)	Chemicals	1,643
Sony (Ja)	Electrical, electronic equipment	1,146
Sulzer (Swi)	Engineering	903
Sumitomo Shoji Kaisha (Ja)**	Trading, mining	..
Svenska Kullagerfabriken (Swe)	Bearings, engineering	1,345
Teijin (Ja)	Textiles, synthetics	984
Textron (US)	Helicopters, apparatus	1,858
Tokyo Shibaura Electric (Ja)	Engineering	4,022
Toyota Motor (Ja)	Motor vehicles	5,547
Tube Investments (UK)	Pipes, aluminium, engineering	993
Universal Oil Products (US)	Petrochemicals, plastics	611
Vallourec (Fr)	Steel, pipes	931
Vickers (UK)	Aircraft, shipbuilding equipment	521
Zanussi (It)	Appliances, industrial equipment	535

For footnotes and sources, see Table 2, pp. 38-9.

CORPORATIONS SIGNIFICANTLY INVOLVED IN SOCIALIST COUNTRIES—*continued*

Assets in 1973* $m.	Foreign Affiliations in Capitalist World§	Foreign Content in %≠	Socialist Partner Countries‡
..	7 (8)	42 *S*	Ch, Cz, Po, **USSR**, Yu
967	24 (32)	63 *F*	Bu, Cz, **NK**, Po, Ro, **USSR**, **Yu**
821	33 (84)	63 *F*	Bu, Ch, **Cz**, **GDR**, Po, Ro, USSR, Yu
1,249	19 (49)	90 *S*	Bu, **Po**, Ro, USSR, **Yu**
1,150	17 (52)	22 *S*	Bu, Cz, GDR, Ro, **USSR**, Yu
1,834	46 (62)	45 *S*	Bu, Cz, USSR
2,124	8 (11)	21 *S*	Bu, Ch, Po, **USSR**
5,059	7 (8)	36 *S*	**Ch**, Cz
647	28 (33)	62 *F*	Bu, Ch, GDR, Hu, Po, **USSR**, Yu
1,150	25 (54)	35 *S*	Cz, GDR, **Hu**, **Po**, Ro, **USSR**, **Yu**
746	14 (50)	40 *F*	Cz, USSR
908	33 (104)	68 *F*	Bu, Ch, Ro
1,491	13 (48)	..	Po, **USSR**
595	12 (31)	..	Bu, **Ch**, **Po**, USSR
1,344	29 (116)	42 *F*	Bu, **Cz**, GDR, **Hu**, Po, Ro, **USSR**, Yu
1,329	6 (12)	23 *S*	Hu, Po, **USSR**, Yu
1,132	13 (29)	33 *F*	**Cz**, Hu, **USSR**, Yu
1,366	39 (80)	83 *F*	Bu, GDR, **Hu**, Po, **Ro**, **USSR**
692	34 (62)	70 *F*	GDR, Po, **USSR**
628	36 (58)	75 *F*	**GDR**, **USSR**
1,494	10 (16)	29 *F*	Po, USSR
1,826	13 (56)	75 *F*	USSR, Yu
1,279	11 (12)	49 *S*	Ch, Cz
1,436	22 (44)	88 *F*	Bu, Ch, Po, **Ro**, USSR, Yu
..	7 (8)	41 *S*	GDR, Hu, **Po**, **Ro**, **USSR**
1,638	40 (92)	97 *F*	Bu, Ch, **Cz**, GDR, Hu, Po, Ro, USSR, **Yu**
1,323	5 (5)	..	**Ch**, Cz, **Ro**, USSR
1,310	19 (58)	25 *S*	Po, USSR, Yu
5,289	5 (10)	13 *S*	**Ch**, Cz, **GDR**, **USSR**, Ro, **Yu**
3,697	5 (5)	30 S	**Ch**, Cz, Hu
843	26 (162)	35 *F*	Ch, GDR, Hu, USSR
396	19 (44)	..	GDR, Po, **Ro**, USSR, Yu
815	9 (11)	29 *F*	**USSR**
599	19 (62)	45 *F*	Bu, GDR, Po, USSR, Yu
406	11 (21)	..	USSR

TABLE 4 STATE-OWNED MULTINATIONAL INDUSTRIAL
COMMERCIAL DEALINGS WITH

Name (and Parent Country in brackets*)	Industry	Sales in 1973† $m.
Aerospatiale (Fr)	Aircraft	890
Alfa Romeo (It)	Motor Vehicles	605
British Steel (UK)	Iron and steel	4,290
ELF Group (Fr)	Petrochemicals	2,867
Elin-Union (Au)	Metals, engineering	..
ENI (It)	Petrochemicals, engineering	4,280
Renault (Fr)	Motor vehicles, machinery	4,656
Salzgitter (FRG)	Steel, shipbuilding	1,852
Statsföretag (Swe)	Mining, steel, paper	1,288
VÖEST-Alpine (Au)	Metallurgy, engineering	1,511

For footnotes and sources, see Table 2, pp. 38-9.

Western technology. Their total sales in 1973 exceeded $525,000m., which was more than the industrial output of the 14 Socialist countries put together.

These multinationals also represent an extreme case of capital concentration under capitalism. 'Capital', Marx once emphasized, 'comes dripping head to foot, from every pore, with blood and dirt.'[30] One wonders what Marx would say today in the face of the Communist regimes' enthusiastic collaboration with such 'monopolies' which have accumulated nearly $500,000m. worth of assets – and if the assets of the 50 multinational banks dealing with the Socialist countries (see Table 13, pp. 122-5) are added, the figure comes to the staggering total of $1,430,000m. If the Communist Parties in the Western countries were in a position to seize this fortune, there would be enough to make each of the 900,000 registered Party members outside Italy a millionaire, and there would still be plenty left over for princely consolation prizes to all the 1,500,000 Italian Communists!

[30] K. Marx, *Capital*, New York, International Publishers, 1967, vol. 1, p. 760.

ENTERPRISES SIGNIFICANTLY INVOLVED IN SOCIALIST COUNTRIES

Assets in 1973† $m.	Foreign Affiliations in Capitalist World§	Foreign Content in %≠	Socialist Partner Countries‡
..	3 (4)	..	Ch, Ro, USSR, Yu
1,245	15 (15)	55 *F*	Cz, USSR
3,561	15 (40)	23 *F*	Bu, **Ch**, **Po**, Ro, USSR, Yu
2,750	16 (18)	..	**USSR**, Yu
..	8 (9)	60 *F*	Bu, **GDR**, NK, **Po**, USSR, Yu
8,708	48 (111)	18 *E*	Bu, Ch, Cu, Cz, GDR, NV, **Po**, Ro, **USSR**, Yu
1,818	27 (49)	40 *S*	Cz, Hu, NV, **Po**, **Ro**, **USSR**, **Yu**
2,690	13 (25)	20 *F*	**Po**, Ro, **USSR**, **Yu**
2,020	13 (30)	..	Po
1,971	9 (12)	41 *F*	Cu, Cz, **GDR**, Hu, **Po**, Ro, **USSR**, Yu

As is roughly indicated in Tables 2-4, the extent of business dealings with the Socialist countries varies from one multinational to another. In the case of some corporations the scale of business operations is most impressive. The multinationals which have recently completed or undertaken deals totalling in excess of $500m. include Brown, Boveri, Control Data, Creusot-Loire, ENI, Fiat, General Electric (US), Klöckner-Humboldt-Deutz, Krupp, Mannesmann, Mitsubishi, Mitsui & Co., Montedison, Occidental Petroleum, Pechiney-Ugine-Kuhlmann, Pulman, Renault, Salzgitter, Sumitomo Shoji Kaisha, Teijin, A. Thyssen-Hütte, and Westinghouse Electric.

It must be realized that many smaller multinational corporations (with annual sales below $500m. and/or affiliates in 1-4 foreign countries) have also been active in business dealings with the Socialist countries. Space does not allow their inclusion in the tables, but they will be introduced in the following chapters. Those which warrant being singled out at this stage are (the parent country is given in the first brackets, followed by the number of host capitalist countries and, in the second brackets, of the foreign-located affiliates): Bayerische Motoren Werke (FRG) – 4 (4), John Brown

(UK) – 10 (40), Carborundum (US) – 19 (46), Cie Internationale pour l'Informatique (Fr) – 1 (1), International Computers (UK) – 21 (33), Ishikawajima-Harima (Ja) – 1 (2), Kawasaki Steel (Ja) – 2 (3), Kobe Steel (Ja) – 1 (1), Koehring (US) – 10 (18), Kraftwerk Union (FRG) – 3 (3), Linde (FRG) – 14 (25), McDonnell Douglas (US) – 2 (2), Rubery Owen (UK) – 6 (15), Schöller-Bleckmann (Au) – 10 (11), Toray Industries (Ja) – 2 (2), Verenigde Machinenfabrieken (Ne) – 10 (17) and Wärtsilä (Fi) – 1 (2).

Another sphere of East–West economic relations in which multinationals have come to play an important part is finance. Of the 100 largest multinational banks in the West (each with assets in excess of \$2,000m. in 1973), more than one-half have been involved in financing East–West business deals. This question is considered in detail in Chapter 7 (see especially Table 13, pp. 122-5).

3 Trade

A. GENERAL CHARACTERISTICS

SINCE 1960 there has been a remarkable expansion of East–West trade. Over the period 1960-73 its value grew at the average annual rate of 15.8 per cent, compared with 12.4 attained by the world as a whole. The rapid increase in the Western export of machinery and transport equipment to the Socialist countries is the most notable feature of this expansion, so that their share has risen from one-quarter to one-third of the total. As one would expect, the Western import of these two categories of manufactures from the East has been much smaller, the proportion being less than one-tenth of total imports. For details, see Table 5.

The expansion of East–West trade has been largely due to the initiative of the Socialist countries. Indeed, their trade with the West has been growing faster than that with one another, viz. over the period 1960-73 at the average annual rate of 15.8 per cent, compared with 9.2 in intra-Eastern foreign trade. Consequently, taking the foreign trade of the East as a whole, the share of intra-Eastern trade declined from 68 per cent in 1960 to 57 in 1973, whilst the Western share rose from 19 to 31 per cent during the same period.[1]

The most conspicuous reorientation of trade to the West has occurred in the case of China. The Socialist countries claimed 66 per cent of China's trade in 1960 (74 per cent in 1955), but the proportion dropped to a mere 17 per cent in 1973, whilst the share of the West over the 1960-73 period climbed from 20 to 55 per

[1] United Nations *Monthly Bulletin of Statistics*, 6/1963, pp. xii-xiv and 6/1975, pp. xiv-xvii. The rate arrived at slightly understates the growth of intra-Socialist trade as prices in this trade have, on the whole, not been rising as fast as in East–West trade.

TABLE 5 TENDENCIES IN EAST–WEST TRADE, 1960-1973*

Year	East–West Trade in $m.	East–West Trade *as a % of world trade*	Western Export of Machinery & Transport Equipment to the East in $m.	Western Export ... *as a % of total export to the East*	Eastern Export of Machinery & Transport Equipment to the West in $m.	Eastern Export ... *as a % of total export to the West*
1960	5,770	2.3	759	25.6	205	7.3
1961	6,210	2.3	869	27.2	215	7.2
1962	6,500	2.3	1,055	31.4	250	8.0
1963	7,270	2.4	1,026	27.4	250	7.1
1964	8,690	2.5	1,136	24.7	341	8.3
1965	9,670	2.6	1,345	27.6	342	7.3
1966	11,340	2.8	1,735	30.1	417	7.5
1967	12,190	2.8	2,040	32.5	421	7.1
1968	12,730	2.7	2,075	32.3	455	7.4
1969	14,080	2.6	2,420	34.2	540	7.8
1970	16,330	2.6	2,635	31.5	630	8.1
1971	17,650	2.6	2,760	30.8	810	9.3
1972	22,080	2.7	3,610	30.4	950	9.2
1973	35,620	3.1	5,260	28.6	1,310	8.5

* These figures are based on the United Nations classification. The 'East' includes the 12 European (excluding Yugoslavia) and 4 Asian Socialist countries. The 'West includes the rest of Europe, North America, Japan, Australia and New Zealand and South Africa. Trade between the German DR and the FR of Germany is not included (as it is regarded as 'inner-German' trade). Both exports and imports are valued f.o.b.

Source: Based on United Nations *Monthly Bulletin of Statistics.*

cent.[2] In particular, there has been a spectacular diversion of Chinese trade away from the USSR in favour of the USA. Over the thirteen-year period, the value of Sino–Soviet trade fell drastically from 1,500m. to 200m. roubles, whilst Sino–American trade surged from nil to $875m.[3] At the same time, Soviet–American trade increased from $60m. in 1960 (to $200m. in 1970) and reached $1,500m. in 1973.[4]

In these developments, multinational corporations have gradually

[2] *Current Scene*, Hong Kong, 12/1974, p. 7; K. Leonidov, ('Foreign Trade of the PR of China'), *Ekonomicheskaya gazeta* (Economic Gazette), Moscow, 32/1974, p. 21.

[3] *Current Scene*, op. cit., p. 8; K. Leonidov, op. cit.; *Vneshnaya torgovlya SSSR za 1960 god* (Foreign Trade of the USSR in 1960), Moscow, Vneshtorgizdat, 1961, p. 9.

[4] *Pravda*, Moscow, 1/3/1974, p. 5.

come to play a most obliging part, in particular as suppliers of machinery, equipment and even complete industrial plants embodying advanced technology. In some respects the marketing of their products in the Socialist countries is easier, certainly more so now than it was in the past. As an American specialist in the field said, 'to cover [the FR of] Germany may require 20 salesmen. Because of centralized purchasing in the Soviet Union and other Eastern countries 2 or 3 representatives would suffice. Furthermore overhead costs of advertising internal distribution and consolidated offices are minimal, often amounting to less than 2 per cent of sales, and yet these cover a vast industrial market of over 300m. people.'[5]

There are also several multinational trading corporations specializing in East–West trade, such as Eastern Industrial (UK), Eurintrade (Be), and Satra (US). A multinational advertising firm, Marsteller (US) signed an agreement in 1973 with Vneshtorgreklama (USSR) on co-operation in advertising industrial products in the two countries. In the same year Occidental Petroleum (US), together with its subsidiary Bechtel, signed an agreement with the Chamber of Commerce and Industry of the USSR for the construction of a large International Trade Centre in Moscow, to house 400 foreign companies and organizations accredited to the USSR.[6] Its construction began in 1974 and it is financed by a consortium of American banks headed by the Chase Manhattan Bank. This project symbolizes the new approach by the Western multinationals and the Communist regimes to East–West trade on a grand scale.

B. THE EXPORT OF ITEMS EMBODYING ADVANCED TECHNOLOGY

The range of items exported by multinational corporations to the Socialist countries now covers practically the whole spectrum of manufactures entering world trade. They include semi-finished

[5] E. J. Milosh, 'Imaginative Marketing in Eastern Europe', *Columbia Journal of World Business*, Winter 1973, p. 69.

[6] For country abbreviations used in this book, see footnote 3, p. 2. The extent of the multinational affiliations of the companies mentioned in this book is indicated in the Complete List and Index, pp. 197-232, and further details on the larger parent corporations in Tables 2, 3 and 4, pp. 36-47.

materials, components, instruments, appliances, apparatus, machines, means of transport and other accoutrements needed by nations pursuing accelerated industrialization and experiencing rising standards of living. Although consumer goods now also appear on the list, the bulk of these exports consists of capital goods instrumental to the further development and modernization of the Socialist economies. In this section we shall highlight the latter type of exports embodying advanced technology. We shall concentrate on those which at one stage or another were subject to the Western strategic embargo.

(a) Large-Diameter Pipes and Equipment. The embargo on these pipes (exceeding 48 cm in diameter) was administered by the NATO nations over the period 1962-6. Scurrilous attacks were made in the Socialist countries against the 'International Pipe Cartel', – including such multinational companies as Lorraine-Escaut (Fr), Mannesmann (FRG), Phönix Rheinische Rohrwerke (FRG), Stewarts and Lloyds (UK) and Vallourec (Fr)[7] – as instigators, or at least as willing accomplices of the NATO military-industrial complex.[8] But all that now belongs to history and the Western multinationals have become conspicuous suppliers of oil and gas pipes, as well as of some sophisticated equipment for their installation and maintenance. In fact it may be noted here that Gränges – of Sweden, not a member country of NATO – capitalized on the NATO embargo adhered to by its capitalist brethren and kept on supplying such pipes to the USSR (and in 1970 it concluded an R & D co-operation agreement with the Ministry of Iron and Steel of the USSR on the development of special steel for gas and oil pipelines under harsh climatic conditions).[9] The best known suppliers in recent years have included Comptoir Franco-Belge des Tubes (Fr), Finsider (It), Mannesmann (FRG), Thyssen Röhrenhandel (FRG), Vallourec (Fr), and VÖEST-Alpine (Au). Largely to satisfy Soviet needs, Mannesmann built a factory, at Mülheim, for the manufacture of large-diameter (142 cm) gas pipes, and the first pipe leaving the

[7] Since that time, Lorraine-Escaut and Vallourec have merged to form Usines à Tubes de Lorraine-Escaut et Vallourec Réunies (or briefly 'Vallourec'), whilst Phönix Rheinische Rohrwerke has been taken over by August Thyssen-Hütte.

[8] e.g., see T. Belous, ('International Pipe Cartel'), *Vneshnaya torgovlya* (Foreign Trade), Moscow, 2/1965, pp. 17-21.

[9] *East–West*, Brussels, 6/11/1970, p. 5.

production line in 1970 was 'baptized' with a bottle of Crimean wine. By the end of 1976 Mannesmann and Thyssen Röhrenhandel alone had supplied over $1,400m. worth of pipes to the USSR. Furthermore a variety of equipment for laying down and operating the pipelines has been supplied by Borg-Warner (US), Borsig (FRG), Caterpillar Tractor (US), Constructions Métalliques de Provence (Fr), Cooper Industries (US), Creusot-Loire (Fr), General Electric (US), International Harvester (US), Nuovo Pignone (It) and others.

(b) Scientific Instruments and Measurement and Control Apparatus. A wide range of these items has been supplied by such multinational companies as: Honeywell (US) – control systems for oil pipelines, to the USSR; A. A. Jones and Shipman (UK) – precision grinding machines, to the USSR; Olivetti (It) – electronic control and measurement apparatus, to the USSR; Pye Unicam (UK) – atomic absorption spectrophotometers, to China.

(c) Communications Equipment. This category has embraced radio, television, telephone, telegraph, radar and satellite telecommunication equipment. Television (including colour) transmitting and relay facilities have been exported by Robert Bosch (FRG), Nippon Electric (Ja), Radio Corporation of America (US), Sony (Ja), Thomson-CSF (Fr) and Tokyo Shibaura Electric (Ja). Indeed, there has been some cut-throat competition amongst these companies to thrust their respective wares (based on either PAL or SÉCAM systems, or their versions) – to the amusement of the Socialist countries, especially China and the USSR. Radar equipment has been supplied by Decca Radar (UK) to the German DR, and by Plessey Radar (UK) to Romania. International Telegraph and Telephone (US) and Nippon Electric (Ja) each supplied sets of equipment to the USSR for satellite–ground communication stations, and RCA did the same for China. The installation of the station by RCA in China, to cover President Nixon's visit in February 1972, before the formal strategic embargo had been lifted, caused a good deal of irritation amongst the Japanese and West European companies. It was interpreted as a cunning American trick to capture the Chinese market before the official lifting of the ban.[10] AEG Telefunken (FRG), Cie Générale des Constructions Téléphoniques

[10] *China Trade Report*, Hong Kong, 3/1972, p. 13.

(Fr), L. M. Ericsson (Swe), Lockheed (US), Marconi Instruments (UK), Matsushita Electric Industrial (Ja), Siemens (FRG), Storno (De) and many others have also supplied sophisticated communications equipment to one or more Socialist countries.

(d) Computers. The centrally-planned economies have always been regarded by the Western computer companies as a market of great current and potential capacity, and rivalry amongst them has been very keen. The American embargo pursued up to the early 1970s on the export of the latest computers – which also applied to those produced under licence outside the USA – was regarded in Western Europe as a well-designed stratagem. Namely, it was viewed by some as a clever trick to enable IBM and other American makers to dump their older computers in the East, thereby creating new markets in the capitalist world for their later models – in each case at the expense of the West European export of current production. However, in recent years third-generation computers have been exported by practically all the best known Western makers, such as Compagnie Internationale pour l'Informatique (Fr), Control Data (US), General Electric (US), Honeywell (US), IBM (US), International Computers (UK), NCR (US), Olivetti (It), Saab-Scania (Swe), Siemens (FRG) and Sperry-Rand (US) to practically all the Socialist countries. Furthermore, equipment, licences and know-how have been supplied by some of these and other companies for the manufacture of the most complex elements or sub-assemblies. Thus Poland is now producing integrated circuits with the aid provided by Ferranti (UK) and semiconductors, thyristors and rectifiers – by Westinghouse Electric (US). According to some reports IBM, Olivetti and Sperry-Rand may build complete plants in the USSR for the production of the most modern computers.[11]

(e) Ships. Many Western shipbuilding companies have been amongst the earliest advocates of the relaxation and abolition of the strategic embargo, as the contracts offered by the Socialist countries have usually been large and most tempting. The multinational firms which have recently concluded deals for the delivery of freighters

[11] A. Dembiński and B. Kempiński, *Komputery w krajach socjalistycznych* (Computers in the Socialist Countries), Warsaw, CIINTE, 1969, p. 15; C. Levinson, *International Trade Unionism*, London, Allen & Unwin, 1972, p. 157; *Der Spiegel* (Mirror), Hamburg, 3/6/1974, p. 1.

include Hitachi (Ja) – to China (the value of the contract: $16m.), Weser (FRG) – to Poland ($30m.) and Sunderland Shipbuilding (UK) – to Yugoslavia ($65m.). During 1973-4 Wärtsilä (Fi) received orders for the delivery of two icebreakers ($100m.) to the USSR, whilst Howaldtwerke-Deutsche Werft (FRG) and Ishikawajima-Harima Heavy Industries (Ja) contracted to build large tankers of 120,000 – 144,000 dwt for Poland ($100m.) and Yugoslavia ($42m.) respectively. During the same period, International Hydrodynamics (Ca) undertook to deliver two pocket submarines to the USSR (for $4m.).

(*f*) *Aircraft.* The Socialist countries have recently become a buoyant market for Western aircraft. Many corporations which have 'suffered' financially from the slow-down in the arms race have enthusiastically embraced this godsend. Boeing (US) has sold B-707s to China and Romania, B-727s to Yugoslavia and at the time of writing it was negotiating with the USSR for the sale of B-747s. British Aircraft Corporation (UK) has supplied BAC-111 airliners to Romania and Handley Page Aircraft (UK) – HPH passenger aircraft to China, but a larger deal was represented by the sale of 38 Trident jet aircraft by Hawker-Siddeley (UK) also to China during 1971-4 for $287m. Another supplier of aircraft to China has been Vickers.[12] When Sir Alec Douglas Home visited Peking in October 1972, Mr Chou En-lai was reported to have made complimentary remarks about the aircraft produced by the British companies but disparaging references to the Soviet-made planes, such as Ilyushin-62.[13] Similarly, McDonnell Douglas (US) has delivered at least nine DC-9 airliners to Yugoslavia and VFW Fokker (FRG) is to supply 50 short-haul jet aircraft (worth $120m.) to Romania. In addition, judging by recent negotiations, Aérospatiale (Fr) is anxious to sell helicopters to Romania and United Aircraft (US) also helicopters to China, whilst Lockheed Aircraft (US) is likely to export Tristar airbuses to the USSR.

[12] As of 31/12/1973 China had 194 civilian aircraft in use or on order. Of these, 57 were of Western make, viz.: Boeing 707 – 10, Handley Page Herald – 2, Hawker-Siddeley Trident 1E, 2E and 3B – 38 and Vickers Viscount – 7. The remaining 137 were Soviet-made, or at least Soviet-designed. See D. Chambers, 'Civil Aviation in the PRC', *Current Scene*, 8/1974, pp. 1-14, esp. p. 12.

[13] *China Trade Report*, 11/1972, p. 5.

(*g*) *Nuclear Equipment.* This category of export at first, naturally, caused the greatest sensation. In 1966 Fairey Engineering (UK) signed a contract for the delivery of a training reactor to Romania and, three years later – for a nuclear decontamination facility, also to Romania (both contracts totalling £450,000). In 1973 Gulf Energy and Environmental Systems (US) undertook to supply Romania with an experimental twin-cored triga reactor worth $4m. (to be operational in 1976) and a year later Kraftwerk Union (FRG) and Metallgesellschaft (FRG) agreed to participate in establishing the Institute for Nuclear Technology at Piteşti. A much larger project is the atomic power station being constructed (over the period 1973-8) by Westinghouse Electric at Krsko in Yugoslavia; the scheduled capacity of the station is 600 MW and it is worth $150m. to Westinghouse which, in addition, is to open a uranium mine in the district to provide nuclear fuel (also see Ch. 5C, p. 92, on the proposed West German–Soviet scheme).

(*h*) *Other Machinery and Equipment.* The remaining exports embodying advanced technology encompass a very wide range of items. We shall only outline those of greatest interest. The largest industrial project undertaken so far in the Socialist bloc is the Kama Truck Works at Naberezhniye Chelny on the Kama River in the USSR (between Moscow and the Urals). It was built during 1971-5 to produce 150,000 heavy-duty (8-20 ton) trucks and 250,000 diesel engines annually. The total cost of the project exceeded 3,000m. roubles – one and a half times more than the giant passenger car factory at Togliattigrad constructed by Fiat during 1968-71. The Kama Works have been equipped with some 50,000 machine tools, the largest foundry in the world, ultra-modern presses, furnaces, rolling mills, electronic computing units and assembly lines totalling 300 km in length. The complex has been described by Soviet officials as the largest and most modern truck factory in the world (as, indeed, it is) and a tribute to the vision and resourcefulness of the Soviet leaders and people building communism. In fact, it is a monument not so much to the Soviets as to the Western multinational corporations. The list of the suppliers reads like an extract from *Who Owns Whom.* The value of the contracts (including licences) to the Western companies exceeded $1,000m. Their total number was 150, mainly American, West German, French and

British (plus some Italian, Swedish and Swiss) firms. Renault (Fr) acted as the prime contractor for planning and constructing the engine-building installations ($400m.), Swindell-Dressler (US) for building the huge foundry plant ($200m.) and Liebherr-Verzahntechnik (FRG) for equipping the transmission-machinery division ($165m.). A sample list of 25 other multinationals with deliveries amounting to $1m. or more is given in Table 6.

TABLE 6 DELIVERIES OF MACHINERY AND EQUIPMENT BY WESTERN MULTINATIONAL FIRMS FOR THE KAMA TRUCK WORKS IN THE USSR

Western Supplier*	Description of the Delivery	Value in $m.
Abex Denison (US)	Hydraulic presses	1
Albany International (US)	Forging machines and tooling	3
American Chain & Cable (US)	Handling and control equipment	5
Amtec-France (Fr)	Turning multi-spindle machines	2
E. W. Bliss (US)	Automatic production line	20
Carborundum (US)	Shot-blasting equipment	10
Chromaloy-Kessler (US)	Patterns and tooling for steel castings	3
Cie Française de Convoyeurs (Fr)	Conveyor system	13
Dryzys (Fr)	Finishing lines	19
Dymo (UK)	Machines and tools for die-casting	1
EFCO (UK)	Metal-finishing equipment	114
Ex-Cell-O (US)	Equipment for cylinder linings	14
Fata (It)	Equipment for aluminium foundry	22
Girling (UK)	Automatic line for brake shoes	3
IBM (US)	Computer installation	5
Ingersoll Milling & Manufacturing (US)	Engine block machining line	22
Ingersoll-Rand (US)	Engine assembly equipment	4
Maschinenfabrik Sack (FRG)	Equipment for automatic filters	3
Mauser-Schärer (FRG)	Equipment for differential casings	6
Mitsubishi (Ja)	Gear manufacturing equipment	33
Rheinstahl (FRG)	Production lines and equipment	85
Simon-Carves (UK)	Mill room, control systems, etc.	57
Sonocom (Fr)	Automatic presses	2
Svenska Fläktfabriken (Swe)	Gas-treatment equipment	10
Tyler (US)	Moulding machine systems	30

* For their multinational affiliations, see the Complete List and Index, pp. 197-232, and for further details of parent companies, Tables 2, 3 and 4, pp. 36-47.

Sources: Based on daily and periodical literature published in Socialist and Western Countries.

Other contracts concluded by multinational firms in recent years, involving sophisticated items and large values ($20m. or more), may be briefly noted:

(i) Cie Electro-Mécanique (Fr) – electrical and electronic equipment for steel rolling mills, to Poland ($50m.);
(ii) Dowty (UK) – coal-mining equipment, to China ($29m.);
(iii) Dresser Industries (US) – compressors for petrochemical production, to the USSR ($27m.);
(iv) General Electric (US) – 65 modular gas turbine compressors, to the USSR ($250m.);
(v) General Motors (US) – 110 locomotives, to Yugoslavia ($38m.);
(vi) Gildemeister (FRG) – machinery and equipment for the manufacture of fuel apparatus for tractor diesel engines, to the USSR ($100m.);
(vii) International Harvester (US) – construction machinery and equipment, to the USSR ($100m.);
(viii) Karlstads Mekaniska Verkstad (Swe) – machinery and equipment for the manufacture of cellulose, to the USSR ($53m.);
(ix) Siemens (FRG) – special electrotechnical equipment for hot-rolling strip mills, to the USSR ($50m.);
(x) Svedala (Swe) – mining equipment, to the DPR of Korea ($20m.).

C. DELIVERIES OF COMPLETE INDUSTRIAL PLANTS

In several respects these deliveries are the most impressive form of exports to the East. They usually involve not only the most up-to-date machinery and equipment but also designs, licences, know-how and the training of specialists to manage and operate the plants. Although in the export of the type of items described in the preceding Section firms without multinational affiliations may play an important part, complete plants are almost exclusively supplied by multinational corporations. These orders involve large and varied resources, intricate technologies, a reliable network of suppliers, big thinking, flexible management and (preferably) long experience in the field. Multinational firms, of course, have a unique capacity on this score, and they have taken up the challenge of the offering opportunities. Examples of the more important plants from technical and economic standpoints, delivered or contracted for in the early 1970s, are given below:

(i) Asahi Chemical Industrial (Ja) – for the production of acrylonitrile monomer, to China ($30m.);
(ii) BASF (FRG) – for hydroxylamine (used in synthetic fibres), to the USSR ($12m.);
(iii) Büttner-Schilde-Hass (FRG) – for gypsum, to the USSR ($35m.);
(iv) Cie Centrale d'Etudes Industrielles (Fr) – for carbon sulphide, to Poland ($26m.);
(v) ENSA (Fr) – for polymers, to the USSR ($30m.);
(vi) General Tire & Rubber (US) – for tyres, to Romania ($35m.);
(vii) GEXA (Be) – for fertilizers, to Hungary ($26m.);
(viii) Linde (FRG) – for ethylene, to Hungary ($38m.);
(xi) Schöller-Bleckmann Stahlwerke (Au) – for yeast (4 plants), to Cuba ($25m.);
(x) Teijin (Ja) – for polyester fibres, to China ($19m.).

Some of the deals offered by the Socialist countries are so complex that even large Western companies have to form consortia in order to complete their projects. Thus the contract concluded in 1973 for the supply of a $25m. polypropylene plant to China involved C. Itoh & Co and Mitsui Petrochemicals, both of Japan. A larger project, a $46m. rubber manufacturing factory for the USSR, was undertaken by a West German consortium consisting of Krupp Maschinenfabriken (heading the consortium), H. Berstorff Maschinenbau, Bühler-Miag, Continental Gummiwerke, and Werner & Pfleiderer or Maschinenfabrik. In some cases even multinational consortia of multinational companies are formed, such as that for the delivery of a $45m. ammonia factory to Hungary during 1971-4 by Kellogg International (US), Coppe-Rust (Be), Norsk Hydro (No) and others.

There have also been larger projects involving either the construction of several costly plants or complex combines. The contracts worth over $50m., completed or signed in recent years, are listed in Table 7. Amongst some multinational corporations handling deals of this order, a new phrase is now current describing East–West transactions as 'super-business'. But even more spectacular are the schemes involving investment–production co-operation, some

TABLE 7 LARGE CONTRACTS FOR INDUSTRIAL PLANTS COMPLETED OR UNDERTAKEN BY WESTERN MULTINATIONAL FIRMS IN THE FIRST HALF OF THE 1970S

Western Supplier*	Type of Plant, or Product to be Manufactured (incl. the Importing Country†)	Approximate Value in $m.
Chemico (US)	Ammonia plants (4) (USSR)	200
Creusot-Loire (Fr)	Ammonia plants (2) (USSR)	210
Demag (FRG)	Cold steel strip mill (Ch)	250
ENI (It)	Petrochemical plants (6) (USSR)	900
Fiat (It)	Passenger cars (USSR)	800
Hurtey (Fr)	Ammonia (2) and urea (1) plants (Ch)	125
Hitachi (Ja)	Electric power plants (2) (Ch)	70
ICI (UK)	Ethylene (Hu)	80
Kawasaki Steel (Ja)	Metallurgical plants (4) (Ch)	380
M. W. Kellogg (US)	Ammonia plants (5) (Ch)	130
Marubeni-Ida (Ja)	Paper (USSR)	115
Mitsui & Co. (Ja)	Ammonia plants (8) (USSR)	400
Montedison (It)	Chemical plants (7) (USSR)	650
Parsons et Whittemore (Fr)	Pulp (USSR)	60
Petrocarbon Developments (UK)	Epichlorhydrin (Po)	60
Prinex (UK)	Cellulose triacetate (USSR)	65
Salzgitter (FRG)	Polyethylene (USSR)	70
F. L. Smidth (De)	Cement plants (2) (Po)	70
Technip (Fr)	Petrochemical complex (Ch)	300
Thyssen Stahlunion (FRG)	Wide steel strip mill (Yu)	100
Tokyo Shibaura Electric (Ja)	Air conditioners (USSR)	70
Toyo Boseki (Ja)	Polyester fibre complex (Po)	200
F. Uhde (FRG)	Polyester (USSR)	70
VÖEST-Alpine (Au)	Ethylene oxide (GDR)	55
Westinghouse Electric (US)	Nuclear power plant (Yu)	150

* For their multinational affiliations, see the Complete List and Index, pp. 197-232, and for further details of parent companies, Tables 2, 3 and 4, pp. 36-47.

† For country abbreviations, see footnote 3, Ch. 1, p. 2.

Sources: Based on daily and periodical literature published in Socialist and Western countries.

of which run into tens of billions of dollars. These are discussed in Chapter 5C, pp. 90-6.

At first the Socialist import programme was concentrated on traditional procurements in the pursuit of basic industrialization.

To some extent this is still continued, especially by the less-developed Socialist countries, such as China. But more recently their import strategy has been increasingly oriented towards the most up-to-date equipment and plants, such as those for the production of the most advanced chemicals. Thus in 1972 the European Socialist countries alone placed orders with Western firms for 160 complete chemical plants worth over $1,700m. (which represented 13 per cent of the chemical plants exported by Western countries). The composition of these plants by value was: oil refineries – 35 per cent, plants for the production of organic chemicals – 18 per cent, for inorganic chemicals – 10 per cent, for artificial fibres – 5 per cent, for industrial gases – 3 per cent and 13 per cent for other chemicals.[14] But even China, having recovered from her disruptive Cultural Revolution, has set out on a 'technological leap'. In 1973 alone she ordered 26 complete industrial plants from the West, valued at $1,240m., of which 18 were ammonia plants.[15]

D. IMPORTS FROM SOCIALIST COUNTRIES

Although the Socialist countries are large importers of embodied advanced technology from the West, some of them have achieved high technological levels in a number of fields. In several branches of industrial production they are equal to or ahead of the Western nations – particularly in metal-working machinery, metallurgical equipment, electric generators (especially magneto-hydrodynamic and turbo generators) and other electrical machinery, oil-drilling gear, communications equipment, welding apparatus, shipbuilding, certain types of aircraft and helicopters and nuclear equipment and fuels. These countries have become exporters of sophisticated items not only to less-developed areas but also to the industrialized West.

Many readers will be surprised to know that multinational corporations are now amongst the importers of Socialist-produced materials, tools, machinery, means of transport and even industrial plants. It is rather ironical that some of the items imported by them were at one stage on the Western strategic lists, barred from being

[14] *Rynki zagraniczne* (Foreign Markets), Warsaw, 26/8/1972, p. 6.
[15] *Rynki zagraniczne*, 28/3/1974, p. 3.

exported to the Socialist bloc. Western imports of Soviet oil have not only become substantial and taken for granted, but its marketing has also been facilitated by multinational corporations, including oil companies, and in fact it is the Soviets who dictate conditions now. Bomin (FRG), the ELF Group (Fr), ENI (It), Union Carbide (US), Veba (West Berlin) and other petrochemical multinationals have been eagerly buying Soviet oil and more recently pleading for larger deliveries. After the 30-year-old ban on Soviet oil was lifted in Britain in 1971, British Petroleum undertook to refine it for the Soviet-controlled distribution network 'Nafta' (with over 400 service stations in England). Royal Dutch-Shell acts as a Western outlet for Romanian oil and products. There are also larger schemes of co-operation under which Soviet oil and gas, and more recently Chinese oil, are marketed in the West by multinational companies (see Ch. 5C, pp. 91-6).

The Socialist countries have a very well-developed production capacity for metal-working machinery of practically every type, including automatic, semi-automatic, numerically-steered, laser-equipped and other special-purpose varieties. Czechoslovak, Hungarian, Polish, Soviet and Yugoslav metal-working machines and tools have been in use for years in the plants of such companies as ASEA (Swe), British Leyland (UK), British Steel (UK), Fiat (It), Ford Motor (US), General Electric (US), General Motors (US), Gutehoffnungshütte (FRG), Hitachi (Ja), Krupp (FRG), Mitsubishi (Ja), Montedison (It), Renault (Fr), Rheinstahl (FRG), Siemens (FRG), Toyota Motor (Ja), VÖEST-Alpine (Au), Volkswagen (FRG), and Volvo (Swe).

According to recent reports, General Electric (US) and General Motors have purchased Soviet electronic and computer components,[16] and Hungarian computer software and telecommunication equipment has been taken by AEG Telefunken (FRG), Cie Internationale pour l'Informatique (Fr), Philips (Ne) and Siemens (FRG); also from Hungary, Royal Dutch-Shell (Ne-UK) has purchased heavy-duty rubber conveyor belts and oil-drilling hoses and Volvo has bought containers.[17] Amongst the customers for the

[16] *Die Wirtschaft des Ostblocks* (Economies of the East), Bonn, 21/5/1974, p. 10; *Soviet News*, Soviet Embassy in London, 16/7/1974, p. 266.

[17] *Hungarian Exporter*, Budapest, 1/1974, p. 12; 2/1974, pp. 4-5; 5/1974, p. 10.

Czechoslovak unique spindleless spinning machines are such entities as Courtaulds (UK) and Frotierweberei Vossen (FRG),[18] and for the Polish textile dyeing machines – Kleinewefers Krefeld (FRG).[19] A wide range of technologically advanced machinery and equipment has been imported from the USSR: electric motors (including turbo-generators) – by Innocenti (It), Rauma-Repola (Fi), Technip (Fr) and J. M. Voith (Au);[20] metallurgical presses – by ASEA (Swe), Creusot-Loire (Fr), Pechiney-Ugine-Kuhlmann (Fr) and Wärtsilä (Fi);[21] mining equipment – by Gutehoffnungshütte (FRG) and Rheinstahl (FRG);[22] and welding machinery (including electro-slag welders) – by Cockerill (Be), Hitachi (Ja), Ishikawajima-Harima (Ja), Misubishi (Ja), Mitsui & Co (Ja) and Svenska Kullagerfabriken (Swe).[23]

Socialist means of transport is another object of the multinationals' interest evident in recent years. Ships have been purchased by Cie Maritime Belge (Be) and Norexim (No) from the USSR, by Gränges (Swe) from Yugoslavia, by Hapag-Lloyd (FRG), KNSM (Ne) and P & O (UK) from Poland and by Svenska-Lloyd (Swe) from the German DR, whilst Rockwell International (US) is marketing Soviet aircraft (YAK-40) in the USA.[24]

But there are also cases of industrial plants which have been modernized, equipped or fully constructed by the Socialist countries for multinational corporations, as is illustrated by the following examples:

(i) Oil refineries belonging to the ELF Group (Fr) have been modernized and expanded by the USSR.[25]
(ii) A rolling mill, owned by Hoesch (FRG) has been equipped with rolls by the USSR.[26]

[18] *Czechoslovak Foreign Trade*, Prague, 3/1972, p. 21.
[19] *Polish Foreign Trade*, Warsaw, 7/1973, p. 20.
[20] *Foreign Trade*, Moscow, 4/1972, pp. 36-7, and 6/1972, p. 16.
[21] *East–West Commerce*, London, 5/1973, p. 8; *Ekonomicheskaya gazeta*, 29/1974, p. 22.
[22] *Die Wirtschaft des Ostblocks*, 9/10/1973, p. 4; *Ekonomicheskaya gazeta*, 7/1974, p. 21.
[23] *Ekonomicheskaya gazeta*, 7/1974, p. 21; *Foreign Trade*, Moscow, 5/1972, p. 48.
[24] *Die Wirtschaft des Ostblocks*, 30/1/1974, p. 14; *East–West*, Brussels, 25/6/1970, p. 6 and 9/2/1972, p. 4; *East–West Commerce*, 4/1972, p. 5.
[25] *Foreign Trade*, 7/1972, p. 10.
[26] *Foreign Trade*, 12/1973, p. 51.

(iii) A complete automatic foundry has been delivered to Elin-Union (Au) by Poland.[27]

(iv) A complete electric smelting plant has been constructed for Svenska Kullagerfabriken (Swe) by the USSR.[28]

(v) Complete cold-rolling tube mills have been supplied by the USSR to the Japanese multinational companies – Kanematsu Gosho, Kobe Steel, Mitsubishi Metal, Sumitomo Metal Mining, and Tokyo Shibaura Electric (at least 15 mills in all), as well as to several multinationals in France, the FR of Germany, Sweden and the USA.[29]

(vi) A nuclear power station is being constructed for Imatra-Voima (Fi) at Loviisa by the USSR (to be completed in 1976). The value of the Soviet deliveries, including a 440 MW pressurized water reactor and two turbogenerators, is to exceed $50m. Another plant, in the Helsinki area and to be completed in the late 1970s, is under construction in co-operation with some Western multinational firms. The Soviets also signed a contract in 1974 for the supply to Wärtsilä (the largest Finnish shipyard) of a reactor for a nuclear icebreaker under construction. In addition the USSR has undertaken to supply enriched uranium to the Finnish companies, as well as to other multinationals and institutions in the FR of Germany (notably Rheinisch-Westfälisches Elektrizitätswerk), Japan (Tokyo Shibaura Electric), Austria, Canada, France, Spain and Sweden.[30]

Finally, it may be noted here that many Western multinational industrial and trading corporations have been importing a wide range of other products either for their own use or for resale or marketing in capitalist countries. Some of these imports may be reluctantly agreed-to counter-purchases, tied to their exports to the Socialist partners. Thus Honda Motor (Ja) and Nissan Motor (Ja) have purchased Chinese metal products, Marubeni-Ida (Ja) – Hungarian textiles, Morganite Resistors (UK) – Hungarian electronic equipment, C. Itoh & Co. – Chinese silk and other textiles, Winn Industries (UK), through its associate company, Neotype – Soviet

[27] *Polish Foreign Trade*, 8/1973, p. 20.
[28] *Rynki zagraniczne*, 29/12/1973, p. 10.
[29] *Foreign Trade*, 6/1972, pp. 32-4.
[30] *Die Wirtschaft des Osblocks*, 19/3/1974, p. 8; *Eastern Europe Report*, 15/6/1973, p. 167; *Minerals Yearbook 1970*, Washington, US Bureau of Mines, 1972, vol. I, p. 1151; *Planovoe khoziaistvo* (Planned Economy), Moscow, 5/1974, p. 85.

printing machines, Occidental Petroleum (US) – Soviet chromium and nickel, Rank Xerox (UK) – Soviet electric motors, Siemens (FRG) – Hungarian telephone equipment and Czechoslovak teleprinters, Toyo Menka Kaisha (Ja) – Czechoslovak textiles, and United States Steel (US) – Chinese tin.

The following multinational trading companies have been handling the distribution of Socialist products in Western countries: Ataka & Co. (Ja) – Soviet metal-working machinery, Atalanta (US) – Chinese foods, Eurintrade (Be) – Soviet metal products and machines, La Salle Machine Tool (US) – Soviet machine tools, Satra (US) – Soviet cars, hydrofoils and tractors, Sears Roebuck Overseas (US) – Eastern European and Soviet consumer goods and raw materials, Time Products (UK) – Soviet watches, Tokyo Boeki (Ja) – Eastern European and Soviet metal-working machinery. Up to 1973, De Beers (the South African diamond concern) handled the marketing of Soviet diamonds through its network in the capitalist world; however in that year the Soviets established a joint venture, 'Russalmaz', in Belgium for the purpose (see Ch. 6B, p. 105).

Goods from the Socialist countries may also be imported by Western multinational companies as a consequence of production and marketing co-operation or joint ventures (for details, see Chs. 5 and 6, pp. 79-114).

4 Licences

A. FROM DIVERGING TO CONVERGING INTERESTS

MULTINATIONAL corporations have traditionally been noted for their predilection for industrial secrecy and jealously guarded patents.[1] Their attitude to the Socialist countries for a long time was generally marked by hostility and grievance, which was conditioned not only by ideological sentiments but particularly by the Socialist poaching of their technology without permission or appropriate remuneration (see Ch. 1A, p. 3). With the steeply rising costs of research and development (R & D),[2] and the Socialist export drive and even the dumping of goods produced on the basis of Western technology, their disgust became the more intense.

To orthodox Marxists, scientific and technical knowledge amounts to a social heritage, and consequently royalties to inventors and particularly patent-holding enterprises are socially unacceptable – as they represent a form of exploitation and lead to inequalities of income and to monopolies. The practical expression of this view was found in the appropriation of Western inventions in many cases without due compensation, and this principle was systematically

[1] According to a Socialist source, the proportion of the capitalist countries' export protected by patents and trade marks was 50 per cent in 1920 and rose to 75 per cent by the mid-1960s. M. Mazur, ('Foreign Licences and Know-How in Economic Development'), *Gospodarka planowa* (Planned Economy), Warsaw, 4/1974, p. 267.

[2] e.g., according to one Western authority on the history and philosophy of science (D. J. de Solla Price, *Science since Babylon*, New York, Yale U.P., 1961, pp. 120-21), to double the number of scientists the supporting staff must be increased 8 times; to increase the GNP by 3 per cent, a 10 per cent increase in the R & D outlay is essential, i.e. the cost of R & D rises as the cube of the resultant production. According to a Socialist source [A. Bodnar and B. Zahn, *Rewolucja naukowo-techniczna a socjalizm* (Scientific and Technical Revolution and Socialism), Warsaw, KiW, 1971, p. 154], the cost relation research: development, increased from 1:3 in the 1950s to 1:10 in the 1960s; similar cost ratios appear to apply to the Socialist economies, too (see pp. 73-4).

applied in the intra-Comecon transfer of technology under the 'Sofia Rules' introduced in 1949. It may be observed here in passing that before the early 1960s the Socialist countries were essentially preoccupied with basic industrialization, and at lower levels of economic development the need for sophisticated technology is not urgent. In retrospect it appears that the extent of their exploitation of Western technological achievements had not been as widespread as had been implied in popular claims in the West.

However, Socialist attitudes began to change in the late 1950s.[3] Most of these countries were entering higher stages of economic development, and they were further prodded by the scientific and technical revolution and the need for the utilization of technological progress as a source of economic growth. They have gradually reconciled themselves to paying for Western licences, treating it as a reasonable contribution to covering a portion of the R & D involved. In 1965 the USSR acceded to the International Union for the Protection of Industrial Property and in 1973 to the International Union for the Protection of Literary and Artistic Works, and other European Socialist countries (which had joined them before the Communist takeover) have decided to adhere to the international conventions more strictly.

This departure from previous attitudes and practices has been partly conditioned by the desire to improve relations with the West and Western business in particular, and partly – no doubt – by the fact that these Socialist nations also have reached high technological levels in some fields and have become anxious to sell their patents to capitalist countries. To place the acquisition as well as sale of licences on a systematic basis, special enterprises have been established for the purpose or (in the case of Romania) designated existing foreign trade enterprises have been given the responsibility: in Bulgaria – *Tekhnika*, Czechoslovakia – *Polytechna*, the German DR – *Limex*, Hungary – *Licencia*, *Nikex*, *Novex* and *Tesco*, Poland – *Polservice*, Romania – *Industrialimport* and *Romchim*, the USSR – *Litsensintorg* and in Yugoslavia – *Patentcentar*.

In fact, the Comecon countries have gone further and since 1967 have been increasingly applying the commercial principle in the

[3] The Yugoslav quest for Western licences began in the early 1950s. Special legislation was passed for the purpose in 1954.

exchange of technology amongst themselves. But it is significant that they had begun this practice some 5-10 years earlier in their relations with the capitalist world. The fact that these countries have to pay for the licences obtained from other Comecon members has further been prompting them to turn to the West.

In contrast to the European Socialist countries, China, the DPR of Korea and the DR of Vietnam have not been as eager to acquire, and pay for, Western (especially American) licences, which can be largely explained by their lower stage of economic development and stricter adherence to orthodox Marxist thinking. However, even they appear to be changing their attitudes, in practical terms at least.[4] In 1972 China agreed to receive and pay for the licence provided by Bechtel (US) through the Japanese Taisei Construction Co. She also reached a royalty agreement with the Standard Oil Co. of Ohio (US) in 1973 for the production of acrylonitrile a basic material for synthetic fibre) and in 1974 with Chemische Werke Hüls (FRG) for the manufacture of ethylene oxide.[5]

In these departures from previous policies, the Socialist countries have met with remarkable co-operation from Western multinational corporations – which are not only willing but, indeed, anxious to sell licences and know-how. The corporations' response is governed by cold business calculation. Firstly the marketing of goods in the Socialist centrally planned economies is often complicated and uncertain. This is particularly so in the case of consumer goods for the import of which official priorities are usually very low. Thus selling licences may be a sensible alternative to the direct export of products.

Secondly, in contrast to previous practice, the Socialist countries are increasingly inclined to buy licences on the understanding that payment will be made in accordance with the size of the output sold, and such output may be distributed in other Socialist markets as

[4] None of the three countries, plus Mongolia and Albania were, at the time of writing, members of the International Union for the Protection of Industrial Property or the International Union for the Protection of Literary and Artistic Works.

[5] *China Trade Report*, Hong Kong, 8/1972, p. 5 and 5/1973, p. 9; *Euro-Commerz* (Euro-Commerce), West Berlin, Jan, 1974, p. 22. For country abbreviations, see footnote 3, p. 2, and for foreign affiliations of the companies – the Complete List and Index, pp. 197-232 (further details of the larger parent multinationals can be found in Tables 2, 3 and 4, pp. 36-47).

well. In effect, royalties may be quite substantial. Thirdly, sales of licences often lead to larger consequential exports of materials, components, machinery and equipment – of which the Western licensor, or its affiliates, is likely to be the only supplier. According to Business International, in 98 per cent of cases (by value) sales of Western licences to the Eastern European countries are followed by other sales.[6] In Poland the purchase of a licence leads to imports worth 6-8 times the original outlay on the licence.[7]

Finally, the corporations are not too much concerned about the loss of their technological lead. In many cases they sell only relatively dated technology, and furthermore – owing to their cumbersome institutional set-up and bureaucratic procedures – the Socialist countries are rather inert in applying the acquired licences in production. To start with, experience shows that it takes two years on the average to negotiate a licence sale to a Socialist country.[8] But this is only the beginning, and a sequence of delays usually follows. Thus in Hungary, the lag of time between the acquisition of a licence and its practical application ranges from one to six years;[9] in Poland, of the 87 licences purchased in 1967, only 14 were utilized within a year, 11 – in two years, 23 – in 3-5 years and 3 – in 6 or more years,[10] and similar delays have been reported in Bulgaria and Romania.[11] At the same time, using the proceeds from the licence sale, the corporations finance their next round of R & D, so that they can still steal a march on the Socialist licensees.

Licences have come to occupy an important place in international economic relations. The total number of licence contracts now concluded annually is about 40,000, valued at $2,000m., and trade in licences has been rising about three times as fast as merchandise trade. Taking the Socialist countries as a whole, their share in world licence turnover is about 7 per cent.[12] This percentage is low, considering that these countries' share in world trade is 12

[6] *Eastern Europe Report*, Geneva, 28/12/1973, p. 386.
[7] M. Mazur, op. cit., p. 268.
[8] *Eastern Europe Report*, 28/12/1973, p. 386.
[9] *Figyelö* (Economic Observer), Budapest, 1/3/1972, p. 4.
[10] Z. Madej, *Nauka i rozwój gospodarczy* (Science and Economic Development), Warsaw, PWE, 1970, p. 180.
[11] *Eastern Europe Report*, 11/8/1972, p. 35; *Finanţe şi credit* (Finance and Credit), Bucharest, 12/1971, pp. 21-2.
[12] M. Mazur, op. cit., pp. 270-71.

per cent and in the world's industrial output over 35 per cent. The low percentage can be explained by several factors, viz. many Socialist countries (especially the Asian members) are still in early stages of economic development, much of the technology within Comecon is still exchanged on a free basis and, in general, there are still strict controls over imports involving the expenditure of hard currencies, and moreover the export of Socialist licences is small.

However, the Socialist countries' trade in licences has been growing 3-4 times faster than their visible trade. In relation to the West they are, naturally, much more important as importers than exporters of licences. As importers they mostly turn to multinational corporations, but more recently they have been selling licences to them, too. We shall examine these dealings in the following two sections.

B. THE SALES OF LICENCES TO SOCIALIST COUNTRIES

The Socialist purchases of Western licences began in the 1950s but they have assumed greater proportions more recently – especially since the late 1960s – so that more licences were acquired over the period 1970-5 than in the preceding 15 years. Yugoslavia has been the largest purchaser (about 500), followed by Czechoslovakia, Hungary, Poland and the USSR (250-300 each). The annual proceeds to the West from these sales in the mid-1970s were in the order of $500m. The total number of licences sold by the West to the East over the period 1960-75 exceeded the figure of 2,000, to which total multinational firms (including their affiliates) contributed three-quarters. The purposes for which the licences are sold to the East now cover a very wide range, viz. metallurgy, machine-building, means of transport, electrical engineering, communications equipment, building materials and consumer goods. The following general observations on the trends are worth noting.

At first the Socialist licence quest was concentrated on heavy industry, heavy inorganic chemicals and heavy means of transport. But then the emphasis shifted to the technologically most dynamic industries producing automatic metal-working machinery, lighter chemicals (pharmaceuticals, plastics, synthetic fibres), motor vehicles (trucks, buses, passenger cars), aircraft and electronic equipment (control systems, computers, electronic data processing). The second significant tendency concerns the relation between producer and consumer goods. The overwhelming emphasis on the production of capital equipment in the past has in recent years been relaxed somewhat in favour of consumer goods. This has been most noticeable in Yugoslavia, Hungary and Czechoslovakia, where the role of the market mechanism is greater and the authorities are more sympathetic to the consumer. Similarly, whilst originally licences were directed primarily towards import-replacement, more recently increasing attention has been given to export-oriented production.

Some of the best-known licences provided by the multinationals to the Socialist countries cover a number of related processes and may include many sub-licences. Examples may be given by reference to the motor vehicle industry. The manufacture of passenger cars in Bulgaria and Romania is based on licences supplied by Renault (Fr), in Poland and the USSR – by Fiat (It) and in Yugoslavia – by Fiat and Volkswagen (FRG).[13] Buses in Poland are produced on the basis of licences supplied by Berliet (Fr) and British Leyland (UK) and (some) Soviet and Yugoslav trucks – by Daimler Benz (FRG). Deliveries of complete plants often require the supply of licences and know-how, which may yield licensors substantial income. Thus the $29m. contract signed in 1973 by a Japanese company for the construction of a synthetic fibre plant also involved $8m. worth of technology (for the production of acronitrile) provided by the Standard Oil Co. of Ohio (US).[14]

Following are examples of licences sold by the multinationals in other technologically dynamic branches of industry. Aerospatiale (Fr) in conjunction with Westland Helicopters (UK) have supplied technology to Yugoslavia for the manufacture of helicopters, British Leyland (UK) and Henschel (FRG) – to Poland for small aircraft whilst Boeing (US) has sold a licence to the USSR for the produc-

[13] According to recent reports, Volkswagen may also supply licences and know-how to China and Romania.

[14] C. H. Phillips, 'Breakthrough in U.S. – China Business Relations', *Columbia Journal of World Business*, Winter 1973, p. 93.

tion of passenger aircraft doors. The manufacture of communications equipment, highly sophisticated electronic components and even computers is in many cases based on Western licences. Cie Générale des Constructions Téléphoniques (Fr) has sold a licence to Poland for producing modern cross-bar telephone exchanges, Standard Telephone & Cables (UK) – to Czechoslovakia for an off-line transmission device for the automatic detection and correction of errors and Philips (Ne) – to Poland for television set transformers, Ferranti (UK) – also to Poland for integrated circuits and International Computers (UK) – to Czechoslovakia for computer-controlled fast printers. Medium third-generation computers are produced in Romania partly on the basis of technology supplied by Cie Internationale pour l'Informatique (Fr).

Other examples of licences supplied by the multinationals in recent years are given in Table 8. The reader will note the wide range of technology so provided and the calibre of the licensors.

There is little doubt that the licences acquired from the Western companies are of great technological and economic benefit to the Socialist countries. Thus the proportion of Hungarian machinery exported to the West which is manufactured with the aid of Western licences is 22-25 per cent.[15] In Poland nearly one-tenth of industrial output is produced on the basis of Western licences, and experience has shown that expenditure on licences yields export earnings 4.6 times larger.[16] In the USSR the total benefit accruing to the economy from foreign licences is 10 times or more the original outlay on them.[17]

The acquisition of a licence from a large company often involves a technological package deal. It may include the provision of technical documentation, models and specimens, know-how, the training of specialists (in the licensor's plant) and technical aid and supervision in the construction of the necessary facilities. Such coincidentals not only reduce the technological gap but also save domestic resources. It appears that technology obtained through Western licences, rather than from domestic R & D, accelerates technological

[15] T. Sebestyen, ('Problems of the Acquisition of Licences and Know-how'), *Figyelö*, 6/2/1974, p. 1.

[16] M. Mazur, op. cit., p. 272.

[17] M. L. Gorodisski, *Litsentsii vo vneshnei torgovle SSSR* (Licences in Soviet Foreign Trade), Moscow, MO, 1972, p. 20.

TABLE 8 LICENCES SOLD BY WESTERN MULTINATIONAL FIRMS TO SOCIALIST COUNTRIES IN THE FIRST HALF OF THE 1970S

Western Licensor*	Industrial Application in the Licensee Country†
Alsthom (Fr)	Insulation for electrical rotary machines (Hu)
British Petroleum (UK)	Lubricating oils (Po)
Brown, Boveri (Swi)	High-tension switches (Hu)
Chemische Werke Hüls (FRG)	Ethylene oxide (Ch)
Deutsche Babcock & Wilcox (FRG)	Steam boilers (Ro)
Girling (UK)	Shock absorbers (Hu)
Globe Union (US)	Batteries (Yu)
B. F. Goodrich (US)	Tyres (Yu)
ICI (UK)	Powdered pigments (Hu)
Marubeni-Ida (Ja)	Synthetic yarns (Po)
Perkins Engines (UK)	Medium diesel engines (Yu)
Poclain (Fr)	Hydraulic excavators (Yu)
Rubery Owen (UK)	Container handlers (Bu)
Saab-Scania (Swe)	Welding machines (Yu)
San Giorgio (It)	Automatic machine tools (Hu)
Siemens (FRG)	Recovery of pulverized paints (Hu)
Singer (US)	Sewing machines (Po)
SNIA Viscosa (It)	Nylon cord for tyres (Po)
Sulzer (Swi)	Marine diesel engines (Bu)
Svenska Fläktfabriken (Swe)	Pulp equipment (Po)
Teijin (Ja)	High-tensile nylon thread (Cz)
Toray Industries (Ja)	Nylon (Po)
Toyo Engineering (Ja)	Ethylene (Cz)
Universal Oil Products (US)	Ethyl benzine (USSR)
Wascator (Swe)	Washing machines (Yu)

* For their multinational affiliations, see the Complete List and Index, pp. 197-232, and for further details of parent companies, Tables 2, 3 and 4, pp. 36-47.

† For country abbreviations, see footnote 3, Ch. 1, p. 2.

Sources: Based on daily and periodical literature published in Socialist and Western countries.

progress in the industries where it is applied by 7-8 years.[18]

As in the West, the cost of R & D in the Socialist countries is very high. According to an East German economist, the doubling of scientific knowledge necessitates a sixteen-fold increase in the number of research workers and a thirty-fold increase in the total

[18] A. Bodnar and B. Zahn, *Rewolucja naukowo-techniczna a socjalizm* (Scientific and Technical Revolution and Socialism), Warsaw, KiW, 1971, p. 158.

R & D outlays.[19] A 'horizontal' transfer of technology from the West – as distinct from a 'vertical' flow based on domestic R & D – represents a saving of resources. The resources so economized may be devoted to the further perfection of the technology acquired or to other uses.

C. PURCHASES OF SOCIALIST LICENCES

Although the Socialist countries are mainly buyers of licences from the West, in recent years they have also become sellers. By the mid-1970s they had sold about 700 licences mostly involving minor specialized (but not necessarily of low sophistication) inventions, not in the same class as those purchased from the West. To the total figure, Czechoslovakia contributed more than one-half, followed by the USSR, Hungary, the German DR, Poland and Yugoslavia (in that order), the remaining Socialist countries playing a minor role.

Compared with Czechoslovakia (and Yugoslavia), the USSR is a recent entrant to the Western licence market. Western visitors to the Trade Fair in Frankfurt/M in June 1970 were startled to see the USSR's offer of 400 licences for sale; so far the Soviets have sold licences to firms in at least 35 countries.[20] There are now several firms in Western countries handling the sale of Soviet licences, such as Finsilta (It), Heine Brothers (Australia), Patent Management (US) and Sofracop (Fr).

The sophistication and magnitude of the inventions made in the more advanced Socialist countries have been increasing rapidly. Taking the seven European Comecon countries (i.e. without Albania and Yugoslavia), their average receipts per licence sold to the capitalist world in the 1960s was only one-eleventh of what they paid per purchased licence, but by the early 1970s this ratio had improved to one-quarter.[21] The annual earnings from the sale of

[19] G. M. Dobrov, *Aktuelle Probleme der Wissenschaftswissenschaft* (Current Problems of Scientific Knowledge), East Berlin, Dietz Verlag, 1970, pp. 8-9.

[20] *East-West*, 8/7/1970, p. 5; *Sotsialisticheskaya industriya* (Socialist Industry), Moscow, 15/3/1974, p. 2.

[21] R. Osterland, ('More Intensive Exchange of Scientific and Technical Achievements through Integration'), *Die Wirtschaft* (The Economy), East Berlin, 37/1972, p. 27.

Socialist licences to the West in the mid-1970s amounted to $40m. (compared with some $500m. spent on Western licences).

The fields in which the Socialist countries have technology for sale which is of interest to Western firms include above all the following:

(i) *Metallurgical processes* – Bulgaria, Czechoslovakia, Hungary, Poland, Romania, the USSR and Yugoslavia.
(ii) *Electrical engineering* – Bulgaria, Czechoslovakia, Hungary, Poland, the USSR and Yugoslavia.
(iii) *Metal-working machinery* – Czechoslovakia, the German DR, Hungary, the USSR and Yugoslavia.
(iv) *Textile machinery* – Bulgaria, Czechoslovakia, the German DR and Hungary.
(v) *Pharmaceuticals* – Czechoslovakia, the German DR, Hungary and the USSR.
(vi) *Petrochemicals and other chemicals* – the German DR, Romania, the USSR and Yugoslavia.
(vii) *Food and feed processing* – Bulgaria, Hungary, Poland and the USSR.
(viii) *Medical apparatus* – Czechoslovakia, Hungary, Poland and the USSR.
(ix) *Soldering and welding* – Hungary and the USSR.
(x) *Coal mining and processing* – Hungary and the USSR.

Most of the buyers of Socialist licences are medium or smaller, independent firms. Multinational corporations have acquired about one-tenth of the total number of 700 – compared with three-quarters of the 2,000 sold to the Socialist countries. By value, the multinationals' acquisition from the East is probably less than 5 per cent of what they have sold to the East, the proportion being much higher in the case of Czechoslovakia, Hungary, the USSR and Yugoslavia while in the case of the German DR it is probably as high as 30 per cent (or may be even more).

A sample list of the Socialist licences purchased by the Western multinationals is given in Table 9. Some of these licences, as well as others not included in the table, represent inventions of major consequence which have been acquired by more than one firm. Thus the Bulgarian licence for the electrolytic refining of copper at high current densities has been purchased by firms in Italy, Japan, Spain,

Sweden and the USA (not to mention such less-developed countries as Brazil, Chile, India, Peru and Zambia). The highly successful Czechoslovak invention of a spindleless spinning machine has also been acquired by (in addition to San Giorgio) Toyota (Ja) and by firms in 20 other countries. The Hungarian process for the extraction of protein from grasses for animal feeding has also been bought by Alfa-Laval (Swe), Anhydro (De), Schöller-Bleckmann (Au) and others. The Polish method for forging crankshafts, purchased by Sulzer, has also been in use in other firms in the FR of Germany, Japan and the United Kingdom.

The Soviet technology for liquid self-hardening mixtures, used in the production of casting rods and moulds, has been adopted by Kobe Steel (Ja) and companies in Denmark, France, the FR of Germany, Italy, Sweden, the United Kingdom, the United States and elsewhere. Another major Soviet invention, for the evaporation cooling of blast furnaces, has been most successfully applied not only by Kobe Steel but also by Broken Hill Pty (Australia), Gutehoffnungshütte Sterkrade (FRG) and in such countries as Belgium, Canada, France, Italy, Luxemburg, the United Kingdom and the United States. The metal used in the construction of steel frames for the Anglo-French *Concorde* supersonic airliner is produced on the basis of a Soviet licence for electroslag refining used not only by Cie Electro-Mécanique (Fr) but also by Creusot-Loire (Fr), Svenska Kullagerfabriken (Swe) and others.

The Socialist countries attach a good deal of importance to the sale of their technology to the multinationals and other firms in the West. They are prompted not only by their desire to earn hard currency but also by broader considerations of a psychological and political nature. They are anxious to correct the view prevalent in the West that the Socialist countries are technologically stagnant. In fact the ambitions of Socialist leaders go further, in their determination to demonstrate that socialism is not only a superior social system but it also has the capacity – now that high priority is assigned to technology – to catch up and surpass capitalism technologically. A Soviet specialist in the field noted a few years ago:

> Indeed, in the economic competition between the two systems, scientific and technological progress in the Socialist countries not only

TABLE 9 SOCIALIST LICENCES PURCHASED BY WESTERN MULTINATIONAL FIRMS

Western Licensee*	Socialist Licensor Country	Industrial Application
Anger Plastic VM. (Au)	USSR	Double-walled plastic tubes
Ataka & Co. (Ja)	German DR	Steel bar fagotting machines
Bausch & Lomb (US)	Cz'slovakia	Soft contact lenses
Bignier-Schmidt-Laurent (Fr)	German DR	Contact plates for oil processing
British Steel (UK)	Bulgaria	Protective coating for graphite electrodes
Brown, Boveri (Swi)	Romania	'Vulcan' type of pumps
Chesterfield Tubes (UK)	Hungary	Large steel cylinders
Cie Electro-Mécanique (Fr)	USSR	Electroslag refining
Continental Engineering (Ne)	Hungary	Sorbitol (for vitamin C)
Creusot-Loire (Fr)	Poland	Carousel furnaces
Demag (FRG)	USSR	Metal-cutting machines
Elanco (It)	Hungary	Respiratory diseases medicine
Ingersoll Milling Machine (US)	USSR	Graphite electrodes
Joy Manufacturing (US)	USSR	Pulsed water-flow gauges
Kabel und Metalwerke H. (FRG)	Hungary	Soldering of aluminium
Klöckner-Humboldt-Deutz (FRG)	USSR	Extraction of non-ferrous metals
Kobe Steel (Ja)	USSR	Cooling of blast furnaces
Mannesmann (FRG)	Cz'slovakia	Automatic mandrel rod changers
Messer Griesheim (FRG)	USSR	Arc steel tube welding
Mitsubishi (Ja)	Hungary	Extracting proteins from grasses
Nissan Motor (Ja)	Cz'slovakia	Rotary stencil printing of textiles
Reynolds Metals (US)	USSR	Casting of aluminium ingots
San Giorgio (It)	Cz'slovakia	Spindleless spinning machines
Sulzer (Swi)	Poland	Forging of crankshafts
Utvecklings (Swe)	Hungary	Improving low-carbon steels

* For their multinational affiliations, see the Complete List and Index, pp. 197-232, and for further details of parent companies, Tables 2, 3 and 4, pp. 36-47. Country abbreviations are explained in footnote 3, Ch. 1, p. 2.

Sources. Based on daily and periodical literature published in Socialist and Western countries.

> strengthens socialism, it also has an international political and social resonance.[22]

Two Polish economists further asserted:

> Utilizing their social and political potential, it is certain that the Socialist countries will develop such technological, economic and social levels of attainment as will confirm the superiority of socialism even in the era of the post-industrial society. They will evolve a socialist industrial civilization with high cultural values, distinct from those under capitalism.[23]

These considerations largely explain the fact that the number of patents registered by the Socialist countries in the capitalist world has more than doubled since the early 1960s. In the mid-1970s their annual applications exceeded 20,000, of which one-half was actually granted. These figures are about twice as high as those representing patents applied for by capitalist countries and granted in the East.[24] Furthermore a good deal of publicity is given in Socialist literature to the sale of licences to capitalist firms, particularly if well-known Western multinational corporations are involved.

[22] A. Pokrovsky, 'Some Sociological Aspects of the Scientific Technological Revolution in the Capitalist World', *International Affairs*, Moscow, 2/1971, p. 30.

[23] A. Bodnar and B. Zahn, op. cit., p. 233.

[24] Author's estimate based partly on K. Jankowski, *Polityka patentowa w krajach RWPG* (Patent Policy in the Comecon Countries), Warsaw, CIINTE, 1970, pp. 12, 14.

5 Industrial Co-operation

A. THE ECONOMIC BACKGROUND

INDUSTRIAL co-operation is a rapidly expanding sphere of East–West economic and technological collaboration and it is a more systematic and lasting form of inter-enterprise dealings than conventional trading relations. This association consists in reciprocally matching or joint pursuits in such fields of interest to the partner enterprises as research and development (R & D), know-how, investment, production, the construction of projects, the training of specialists and marketing.

The development of these ties dates since the early 1960s (since the mid-1950s in the case of Yugoslavia). They have proved most successful in those branches of industry or in the case of those products where technologies or manufacturing processes are horizontally or vertically segmentable, so that different phases of industrial activities can take place in separate locations. This co-operation is now facilitated by several specialized agencies and enterprises in the East as well as in the West (such as Inter-Co-operation in Hungary and Maxwell Stamp Associates in Britain) and at the official levels co-operative imports have in many cases been exempt from tariffs and quota restrictions under bilateral agreements. Industrial co-operation holds great potential for further development, and the Secretariat of the Economic Commission for Europe has recently recommended the creation of an East–West Industrial Co-operation Centre to perform a clearing-house function for current and prospective partners at the enterprise level.[1]

The total number of East–West co-operation agreements concluded by the mid-1970s amounted to about 1,700. On the Eastern side Hungary, Yugoslavia and Poland have been interested most in

[1] *Analytical Report on Industrial Co-operation among ECE Countries*, Geneva, ECE, 9/4/1973, Annex 2, p. 32.

this co-operation (with some 600, 400 and 300 agreements respectively), followed by Czechoslovakia, the USSR, Bulgaria and the German DR. In the past, other Socialist countries showed little interest but according to recent reports China appears to be entering this field too.[2] The annual value of deliveries arising out of East–West industrial co-operation agreements is probably now around $1,000m.

In these agreements multinational corporations figure most prominently. Together with their affiliates, they account for four-fifths of the total number. The initiative usually comes from the Socialist side – mostly state administrative or trading agencies, and now increasingly the enterprises concerned. But more recently the multinationals have in many cases made the first move. On the whole, the latter are in a stronger bargaining position owing to their superior technology, financial resources and marketing channels in hard-currency areas.

The multinationals' interest has increased particularly since the late 1960s and their representatives are now the most active participants in East–West conferences on industrial co-operation. Thus at the East–West Congress of Industrial Co-operation held in Warsaw in April 1974, of the 500 participants over 250 represented Western multinational companies including such entities as AEG Telefunken (FRG), Alfa-Laval (Swe), Berliet (Fr), Bristol-Myers (US), Corn Products (US), Dow Chemicals (US), Du Pont (US), Elin-Union (Au), Fiat (It), General Motors (US), Gildemeister (FRG), Heurtey (Fr), Honeywell (US), Metallgesellschaft (FRG), Monsanto (US), Nissho-Iwai (Ja), Oetker (FRG), Pepsi-Cola (US), Schöller-Bleckmann (Au), Singer (US), Svenska Kullagerfabriken (Swe), Thomson-CSF (Fr), United Aircraft (US), VÖEST-Alpine

[2] In the early 1970s China apparently had a number of co-operative arrangements with several Japanese companies and in 1972 she negotiated a co-operation agreement with Toyo Kogyo for the manufacture of rotary engines. In 1974 it was reported that she was negotiating with the United Aircraft Corporation (US) for the purchase of a fleet of medium-heavy military helicopters for (Sino–Soviet) border patrol duties and/or a possible production co-operation agreement; previously the UAC had sold $40m. worth of jet engines and spare parts for Boeing 707 and for both transactions the US Government had granted export licences. *China Trade Report*, Hong Kong, 1/1972, p. 9; 1/1974, p. 6 and 2/1974, p. 4; C. H. Phillips, 'Breakthrough in U.S. – China Business Relations', *Columbia Journal of World Business*, Winter 1973, p. 93.

(Au), Volvo (Swe) and Westinghouse Electric (US).[3]

The branches of industry in which inter-enterprise co-operation has assumed considerable importance are (roughly in this order of incidence): engineering – mechanical, electrical, electronic, metal-working machinery – chemicals, motor vehicles, metals and measurement apparatus; in contrast to their previous attitude, the Socialist countries are increasingly inclined to include consumer goods (including consumer durables and other luxuries) as the object of co-operation.[4] All these branches of industry are noted for rapidly changing technologies and the most dynamic development, and they indicate the direction of Socialist interest in Western technology. Up to about 1970 co-operation agreements were typically negotiated for 2-5 years. But more recently there has been a tendency for the agreements to extend over 4-8 years (whilst 10 years and more are not unknown), and in many cases the association is continued by the renewal of the expired contracts.

B. TYPES AND CASES

The precise form of the co-operative relations in individual cases is governed by a variety of factors and circumstances – in particular the level of technology each partner commands, the size of each partner, the types of product(s) involved, and their bargaining power in general. Although these forms are still in the process of evolution, it is possible to distinguish between the following contrasting types.

(a) Short-term and Long-term Co-operation. Some co-operation agreements may cover only a particular scheme, such as the joint development and testing of a prototype or the construction of a plant, and once the undertaking is completed the association is

[3] *Rynki zagraniczne* (Foreign Markets), Warsaw, 2/4/1974, p. 3 and 6/4/1974, p. 1. For country abbreviations, see footnote 3, p. 2, and for the extent of foreign affiliations of the companies – the Complete List and Index, pp. 197-232 (further details of the larger parent companies, Tables 2, 3 and 4, pp. 36-47).

[4] According to a study carried out by the Economic Commission for Europe, covering East–West European industrial co-operation in 1972, the percentage distribution was as follows: mechanical engineering (excluding machine tools) – 22.3, chemicals – 19.3, transport equipment – 17.3, electrical engineering and electronics – 16.3, machine tools – 8.4 and other (agriculture, metallurgy, light industry and miscellaneous) – 16.4. *Analytical Report on Industrial Co-operation Among ECE Countries*, 14/3/1973, p. 7.

terminated. On the other hand, the partnership may assume a continuous form extending over several years or indefinitely. Production co-operation is usually of this type. Thus the contract signed in 1974 between Schlömann (FRG) and Škodaexport (Cz) for the joint provision of technology and installations for a high-capacity steel billet mill in Katowice, Poland, illustrates the former while the agreement concluded in 1973 between Oxy Metal Finishing International (Swi) and Metalexport (Po) for the manufacture of galvanized metal and plastic coverings for cars and bicycles is an example of the latter.

(b) Co-operation in the Early and in the Advanced Stages of Industrial Activities. The partner enterprises may agree on the simpler forms of co-operation such as mutual aid in R & D, or the training of specialists, or specialization in and mutual deliveries of, a simple material or component. Alternatively, co-operation may be directed to the advanced stages of production necessitating sophisticated technology and involving sub-assembling or the assembling of the complete product. The agreement entered into by Tokyo Shibaura Electric (Ja) with CKD Blansko (Cz) in 1973 for the development and design of turbines is an example of an earlier stage whilst that by Logabax (Fr) with Metronex (Po), also in 1973, for the manufacture of mosaic key printers for digital computers – of a higher stage of production.

(c) Input–Output Co-operation. This is about the most common basis. One co-operant supplies the initial equipment (and perhaps credits) and subsequently certain components, both usually of an advanced technical content, and perhaps a licence and know-how. The other partner provides buildings, most raw materials and labour and it also produces some components. The first partner is then paid in the form of the sub-assemblies or the complete product. An illustration is afforded by the agreement signed in 1973 between Suntory (Ja) and Vinipex (Bu) for the provision of technology and the construction of a malt factory in Bulgaria and the subsequent export of malt to Japan. The agreement between Waagner-Biro (Au) and Trans-Elektra (Hu) exemplifies a case where production (of steam power plant equipment) is carried on on the basis of advanced technology developed by the Socialist partner.

(d) Uni-Directional, Bi-Directional and Multi-Directional Co-

operation. The association may merely consist in sub-contracting – involving the production of a component or construction of a portion of a plant as commissioned by the chief contractor. This is only an early stage, technically not accepted as co-operation and the Socialist countries resent being reduced to sub-contractors – particularly when simpler products or technologies are involved. However, most common now is bilateral co-operation with reciprocal deliveries of technology and components. In some cases, more than two partners may co-operate in the manufacture of a complete product. Maschinenfabrik-Augsburg-Nürnberg (FRG) and Györ Automotive Works (Hu) co-operate in the bilateral sense in producing large trucks. A quadrilateral type of co-operation is represented by the joint manufacture of cash registers involving Anker Werke (FRG), Anker Datentechnik (Au), ZVS Works (Cz) and IGV Enterprise (Hu).

(e) Vertical and Horizontal Co-production. These types of co-production are based on agreed (or virtually imposed) specialization according to the complexity of the process or component – usually reflecting different stages of the manufacture of the complete product. In the case of 'vertical' co-production, one partner produces relatively simple components or materials, whilst those involving more advanced technology are produced by the other. The latter partner may also take the responsibility for the further finishing of the components or sub-assemblies received and the assembly of the complete product. A portion of the complete output may then be handed over to the less advanced partner. On the other hand, 'horizontal' co-production is typical of technologically 'equal' partners, where each – even though specializing – produces components or sub-assemblies of a similar degree of technical sophistication. Under the arrangement between Metrawatt (FRG) and Iskra-Otoce (Yu) for the production of measurement apparatus, the Yugoslav partner produces simpler measuring elements whilst the West German firm supplies more complex metering instruments and related equipment. On the other hand, the agreement between British Steel Founders and Engineers (UK) and Polimex (Po) for the joint production of medium-size cranes is essentially of a horizontal nature.

(f) Production and Marketing. East–West industrial co-operation is commonly identified with production co-operation, and from the technological point of view that is what really matters. But there are

also instances limited to marketing only. The Eastern partner (usually a foreign trade enterprise) undertakes to act as a distributor of the Western corporation's products in its own Socialist country or perhaps in Comecon as a whole. In exchange, the corporation may use its marketing channels in the capitalist world to distribute the related products of a Socialist enterprise. However, in most cases now agreements on production co-operation are also supplemented with provisions for the marketing of the complete product. The Eastern partner is usually responsible for distribution in Socialist countries whilst the corporation handles the marketing in the rest of the world, especially in hard-currency areas. The agreement between Pechiney-Ugine-Kuhlmann (Fr) and Energoinvest (Yu) is limited to production (aluminium) whilst that between Rheinstahl (FRG) and Mashinoexport (USSR) is essentially directed to marketing (Soviet machinery in the FR of Germany). On the other hand, the agreement between Honeywell Bull (Ne) and Metronex (Po) and Pnefal (Po) for the joint production of equipment for the automation of industrial processes also includes co-operative arrangements for the marketing of the output in Western and Comecon countries.

(g) Singular and Complex Co-operation. The partners may choose to co-operate only in a well-defined narrow field, in which case each side is responsible only for a single type of task or component. On the other hand, the pursuits of the partners may be co-ordinated over a wide range of activities that may include R & D, the training of specialists, production, marketing and servicing of the final product. In addition to specialization, joint pursuits may also be included. The co-operation agreement between Kanthal (Swe) and Csepel (Hu) is limited to the production of resistor wire in Hungary, with technology provided by the Swedish partner. On the other hand the agreement between International Harvester (US) and Metallurgical Works Stalowa Wola (Po) involves the manufacture of caterpillar bulldozers, loaders and machines for laying large-diameter oil and gas pipelines; the American partner has supplied a licence and there is joint production of parts and assemblies and there are joint R & D and marketing arrangements.

(h) Co-operation in the Partner Countries and in Third Countries. Typically, East–West industrial co-operation covers production

which is carried on by the Western corporation in its parent or subsidiary country and the Eastern partner in its own Socialist country. It may also include the exchange of specialists and the joint construction of projects in either or both partner countries. But a development which is assuming significant importance is co-operation extending beyond the partner countries. It mostly takes the form of joint construction of roads, dams, power stations and even industrial plants. The fact that the corporations have multinational affiliations facilitates this partnership. Thus Alsthom (Fr) co-operated during 1973-4 with Ganz Electric Works (Hu) in installing four bulb-turbines at the Kisköre power plant in Hungary. Buttner-Schilde-Haas (FRG) recently participated with Petrom (Ro) in deliveries of equipment and the construction of a complete plant in the DPR of Korea for the production of polyacrilonitril fibres. During 1971-2 Capital Plant (International) (UK) co-operated with Technoexport (Cz) as the main foreign contractor and Naftagas (Yu) as the local builder in the construction of a lubricating plant in Novi Sad in Yugoslavia. A co-operation agreement signed in 1970 between Creusot-Loire, Sollac and other French companies on the one hand and Energomashexport, Mashinoexport and other Soviet enterprises on the other provides for Soviet participation in the construction of a huge ($1,400m.) metallurgical complex at Fos-sur-Mer (near Marseilles) in France; the Soviet side is supplying a licence, know-how, designs and equipment for blast furnaces and also diesel locomotives. VÖEST-Alpine (Au) and Polimex-Cekop (Po) have a long-term agreement on the joint construction of chemical and cellulose plants in less-developed countries.

Most of these types of co-operation are overlapping but all in all input–output arrangements and co-production involving specialization are most common – representing more than one-half of the total number of agreements. There has been a tendency away from short-lived to longer-term association, from uni-directional sub-contracting to bi-directional and multi-directional co-production of a horizontal nature, and from simple to more complex co-operation, including the joint construction of industrial plants and other projects in third countries. It appears that these tendencies will continue, in the near future at least.

TABLE 10 EAST–WEST INTER-ENTERPRISE INDUSTRIAL CO-OPERATION AGREEMENTS OPERATIVE OR CONCLUDED IN THE FIRST HALF OF THE 1970S

Western Multinational Firm*	Eastern Partner†	Field of Co-operation
Brown, Boveri (FRG)	Elektrim (Po)	Thermal overload relays
Elliot Machine (US)	Energomashexport (USSR)	Compressors
English Electric (UK)	Ganz Electric Works (Hu)	Large transformers
Fagesta (Swe)	Metalexport (Po)	Tools for motor vehicles
Farbwerke Höchst (FRG)	Budaprint (Hu)	Textile printing
Fernseh (FRG)	Elektroimpex (Hu)	Sound frequency equipment
Fiat (It)	Universal Tractors (Ro)	Agricultural diesel engines
Ford Werke (FRG)	Fadip (Yu)	Parts for passenger cars
Honeywell (It)	Elektronska Industrija (Yu)	Computers
Intern. Computers (UK)	Videoton (Hu)	Computers
Kockum (Swe)	Fadroma (Po)	Heavy tip trucks
Koehring International (Ne)	Bumar (Po)	Hydraulic machinery
Krupp I. und S. (FRG)	Impexim (Ro)	Mining machinery
Kvernlands Fabbrik (No)	IMT Tractors (Yu)	Ploughs
Nestlé (Swi)	Monimpex (Hu)	Dessicated soups
Nicolas (Fr)	Automotive Works (Po)	Heavy trailers
Oréal (Fr)	Formakhim (Bu)	Typewriters
Perkins Engines (UK)	Ursus Tractors (Po)	Tractors
Roamer Watch (Swi)	Orások Szovetskezete (Hu)	Ladies watches
Rubery Owen (UK)	Buzuluk (Cz)	Equipment for piston rings
SACMM (Fr)	Polmatex (Po)	Shuttleless rapier looms
Sanyo Electric (Ja)	Diora (Po)	Car electric parts
Siemens (FRG)	Iskra (Yu)	Control equipment
Unilever (Ne)	Saponija (Yu)	Detergents
Volvo (Swe)	Ikarus (Hu)	Buses

* For their multinational affiliations, see the Complete List and Index, pp. 197-232 and for further details of parent companies, Tables 2, 3 and 4, pp. 36-47.

† For country abbreviations, see footnote 3, Ch. 1, p. 2.

Sources. Based on daily and periodical literature published in Socialist and Western countries.

Other examples of inter-enterprise industrial co-operation are shown in Table 10. It may be added here that a particular Western multinational company or a Socialist enterprise may co-operate with several partners at the same time. On the Western side, Siemens (FRG) appears to have one of the largest networks of co-operative ties with Socialist enterprises – with over 70 agreements in force in 1973 and 35 more in the preparatory stage.[5] In Yugoslavia in 1972 there were at least 10 enterprises which had five or more co-operation agreements with capitalist firms;[6] thus Iskra, producing electronic components, has at least five such agreements, four of which are with multinationals – British Radio (UK), Hoover (UK), Metrawatt (FRG) and Siemens (FRG).

In addition to the types and cases highlighted so far, there are other forms of co-operation which, although not of clearly industrial content, warrant mention.

(i) Hotels. A number of hotels, meant essentially for Western tourists, have been constructed in Bulgaria, Czechoslovakia, Hungary, Poland, Romania and Yugoslavia in co-operation with Western companies, such as Skänska Cementgjuterjet (Swe). Furthermore, most of these, together with some previously built, luxury hotels are managed and operated in co-operation with local enterprises or agencies by Intercontinental Hotels (US) – in Bucharest, Budapest, Prague, Warsaw and Zagreb, and by Holiday Inns (US) – in Ljubljana. In each case these multinational hotels also use their worldwide reservation systems for the purpose.[7]

(ii) Service Stations. Several Western companies have participated in the construction and operation of modern petrol stations. For example, Bayerische Motorenwerke (FRG), British Petroleum (UK) and Shell (UK) have done this in Hungary.

(iii) Beverages. The world's two largest producers of soft drinks – Coca-Cola (US) and Pepsi-Co (US) – have assisted the European Socialist countries (except Albania) in establishing bottling facilities and are supplying concentrates for local filling and distribution.

[5] *Eastern Europe Report*, 22/2/1973, p. 54.

[6] *Privredni pregled* (Economic Review), Belgrade, 30/7/1973, p. 13.

[7] The basis agreed upon for sharing appears to differ from one case to another but, as recently reported in a Western source, Intercontinental Hotels in Budapest pays a franchise fee of at least 3 per cent of its gross income depending on the volume of business. *Eastern Europe Report*, 24/1/1975, p. 23.

Coca-Cola has concluded such agreements with enterprises in Bulgaria, Czechoslovakia, Hungary, Poland and the USSR and Pepsi-Co – with those in Czechoslovakia, the German DR, Hungary, Poland, Romania, the USSR and Yugoslavia. Pepsi-Co's co-operative arrangement with the USSR provides for the delivery of vodka to Pepsi-Co which acts as its distributor in the American market.

(iv) Leasing. This new form of inter-enterprise co-operation which has been rapidly developing in the West since the late 1950s, was strongly opposed by the Socialist countries up to the early 1970s and most of them still apply at least some restrictions. On ideological grounds it is naturally of concern to the Socialist state that a piece of capital equipment found within its borders is not socialized but is legally owned by a foreign capitalist. But ideological convictions appear to be slowly being sacrificed on the altar of economic expediency. Leasing reduces the immediate outlay of hard foreign exchange and enables access to the latest models on the one hand, and offers the Socialist countries an avenue for establishing their capital equipment in difficult and competitive markets in the West. So far Bulgaria and Yugoslavia have liberalized their legislation most, and Hungary, Poland and the USSR have also adopted a more favourable attitude. Western means of transport, electronic equipment (including computers) and specialized machinery (especially if needed in export production) have the best chance of being leased in the East. Thus Siemens (FRG) has leased electronic equipment to Metronex (Po) and Container Transport International (UK) and Strick Co. (US) have leased containers to Sovfrakht (USSR). Several European Socialist countries have also taken first steps towards establishing a foothold for their capital equipment in capitalist countries through leasing. But the drive is being directed not so much to the multinational corporations but rather to medium and small firms. To promote East–West leasing, in 1973 Morgan Grenfell & Co. (UK) and the Soviet-owned Moscow Narodny Bank in London established a joint venture, East–West Trading Co. in London. In the following year, Crédit Lyonnais (Fr) and the Soviet-owned Banque Commerciale pour l'Europe du Nord in Paris announced the formation of another joint company for the purpose – Société pour la Promotion Européenne du Leasing in Paris.

(v) Transit Transport. Some important East–West co-operative transport arrangements have been developed since 1970, involving several Western multinational firms and the USSR in particular on the Eastern side. Of greatest consequence is the Japan – Western Europe route across the USSR, which has radically changed the Japanese competitive position in the Soviet and Eastern and Western European markets – owing to both lower transport costs and shorter delivery periods.[8] In 1970 several major Japanese corporations – notably C. Itoh & Co., Marubeni-Ida, Mitsui & Co. and Sumitomo Shoji Kaisha – signed an agreement with the Soviet Government to allow them to operate container transport using the Trans-Siberian Railway. For this purpose they co-operated in the construction of port and container facilities in the Vostochny port (in Wrangel Bay) to handle 120,000 containers annually. Cargoes of Japanese machinery, industrial equipment, consumer durables and other goods are regularly shipped westwards in 20-ton containers. At about the same time Schenker Trans-Siberian Container Service (FRG) began similar operations from Western Europe to Japan. There are also cases of inter-enterprise co-operation in road transport. Svenska Godscentraler and Linjebus, both of Sweden, signed agreements in 1972 with Sovtrans-Avto and Soyuzvneshtrans, both of the USSR, for transit over Soviet territory for Swedish deliveries to and from Iran. Sovtrans-Avto has also been operating regular truck runs to the Benelux countries, using Rutges International Expeditie Gouda (Ne) as its area agent.

(vi) Offsetting Shipments. That economic common sense can prevail in East–West dealings, in spite of the legacy of mutual prejudice, is further proved by the intriguing oil swaps between Western oil companies and the USSR. The 1967 crisis in the Middle East led to the closure of the Suez Canal. Most of the oil produced by the Western European companies has to be shipped to Western Europe from the Persian Gulf (east of the Suez), whilst most of the Soviet

[8] Using the 'trans-Siberian container bridge' between Japan and Western Europe, transport costs are 20-25 per cent lower compared with sea transport by the shortest route (via the Panama Canal) and the transit period is 20 days compared with 26 days by the sea route. The number of containers transported between Japan and Western Europe increased from 4,000 in 1971 to 51,000 in 1974 and 10 per cent of the Japanese–European container traffic now moves across the USSR. *Rynki zagraniczne*, 20/2/1975, p. 1.

oil has to be transported from the Black Sea or Baltic Sea ports, even though many important Soviet customers are in South and East Asia. To reduce wasteful cross-voyages around South Africa, on several occasions since the late 1960s British Petroleum (UK), Compagnie Française des Pétroles (Fr) and Royal Dutch-Shell (UK) have agreed to deliver oil from the Persian Gulf to specified Soviet customers in Asia (such as Burma and Japan), and Soyuznefteexport (USSR) has made corresponding shipments to designated West European destinations (such as – of all countries – Italy!).[9]

(vii) Motion Picture Co-operative Arrangements. Films made by Western multinational companies – such as Columbia Pictures Industries (US), Paramount Television Productions (US), Rank Organization (UK), Twentieth Century-Fox Film (US) and Warner Brothers (US) – are increasingly shown in the European Socialist countries (but these multinationals are less inclined to facilitate the distribution of Socialist films in the West). Columbia Pictures and Paramount co-operated with Mosfilm (USSR) in shooting the $25m. film 'Waterloo' (to which the Soviet side contributed $10m.). The two television transmission systems 'Eurovision' and 'Intervision', operating in Western and Eastern Europe respectively, have a co-operation agreement on mutual retransmission of programmes.

C. LARGER DEVELOPMENTAL SCHEMES

Since the early 1970s many multinational corporations have also embarked upon broader schemes of production and marketing, mostly involving the development of natural resources in some Socialist countries. The USSR and China have become the prime targets, owing to their size and large deposits of untapped resources, but Mongolia, Poland and Yugoslavia have also aroused a good deal of interest. Such projects require massive investments in terms of finance, equipment and technology of an order obviously beyond the present capabilities of the Socialist countries. Some of these schemes are so vast that they are beyond the capacity of even the largest Western corporations and have to be tackled by joint effort. We shall now outline these schemes by countries, highlighting the

[9] R. E. Ebel, *Communist Trade in Oil and Gas*, New York, Praeger, 1970, pp. 101, 102, 182.

part being played by the Western multinationals.

(*a*) *Finnish–Soviet.* In 1972 a $140m. contract was signed for the modernization and expansion of a large paper-mill complex at Svetogorsk (near the south Finnish border) by a consortium of Finnish firms led by Ahlström. Two years later, negotiations were conducted for another scheme – the largest in the history of Finnish–Soviet relations – involving the construction of two metallurgical complexes for copper and nickel near Norilsk, at the mouth of the Yenisei; the value of the project is estimated to be nearly $300m., and Finnish companies – including Ahlström and Rauma-Repola – are to be responsible for 70 per cent of the equipment and construction work.[10]

(*b*) *French–Soviet.* During 1973-4 contracts were concluded with several French companies for the construction of five petrochemical plants in the USSR. The cost of the plants is $200m., one-half of which is being financed by such French multinational banks as Banque Française du Commerce Extérieur and Crédit Lyonnais. Negotiations were also carried on during 1974-5 with other French firms, headed by Pechiney-Ugine-Kuhlmann, and including Renault and Télémécanique Electrique for a series of plants in the Southern Ukraine and Siberia for the production of aluminium. This will be the largest aluminium complex in the world, to cost $1,700m., with an annual production capacity of 500,000 tons of aluminium. The value of the contracts to the French companies is $1,000m. and some of the output of the complex is to be supplied to them in part-payment.[11]

(*c*) *West German–Soviet.* After two years of negotiations an agreement was reached in 1974 between a consortium of West German firms – Korf-Stahl, Krupp, and Salzgitter – and Metallurg-import of the USSR for the construction of huge metallurgical plants near Kursk, to utilize the local deposits of iron ore and gas. The complex, worth to the German companies over $1,000m., is to be the largest and most modern establishment of this nature in the world and is to be completed by 1980. It is to produce 5m. tons

[10] *East–West Commerce*, London, 4/1972, p. 9; *Soviet News*, Soviet Embassy in London, 17/4/1973, p. 182; *Życie gospodarcze* (Economic Life) Warsaw, 8/9/1974, p. 13.

[11] *Rynki zagraniczne*, 22-27/12/1973, p. 2; *Sotsialisticheskaya industriya* (Socialist Industry), Moscow, 1/3/1974, p. 3.

of pellet concentrates and 2.7m. tons of rolled steel annually by a direct reduction process. This case of co-operation represents one of the ironies of history. Kursk was the theatre of the biggest tank battle of the Second World War, where the Nazi armoured divisions – equipped largely by those same firms – fought and lost in July 1943. Another rather unusual scheme is that of a giant nuclear power complex to be built on ex-German territory near Kaliningrad and to consist of four plants with a combined capacity of 4,800 MW. Negotiations to this effect began in 1972 with such West German firms as Kraftwerk Union and Brown, Boveri (in conjunction with Babcock & Wilcox of the USA) and the total value of the contracts may very well exceed $10,000m. It is envisaged that the scheme will be completed by the late 1980s and in payment half of the electricity produced is to be sent to West Germany via long-distance transmission lines up to Frankfurt/M. A related project, uranium mining in Siberia, is being developed with the aid of equipment supplied by Gutehoffnungshütte.[12]

(d) West European–Soviet. A unique scheme representing a lasting East–West bond, in the figurative as well as literal sense, is the gas network linking the USSR with Finland, the FR of Germany, France, Austria and Italy. The large-diameter pipes and equipment for their laying as well as for the processing, storage and transmission of gas (and oil) have been supplied by such multinationals as Borg-Warner (US), Finsider (It), Mannesmann (FRG), Vallourec (Fr) and VÖEST-Alpine (Au) (see Ch. 3B, pp. 52-3). The total value of these deliveries to the USSR by the mid-1970s exceeded $2,500m. At the same time several Western multinationals, such as ENI (It) and Ruhrgas (FRG) have signed long-term agreements (up to 1990-2000) with Soyuznefteexport and Soyuzgasexport for the supply of gas to the six Western European countries.[13] This scheme represents an interesting case of quadri-angular international co-operation involving Socialist, capitalist and less-developed countries, dictated by distances in relation to markets. Whilst

[12] *Die Wirtschaft des Ostblocks* (Economies of the Eastern Bloc), Bonn, 19/3/1974, p. 6; *Handelsblatt* (Commercial News), Düsseldorf, 28/1/1974, p. 11; 25/3/1974, p. 5; 19/6/1974, p. 11; and 5/9/1974, p. 3.

[13] *Foreign Trade*, Moscow, 4/1974, p. 48; *Handelsblatt*, 12/2/1974, p. 8; *Rynki zagraniczne*, 17/9/1974, p. 2; *Sotsialisticheskaya industriya*, 5/4/1974, p. 3.

the Soviets are supplying gas from the western USSR to Western Europe, they themselves obtain gas from Afghanistan and Iran for their southern outlying provinces.

(e) American–Soviet. Two separate super-schemes have been subject to negotiations since 1972, mostly involving natural gas in Siberia. The first proposed scheme is a twin project designed to exploit Soviet gas in eastern and western Siberia and supply it to the western and eastern United States. In June 1973 agreement of intention was reached between Occidental Petroleum and El Paso on the one hand and the Soviet Government on the other, involving $40,000m. worth of gas over 25 years; the proposal concerns the development of gas resources in Yakutia (north-east Siberia) – including a 3,200 km pipeline to Nakhodka on the Pacific coast, a liquefaction plant, suitable harbour facilities and some 20 tankers for transporting the liquefied gas to the western coast of the USA. However, because of the lack of enthusiasm on the part of the American Government, El Paso has at least temporarily withdrawn from the project and its future at the time of writing was uncertain.

At about the same time, in July 1973, another agreement was reached with the Soviet Government involving a consortium of Texan companies – Tenneco, Texas Eastern Transmission, and Brown & Root – for the development of gas fields in Western Siberia; they proposed to spend about $3,700m. on a 2,900 km pipeline from Urengoy to Murmansk and a gas liquefaction plant at Murmansk, and a further $2,600m. for over 20 tankers to transport the liquefied gas to the eastern coast of the United States. The exploitation is to start in about 1980 and is to continue for 25 years. The future of this project was also uncertain at the time of writing. The second scheme has assumed a more concrete form, largely due to the enthusiasm and persistence of Dr A. Hammer, President of Occidental Petroleum.[14] An agreement of intention between Occi-

[14] Dr Armand Hammer – son of a Jewish intellectual with left-wing convictions who had emigrated to the USA from Czarist Russia for political reasons and later became one of the founding fathers of the American Communist Party – although a graduate in medicine (from Columbia) he turned to business instead. In the 1920s he carried on lucrative business with the Soviets and became a trusted and personal friend of Lenin. During 1957-8 Dr Hammer became the President, Chairman of the Board and the principal shareholder of the ailing Occidental Petroleum which he gradually developed into one of the most dynamic multinational corporations, now with 62 affiliates in 25 foreign countries.

dental and the Soviet Government was signed in September 1973, followed in June 1974 by more specific undertakings concerning co-production of fertilizers and certain other chemicals over a twenty-year period. The scheme, involving investment of $20,000m., is the biggest non-intergovernmental deal concluded in history. Huge plants, to be built near Togliattigrad using gas from the Orenburg fields, are to produce ammonia, carbamide and calcium chloride. The development of necessary port facilities in Odessa and Ventspils (on the Black and Baltic seas respectively) is also included in the project. It is envisaged that the scheme will be in operation in 1978 when the new Soviet plants will begin deliveries of ammonia, urea and potash to the plants of Occidental and its affiliate Bechtel to the tune of $200m.–$500m. annually, in exchange for superphosphoric acid to be produced from phosphates mined (mostly) in Florida. Other American multinational companies to benefit from orders for this scheme include Babcock & Wilcox, Chemical Construction, Chicago Bridge & Iron, General Electric, Honeywell, Ingersoll-Rand, Kaiser Steel, Union Carbide, and Westinghouse Electric.[15] This is certainly an ambitious scheme, promising large profits to both sides. A Western writer, commenting on the deal, remarked: 'If Armand Hammer keeps all the money that Russia promises him, he should be able to hire one of the minor Rothschilds for a butler.'[16]

(f) Japanese–Soviet. Although there were cases of the joint Japanese exploitation of resources (timber in particular) in the USSR in the late 1960s, a more systematic approach and on a larger scale began only in the early 1970s. In April 1974 an agreement was signed under which the Export–Import Bank of Japan undertook to provide long-term credits of $1,050m. to finance the exploitation of coking coal and natural gas in Yakutia and timber resources in the Soviet Far East by such Japanese multinational corporations as C. Itoh & Co., Komatsu, Mitsubishi, Mitsui and Sumitomo. Several more specific agreements have been concluded since; thus according to one the coking coal project is to cover a twenty-year period and in the gas exploration undertaking El Paso (US) is also to parti-

[15] *Eastern Europe Report*, 15/6/1973, p. 165; 10/8/1973, p. 238; 31/5/1974, p. 167. *Rynki zagraniczne*, 2/7/1974, p. 2.

[16] *News Digest – International*, Sydney, 1/1974, p. 18.

cipate. Other schemes under consideration include the Japanese participation in the development of the Tyumen oilfields (in Western Siberia), the construction of a $3,000m. oil pipeline from the Tyumen oilfields to Nakhodka (7,000 km) and oil and gas exploration in southern Sakhalin (the latter project involving some American companies, too). Teijin, and Toray Industries have recently been negotiating barter deals for the construction of polyester, polyethylene and other petrochemical plants in the order of $1,000m. in exchange for Soviet oil.[17]

(g) Japanese–Chinese. The possibility of the exploration and exploitation of the Chinese oil and gas resources has become one of the sensational developments since the early 1970s.[18] On economic and technological grounds China – more than other Socialist countries – needs the Western multinationals, and the world oil crisis has accelerated moves on each side for co-operation in one way or another. In 1972 the Mitsubishi group formed the Japan Drilling Co. which sent its representatives to China and both sides were reported to be eager to embark upon co-operative projects. In the following year, the Energy Development division of the Japan–China Economic Association, headed by the Chairman of Tokyo Shibaura Electric, agreed to co-operate with the Chinese in oil and gas exploration and exploitation. Since that time there has been a proliferation of co-operative projects (mostly of a smaller scope involving medium and small companies).[19]

(h) American–Chinese. Although thought impossible before the early 1970s, the events since that time suggest that there is great potential for production and marketing co-operation between

[17] *Eastern Europe Report*, 8/3/1974, p. 77; 29/11/1974, p. 369; 13/12/1974, p. 377. *Izvestiya*, Moscow, 5/6/1974, p. 3. *Soviet News*, 19/3/1974, p. 104; 11/6/1974, p. 212; 20/8/1974, p. 317; 19/11/1974, p. 317.

[18] China's oil reserves were estimated in 1973 at 50,000m. tons (30,000m. on the mainland plus 20,000m. tons of off-shore reserves), representing about 5 per cent of the world's total. The output of crude oil rose from 20m. tons in 1970 to 60m. tons in 1974 and was expected to increase to 300m. in 1982 and to 500m. in 1985. In the early 1970s oil was produced in six oilfields on the mainland, mostly in Manchuria, and an 800 km pipeline was under construction from the Taching oilfield to Darien. Off-shore fields, especially those in the Gulfs of Pohai and Tonkin, may become important oil-producing areas particularly aimed at export. In 1974 nearly one-quarter of Japanese oil imports was met by China. *China Trade Report*, Hong Kong, 3/1974, p. 10 and 10/1974, p. 2; *Życie gospodarcze*, 3/11/1974, p. 13.

[19] *China Trade Report*, 7/1972, pp. 3-4; 9/1973, p. 7 and 2/1974, p. 7.

American companies and China, and oil and gas are the most promising fields. Discussions or negotiations have been initiated by the Chinese with Continental Oil, Exxon, Mobil Oil, Standard Oil of California, and Zapata. By 1975 several American companies – such as Geo Space, and Rucker – had supplied over $10m. worth of oil and gas exploration equipment and larger deliveries have been under consideration.[20] These are only beginnings and in the future co-operative developmental schemes may raise Sino–American co-operation to levels never dreamt of before, and indeed the whole constellation of relations amongst China, Japan, the USA and the USSR may be radically changed.

(i) Other Developmental Schemes. There has also been a growing number of other East–West developmental projects which at the time of writing were in different stages of negotiation or implementation. The following multinational corporations have, in addition to those already mentioned, in one way or another co-operated with some Socialist countries in oil exploration or development: British Petroleum (UK) – with Bulgaria, Compagnie Générale de Géophysique (Fr) – with China, the ELF group (Fr) – with Yugoslavia, ENI (It) – with Bulgaria, Exxon (US) – with Bulgaria and Oljenprospektering (Swe) – with the USSR. Several Japanese multinationals, viz. Mitsubishi, Mitsui, and Nippon Mining (and other firms) were reported in 1973 to be negotiating for a copper mining project at Rudna, in western Poland, to cost $600m. repayable in copper deliveries to Japan. The same and other Japanese companies have also been considering the development of mineral production in Mongolia on an input–output basis, and there have been discussions on the possible Japanese construction of another 7,000 km Trans-Siberian Railway. General Motors (US) may co-operate in the development of a large truck factory in Siberia, IBM (US) or Sperry-Rand (US) – of a computer manufacturing complex, also in the USSR, and Toyota Motors (Ja) and/or Volkswagen (FRG) – passenger-car plants in China.[21]

[20] *China Trade Report*, 7/1972, p. 4; 6/1973, p. 7; 9/1973, p. 7; and 11/1974, p. 3.

[21] For evidence and further details, see *Die Wirtschaft* (The Economy), East Berlin, 10/1974, p. 31; *China Trade Report*, 9/1971, p. 11 and 6/1973, p. 7; *East–West*, Brussels, 19/7/1972, p. 8; *East–West Commerce*, 31/8/1973, p. 7; *Eastern Europe Report*, 28/6/1974, p. 206 and 23/8/1974, p. 270; *Handelsblatt*, 19/6/1974, p. 36; *Rynki zagraniczne*, 20/9/1973, p. 1.

D. MUTUAL ADVANTAGES

The remarkable expansion of industrial co-operation in its different forms obviously indicates that the participants on each side must derive substantial advantages. We shall first consider the attractions of this co-operation for Western multinational corporations. First, the Socialist countries represent valuable reservoirs of raw material and power resources which, owing to the short industrial history of these countries, have not been depleted. The world fuel crisis, in particular the Arab oil tactics and the prospect of raw material shortages, make additional or alternative sources of supply attractive propositions.

Second, labour represents another resource which is relatively abundant, reliable and inexpensive – important considerations in the case of labour-intensive components. In the past this particularly applied to Bulgaria, Poland, Romania and Yugoslavia, with surplus labour, including skilled manpower, whilst several Western European countries (Belgium, France, the FR of Germany, the Netherlands, Sweden and Switzerland) suffered from labour shortages. Thus Control Data (US) found that the cost of a number of components for electronic equipment and computers produced by Yugoslav enterprises was 25 per cent lower than elsewhere in the West.[22] However, these differentials may not be as large in the future due to the falling reserves and declining growth of manpower in the European Socialist countries, on the one hand, and the large and apparently excessive supply of foreign workers in the Western European countries.[23] Consequently production co-operation may have to shift towards capital and technology-intensive items and

[22] N. Scott and H. Günter (eds), *Transnational Industrial Relations*, London, Macmillan, 1972, p. 25.

[23] The past and predicted five-yearly increases in the working population in the Comecon countries as a whole are: 1961-5 – 12 per cent, 1966-70 – 16 per cent, 1971-5 – 8 per cent, 1976-80 – 6 per cent and 1981-5 – 3 per cent. The working week is expected to be reduced by five hours over the period 1976-85, which will absorb two-thirds of the total increase in employment. The total number of foreign workers in the Benelux countries, France, the FR of Germany and Switzerland in the early 1970s was 6.0m. Based on: *Ekonomika i organizatsiya promyshlennogo proizvodstva* (Economics and Organization of Industrial Development), Novosibirsk, 1/1974, p. 110-11; *Statisticheskii ezhegodnik stranchlenov Soveta Ekonomicheskoi Vzaimpomoshchi 1971* (Statistical Yearbook of the Comecon Countries 1971), Moscow, Comecon Secretariat, 1971, p. 381.

become more horizontal. China, of course, has an ample supply of labour, but whether she will embrace inter-enterprise industrial co-operation on a large scale is not clear at present.

Third, industrial co-operation provides opportunities for specialization and the economies of scale. These considerations are important in the branches of industry involving very large investment outlays on R & D and capital equipment. Production partnership with a Socialist enterprise may enable the Western firm to reduce its overhead costs and instead draw on its partner's production capacity at short notice. Fourth, this co-operation usually provides a more effective control over the technology handed over to the Eastern partner than ordinary licence sale.

Fifth, considering the usual difficulty of entering and operating in the unfamiliar Socialist market, the Eastern partner may prove a guide, philosopher and friend in extending sales locally and perhaps in other Socialist countries as well. Similarly in the case of marketing in capitalist countries, the actual or potential Eastern rival may be turned into a co-operating partner. In addition to the five advantages considered, there are also benefits of a broader or long-run consequence ('externalities'). Industrial co-operation is closer and more lasting than ordinary sales and purchases of goods or licences. As the Socialist countries are noted for planned, orderly and continuous economic development and virtually no industrial disruption or fluctuations on the capitalist scale, such an association may provide an element of stability to the Western partner. Production or marketing co-operation may also lead to other, larger schemes of development and perhaps joint ventures.

Advantages to the Socialist countries are, in general, more varied and compelling. They are of both microeconomic and macroeconomic content and we shall list them briefly.

(i) The possibility of equipping the co-operating Socialist enterprises with modern Western machinery and equipment without direct expenditure of hard foreign exchange.
(ii) The direct assimilation of Western technological processes.
(iii) The application of modern Western management techniques and know-how, which cannot be acquired otherwise.
(iv) Economies of scale consequent upon specialization and production for a wider market.

(v) The improvement in the quality of production as the Socialist enterprise has to meet the demanding requirements of the Western partner operating in competitive buyers' markets.

(vi) The improvement of supplies to the Socialist domestic market with regard to goods previously not produced or in short supply.

(vii) The circumvention of the Western countries' import restrictions as co-operative imports are often admitted under special concessions.

(viii) The establishment of a foothold in, or the extension of, markets in capitalist countries using the Western partner's marketing channels and expertise.

(ix) An improvement in the balance of payments consequent upon the saving of foreign exchange on co-operative supplies of equipment by the Western partner and expanded sales in capitalist markets.

(x) A disciplining factor in general, prodding the Socialist enterprise to more radical and continuous improvements in its methods of production, management, marketing and overall efficiency 'since the weaker partner has to rise to the level of the more advanced partner as it is a condition of mutual success'.[24]

Regarding these advantages, a special note is warranted on Socialist exports to the West. In the Socialist view, the structure of East–West trade has been grossly unfair to the East – not reflecting the latter's progress in industrialization. Thus in 1960 the share of manufactures in total Western exports to the East represented 72 per cent whilst in Socialist exports to the West the proportion was only 32 per cent (and even in 1973 the respective percentages were 72 and 42).[25] This trade has been described as 'vertical', amounting largely to the exchange of Western manufactures for Socialist primary products, and it has been attributed to various forms of discrimination practised in the West. The Socialist countries have been most anxious to earn more hard currencies by exporting industrial products to the West, but export drives via price undercutting have not proved successful in the past, and furthermore on ideological grounds these countries are against cut-throat competi-

[24] *Rynki zagraniczne*, 22-24/7/1971, p. 1.

[25] United Nations *Monthly Bulletin of Statistics*, 3/1963, pp. xvi-xxix; 4/1975, pp. xxii-xli and 7/1975, pp. xxiv-xli.

tion. It is widely held in the East, especially in the European Socialist countries, that industrial co-operation with the West – particularly with companies commanding worldwide marketing channels – now provides about the only realistic way of improving the composition of Eastern exports to the West. In a study of this vital question, a Polish economist pointed out: '... we are endeavouring to create a situation where the entry of Socialist manufactures into Western markets is not looked upon as competition but rather as co-operation.'[26]

[26] F. Kulpa, ('Industrial Co-operation between Poland and Developed Western European Countries'), *Ekonomista* (The Economist), Warsaw, 5/1973, p. 928.

6 Joint Ventures

A. FEATURES AND BENEFITS OF EAST–WEST VENTURES

BY 'joint venture' in its strict legal sense we now understand an integrated, jointly owned and managed enterprise. Thus it is distinct from industrial co-operation where the individuality of the participants in the agreed pursuit or project is essentially retained with regard to ownership and operation. As R. S. Kretschmar Jr and R. Foor state, 'a co-operation agreement becomes a joint venture when both partners have influence over the decision-making process basic to the venture's economic success (equivalent, for business purposes, to equity participation) and when they share in the risks and rewards of the venture.'[1] C. H. McMillan and D. P. St Charles point out that there are three essential elements distinguishing joint ventures from ordinary industrial co-operation agreements, viz. 'pooled assets, joint management and the shared risk'.[2]

Joint ventures are not an exclusive feature of East–West economic relations. Many multinational corporations are parties to such ventures in the capitalist world,[3] and similar entities have also been established by the Socialist countries, especially in Comecon (see Ch. 8B, pp. 138-44). But according to L. G. Franko, of the Centre d'Etudes Industrielles in Geneva, the joint ventures entered into by the multinationals with other capitalist partners are, on the whole,

[1] R. S. Kretschmar, Jr, and R. Foor, *The Potential for Joint Ventures in Eastern Europe*, New York, Praeger, 1972, p. 4.

[2] C. H. McMillan and D. P. St Charles, *Joint Ventures in Eastern Europe: A Three-Country Comparison*, Montreal, Canadian Economic Policy Committee and C. D. Howe Research Institute, 1974, p. 10.

[3] e.g. Bayer (FRG) is reported to be a partner in over 30 such ventures, ICI (UK) – also in 30, Montedison – in 12 and Royal Dutch-Shell – in 25. C. Levinson, *International Trade Unionism*, London, Allen & Unwin, 1972, p. 39.

less durable and successful than those shared with Socialist enterprises.[4]

Most benefits of industrial co-operation (see Ch. 5D, pp. 97-100) also apply to joint ventures, but in addition there are certain advantages peculiar to the latter. Joint venture contracts usually cover long periods, some 15-20 years, and consequently are less disruptive and provide better opportunities for the long-term maximization of gains. Such ventures represent the closest form of inter-enterprise collaboration and enable each party to exercise a closer control over the policies of joint interest.

To a Western firm used to operating on an international scale, a joint venture in a Socialist country may provide an economical basis for extending its production capacity to supply nearby Socialist and capitalist markets.[5] Moreover, a partnership with a Socialist enterprise may provide easier entry to markets further afield – in countries with which the parent country of the multinational company (such as the USA or an ex-colonial power), or the multinational itself, may be unwelcome due to one reason or another. Socialist countries have developed a very good rapport with many nations of the Third World, with which commercial relations are further facilitated by bilateral trade and payment agreements. Algeria, Burma, Egypt, India, Libya, Nigeria, Peru, Syria, Tanzania and Zaire represent obvious illustrations. A joint East–West venture may thus provide a multinational corporation with a means of outflanking its capitalist competitors!

The cash outlay by the Western partner need not be large as the initial contribution may take the form of a licence, know-how or trade-mark, which otherwise may be unsaleable, and over which control can be easily maintained. Then, compared with capitalist countries, there is the advantage of a greater political and economic stability, lower labour costs, virtually no strikes, and the possibility of predicting costs with greater certainty. Experience shows that risk to the multinationals of losing their capital is close to nil –

[4] L. G. Franko, 'Joint Venture Divorce in the Multinational Company', *Columbia Journal of World Business*, May-June 1971, p. 13.

[5] e.g. in 1974 an American corporation was negotiating a joint-venture agreement with Romania for the manufacture of heavy machinery, under which 75 per cent of the output is to be marketed in China. See, N. Holden, 'Co-operating with Romania', *International Commerce*, London, Sep 1974, p. 20.

as the possibility of nationalization is in fact much smaller than in capitalist countries! Although a joint venture association may at first appear more troublesome than industrial co-operation, the former normally offers a greater return than the latter.

On the Socialist side, up-to-date technology and know-how, foreign capital and better access to capitalist markets are the main considerations. A joint venture is superior to the purchase of a licence or industrial co-operation as in the latter two cases the Western partner is not generally interested in passing on all current improvements in technology, whilst in the case of a joint venture he is more likely to be. The close, personal association in a joint venture also brings the benefits of the Western managerial and marketing techniques which cannot be easily acquired otherwise, and there are many other matters of an intangible and sophisticated nature which cannot be effectively dealt with by correspondence.

The inflow of foreign capital, in whatever form, is of a self-liquidating nature as it is primarily directed to export production. The authorities in Yugoslavia – the country with the longest experience in the field of joint ventures – have come to the conclusion that Western equity capital can contribute more to technological progress and the growth of efficiency than ordinary credits.

The provision of skilled employment has been another consideration. This has been particularly the case in Yugoslavia – the Socialist country which has suffered from considerable unemployment – where it has also been hoped that joint ventures would 'bring Tito's divisions back from Western Europe'.[6] This argument has gained additional strength in recent years owing to the disenchantment of several Western European countries with foreign workers. (Other Socialist countries do not, of course, allow the emigration of labour.)

Joint East–West ventures can be located either in the East or in the West. We shall discuss these two types of partnerships in the

[6] During the 1960s unemployment ranged from 200,000 to 330,000 (averaging 7 per cent of the total work force) and in 1973 it reached 380,000 or 7.5 per cent of the total work force. In addition, there were some 650,000 Yugoslavs temporarily working abroad. See E. Primorac and P. A. Della Valle, 'Unemployment in Yugoslavia: Some Structural and Regional Considerations', *Jahrbuch der Wirtschaft Osteuropas/Yearbook of East-European Economics*, vol. 5, 1974, p. 472; *Statistički godišnjak Jugoslavije 1974* (Statistical Yearbook of Yugoslavia for 1974). Belgrade, Federeal Institute of Statistics, 1974, p. 129.

following two sections of this chapter. For historical reasons we shall examine those located in the West first.

B. SOCIALIST JOINT VENTURES IN THE WEST

Although soon after their accession to power the Communist regimes socialized the affiliates of Western companies, they themselves did not mind acquiring assets in the West by establishing joint ventures. These ventures began to appear first in the 1920s[7] and then in the early postwar period, but their number has increased significantly only since the late 1960s. Their total number is now about 300, the most active Socialist countries in this sphere being Yugoslavia, the USSR, Hungary, Poland, Romania and Bulgaria (in that order).

Socialist joint ventures in the West are naturally established and operated in accordance with local bourgeois laws and customs. But in most cases the majority of shareholding is in the hands of the Socialist side. Most of these ventures undertake the marketing of Socialist products in the West (as well as in other capitalist countries) but some are concerned with manufacturing (especially the assembling of Socialist-produced components), construction, catering and certain other services, such as consulting, tourism, transport and the servicing of (Socialist-produced) equipment and vehicles. Joint ventures have also been established in the field of banking and finance (but these are dealt with in Ch. 8C, pp. 144-5).

In most cases Western partners are small or medium trading firms rather than multinational corporations. Nevertheless there are now instances of joint ownership with companies which can be classed as multinational. Thus 'Belarus Equipment of Canada Ltd', established in Toronto in 1973, is owned by the Satra Corporation (US) and Traktorexport (USSR) in the ratio 20:80 respectively.[8] Its function is to import Soviet tractors, provide servic-

[7] The USSR established the following joint-stock companies for the marketing of Soviet oil: 'ABN' – in Sweden, 'Derop' – in Germany, 'Naftarus' – in France, 'Petrolea' – in Italy, 'ROP' – in the United Kingdom and 'Suomalainen' – in Finland. However they were all later wound up.

[8] For the extent of the multinational affiliations of the Western firms mentioned in this book, see the Complete List and Index, pp. 197-232, and for further details concerning the larger parent companies – Tables 2, 3 and 4, pp. 36-47. For country abbreviations, see footnote 3, p. 2.

ing and repair facilities and carry on research on their local suitability and adaptation. There is a twin venture in Toronto under the name 'Belarus Sales of Canada Ltd' – also owned by the same enterprise but this time in the ratio of 80:20 – which is responsible for selling the tractors. Within a year of its establishment the Belarus marketing network covered New Brunswick, Nova Scotia, Ontario, Prince Edward Island, Quebec and its expansion programme included Alberta, Manitoba and Saskatchewan.[9]

'Chemapol Svenska', established in 1970 and based in Stockholm, is 50:50 owned by Beijerinvest (Swe) and Chemapol (Cz). It handles the distribution of Czechoslovak chemicals in Sweden. Rodeco (Romänische–Deutsche Consulting) of Frankfurt/M is a West German–Romanian venture set up in 1971 by Deutsche Gesellschaft für Wirtschaftliche Zusammenarbeit (and two other West German non-multinational firms) and Romanoconsult (Ro), each side owning 50 per cent of the share capital. This partnership is a consulting enterprise providing technical advice mainly associated with the construction of plants in less-developed countries. The West German partners decided to invite Romanian participation because Romania has easily available skilled personnel for the purpose, and furthermore she has very good relations with many developing countries. Another interesting case is represented by 'Russalmaz', formed in 1973 by the Belgian Bunkering and Stevedoring Co. (and two other Belgian non-multinational firms, viz. the Antwerp Diamond Co. and Diacem) and Almazyuvelirexport, Novoexport, and Soyuzpromexport – all three of the USSR. The venture, in which the Belgian side owns 20 per cent of the joint capital and the balance is Soviet-owned, is concerned with the marketing of Soviet diamonds in Western Europe. The USSR now sells about $200m. worth of diamonds in the West.[10]

For further details of these and some other Socialist joint ventures in Western countries, see Table 11. The greatest impact in the West in recent years has been produced by multinational ven-

[9] R. M. Mansfield, 'Belarus Ltd – A Joint East–West Venture in Canada', *Working Paper No. 5*, East–West Commercial Relations Series, Institute of Soviet and East European Studies, Carleton University, Sep 1974, pp. 26-33.

[10] *East–West*, Brussels, 10/9/1973, p. 2.

TABLE 11 SELECTED SOCIALIST

Name and Location	Western* and Eastern Partners†
Arcode, London	Tenant Trading (UK) – Chimimport (Ro)
Belarus Sales of Canada, Toronto	Satra (US) – Traktorexport (USSR)
Chemapol Svenska, Stockholm	Beijerinvest (Swe) – Chemapol (Cz)
East–West Trading, London	Morgan Grenfell (UK) – Moscow Narodny B. (USSR)
Ferchimex, Antwerp	Belgian Bunkering & Stevedoring † (Be) – Soyuzkhimexport † (USSR)
Nafta, Antwerp	Belgian Bunkering & Stevedoring † (Be) – Soyuznefteexport † (USSR)
Rodeco, Frankfurt/M	Deutsche Gesellschaft für Wirtschaftliche Zusammenarbeit † (FRG) – Romanoconsult (Ro)
Romanda, New York	R. B. Anderson (US) – Terra (Ro)
Russalmaz, Antwerp	Belgian Bunkering & Stevedoring † (Be) – Soyuzpromexport † (USSR)
Tjecko-SVEA, Stockholm	Beijerinvest (Swe) – Strojimport (Cz)

* For the multinational affiliations of the Western partners, see the Complete List and Index, pp. 197-232.

† Indicates that there are other partners, too. For country abbreviations, see footnote 3, Ch. 1, p. 2.

TABLE 12 SELECTED WESTERN JOINT

Name and Location	Western* and Eastern Partners†
Astra Pharmaceutica, Sarajevo	Astra (Swe) – Bosnalijek (Yu)
Belinka, Ljubljana	Solvay (Be) † – Belinka (Yu)
Fadip, Belgrade	Dunlop (UK) † – Fadip † (Yu)
Pliva, Zagreb	Ciba-Geigy (Swi) – Pliva (Yu)
Resita-Renk, Bucharest	Zahnräderfabrik Renk (FRG) – Central for Machine-Building (Ro)
Romcontrol Data, Bucharest	Control Data (US) – CIETV (Ro)
Sincontact, Budapest	Siemens (FRG) – Inter-cooperation (Hu)
Tomos, Koper	Citroën (Fr) – Tomos † (Yu)
Unioninvest, Sarajevo	Marlo Italiana (It) – Unioninvest (Yu)
Vega, Ljubljana	Maruman (Ja) – Vega (Yu)

For footnotes and sources, see Table 11 above.

JOINT VENTURES IN THE WEST

Year of Foundation	Western : Eastern Shareholding, in % (and Total Foundation) Capital in brackets)		Field of Operation
1968	50:50	($60,000)	Marketing of Romanian and British chemicals
1973	80:20	(..)	Marketing of Soviet tractors in Canada
1970	49:51	(..)	Marketing of Czechoslovak chemicals in Sweden
1973	50:50	(..)	Financing of East–West leasing
1972	40:60	($115,000)	Soviet-Belgian trade in minerals
1967	40:60	($60,000)	Marketing of Soviet oil in Benelux
1971	50:50	($312,000)	Technical consulting in less developed countries
1971	50:50	(..)	Romanian-US trade and co-operation
1973	20:80	($115,000)	Marketing of Soviet diamonds in the West
1970	49:51	(..)	Marketing of Czechoslovak machinery in Sweden

.. = not available.

Sources. Based on daily and periodical literature published in Western and Socialist countries.

VENTURES IN SOCIALIST COUNTRIES

Year of Foundation	Western : Eastern Shareholding, in % (and Total Foundation) Capital in brackets)		Field of Operation
1973	25:75	($660,000)	Pharmaceuticals
1973	19:81	($6,685,000)	Chemicals
1971	43:57	($2,491,000)	Hydraulic hoses
1972	49:51	($882,000)	Pharmaceuticals
1973	49:51	($7,500,000)	Marine experiment
1973	45:55	($4,000,000)	Peripherals for computers
1974	49:51	($530,000)	Technical advice and servicing
1973	49:51	($11,910,000)	Passenger cars
1973	20:80	($3,200,000)	Air conditioning systems
1969	49:51	($100,000)	Measuring instruments

tures, partly or wholly owned by the USSR, marketing Soviet oil and cars. These, together with other similar Socialist multinational undertakings, are discussed in Ch. 8D, pp. 152-9.

C. WESTERN JOINT VENTURES IN THE EAST

Joint East–West ventures located in Socialist countries are of greater interest because they represent the ownership of capital by private capitalists (foreign at that) where otherwise virtually all means of production have been socialized. Although there were several Western–Soviet companies in existence in the USSR under N.E.P. in the 1920s they were soon liquidated under Stalin (with full compensation to foreign partners).[11] In the modern sense, the origin of the Socialist-based joint East–West ventures is relatively recent, going back to the late 1960s, and so far there are only three Socialist countries clearly permitting them. We shall examine some legal, operational and economic aspects of these ventures and the role played by Western multinational corporations.

[11] Foreign partners were allowed only minority ownership, i.e. less than 50 per cent of the joint capital, contributed in the form of necessary equipment and finance. The joint companies were concerned with export and import as well as the exploitation of certain resources in the USSR and included 'Russangloles' (Russian–English Timber Trading Co.), 'Russgertorg' (Russian–German Trading Co.) and Russgolandoles' (Russian–Dutch Timber Trading Co.). There were also some foreign concessionary companies with the right of manufacturing and exporting their products. At one stage all these joint companies handled up to 10 per cent of Soviet exports and 5 per cent of Soviet imports. Amongst those active in these trading and manufacturing operations was a young medical graduate from the United States, by name Armand Hammer. After 1921 he traded Western medicines and food for Soviet raw materials and confiscated jewellery, paintings and other art treasures. He also ran a successful factory ('A. Hammer Pencil Co.') in Moscow during 1925-30. Although he proposed wider schemes for a joint exploitation of resources they came to nothing, and after his trading and industrial concessions were revoked in 1930 he returned to the USA. His original ambitions were revived after he became the President of Occidental Petroleum and during 1973-4 he signed agreements with the Soviet Government for the joint exploitation of gas and certain minerals in the USSR involving some $20,000m. This scheme, however, is not a joint venture in its strict sense but rather a form of industrial co-operation. See Ch. 5C, pp. 93-4.

Moves Towards Joint Ventures in Hungary, Romania and Yugoslavia

In 1967 Yugoslavia passed legislation allowing joint foreign ownership on her territory and this was followed by several amendments (especially those in 1971, 1972 and 1973) further favouring such partnerships. Hungary and Romania followed suit by passing enabling legislation during 1970-2.[12] Hungary, Romania and Yugoslavia are virtually the only Socialist countries at present permitting joint ventures with capitalist firms within their borders.

Attitudes to Joint Ventures in Other Socialist Countries

In Poland the formation of joint ventures with capitalist partners is not illegal but none has been established yet. A joint-venture agreement was in the process of negotiation with Krupp (FRG) during 1964-5 but it was never actually concluded. Polish authorities have been carefully studying the legislation and experience in the other three Socialist countries and a special act was promised in 1972, but apparently there has been a good deal of scepticism and the promised legislation is not yet forthcoming.

In the USSR, although the question has been widely discussed by economists, lawyers and technocrats, it has not been seriously considered at the official level. Western equity investment in the USSR would contravene the Soviet Constitution and there have been several statements made in the West by such identities as L. Brezhnev and G. M. Gvishiani (Vice-Chairman of the State Committee for Science and Technology) that joint ventures would not be permitted in the foreseeable future.[13] Bulgaria, Czechoslovakia and the German DR are not interested as yet either, as in their view they can obtain all the Western technology and capital they want through industrial co-operation and credits.

The objection to Western ownership in the remaining Socialist

[12] The English translation of the most relevant legislation on joint ventures in the three countries can be found in J. Zoubek, *Prospects for Joint East–West Ventures in East Europe*, Brussels, East–West, 1974, Appendix, pp. x-xlii.

[13] *Eastern Europe Report*, 27/7/1973, p. 215; J. B. Holt, 'New Roles for Western Multinationals in Eastern Europe', *Columbia Journal of World Business* Fall 1973, p. 136.

countries is even stronger on both ideological and historical grounds, and there is no sign of this attitude changing in the near future. But in China an interesting form of foreign investment was introduced in the late 1950s to encourage remittances from abroad. The Chinese residing outside China could invest in the so-called Overseas Chinese Investment Corporations set up by the authorities in areas which had experienced heavy emigration in the past. Under the 1957 regulations these corporations could pay dividends of up to 8 per cent. The share capital could be invested for 12 years and remain the property of the investors, after which it could be repaid in Chinese currency or reinvested.[14]

Conditions of the Formation and Operation of Joint Ventures in Hungary, Romania and Yugoslavia

In all the three Socialist countries the Western partner(s) is (or are) limited to a minority share, i.e. the maximum being 49 per cent.[15] In Yugoslavia foreign investment is allowed only within the framework of an existing Yugoslav enterprise (which does not preclude the creation of a new affiliate), whilst in Hungary and Romania separate new joint-stock companies can be founded, with share capital explicitly or implicitly created. The Western share does not constitute the ownership of private property in the sense understood in capitalist market economies. Neither the titles (the 'shares') nor the assets are easily transferable or marketable. Otherwise this ownership carries the usual rights – in particular to management and profit. In fact in most cases management is shared on a 50:50 basis, in which case the Western partner cannot be outvoted, i.e. a unanimity of decisions is postulated. It appears that the Western share in profits may reach 70 per cent.[16]

As one would expect, joint ventures have made the greatest headway in Yugoslavia. By the beginning of 1974, 91 joint venture

[14] Pauline Lewin, *The Foreign Trade of Communist China*, New York, Praeger, 1966, p. 39.

[15] The Yugoslav legislation provides for the possibility of majority foreign ownership but it requires Parliamentary sanction – which is unlikely in practice.

[16] G. Adler-Karlsson, 'Problems and Perspectives of East–West Economic Contacts', *Acta oeconomica* (Economic Papers), Budapest, vol. 9, no. 3-4, 1972, p. 256.

agreements had been concluded with Western partners (and 31 more were being negotiated). The total capital in these ventures amounted to $870m., of which the Western share represented $210m. or 24 per cent. The average Western investment was $2.3m. per venture. The largest number of ventures was concluded with Italian partners (21), followed by West German (19), American (10), Swiss (9), Austrian (5), French (5) and the rest included partners from Belgium, Britain, Canada, Denmark, Japan, Liechtenstein, Luxemburg, the Netherlands and Sweden.[17] The number of joint-venture agreements signed by Hungary by mid-1974 was two – with West German and Swedish firms – and at least 10 others were being negotiated.[18] At that time Romania had seven signed agreements with American, French, West German, Italian and Japanese companies and 25 proposals were in process of negotiation.[19]

The three Socialist countries are primarily interested in the acquisition of Western technology, capitalist markets for their exports and import-replacement production. But the approach to the implementation of these objectives differs in each country. In Hungary joint ventures are limited to the service sphere – trade, research and development (R & D), consulting and the like. In Yugoslavia, on the other hand, the emphasis is on direct industrial development. Thus in 1973 all but two joint ventures were found in manufacturing, and by value – one-third in the motor vehicle industry; banking, insurance, transport and public services (with the notable exception of R & D) are barred to foreign investors. The Romanian legislation is most liberal on this score as it allows partnerships not only in manufacturing and services but also in agriculture. However, in practice Romanian interest is directed mainly to machine-building (including vehicles), electronics and chemicals.

All the three countries guarantee the safety of the invested capital (against expropriation), the transferability of profits in hard currencies as well as the unrestricted repatriation of the assets after the termination of the joint-venture contract. In Hungary, the Western partner can be indemnified for damages arising from an unexpected action of the Hungarian Government, and in Yugoslavia changes

[17] Based on: *Ekonomska politika* (Economic Policy), Belgrade, 11/11/1974, p. 18; J. Zoubek, op. cit., pp. xliii-li.

[18] *Eastern Europe Report*, 9/8/1974, p. 247.

[19] *Eastern Europe Report*, 15/11/1974, p. 349.

in legislation (should they involve unfavourable effects) may not apply to joint ventures already in existence under previous laws. In Hungary and Romania workers or trade unions have little authority in running domestic enterprises and even less when it comes to joint ventures. Although in Yugloslavia Workers' Councils are normally vested with large powers in the management of enterprises, the 1971 and 1973 legislative amendments provide for the limitation of their authority in joint ventures with a view to attracting more foreign investors. In fact the 1973 enactment, whilst liberalizing conditions for joint ventures, tightened up the terms for industrial co-operation.

Romania offers most favourable tax concessions – there is no tax payable until the venture starts earning income, and then for the first two years the tax rate is only half the usual rate. Moreover, imports needed for the establishment and operation of the venture are duty-free. In Hungary and Yugoslavia if the venture incurs losses, it can draw on its 'reserve fund' and then there are tax reductions granted for the purpose.

By Western standards, the taxation of profits is not exorbitant. In general, they are taxed at the rate of 30 per cent in Romania and 35 per cent in Yugoslavia. In Hungary the tax base is different – 40 per cent on profits representing up to 20 per cent of the venture's net assets and 60 per cent on additional profits. In Hungary the foreign partner's assets are exempt from the 5 per cent annual capital charge (to which Hungarian enterprises and partners are subject). Income tax on foreign personnel is low – generally less than 30 per cent, and in Hungary foreign employees may be exempted from it altogether and are assured of one-half of their salary being repatriated in hard currencies.

There is no compulsory reinvestment of profit,[20] but instead there are generous tax concessions to encourage the local ploughing back of profit. In Romania the tax remission on profits reinvested for at least five years is one-fifth (whilst repatriated profits are subject to a 10 per cent tax). In Yugoslavia, if more than 50 per cent of the profit is reinvested for five years, the tax remission may amount

[20] In Yugoslavia the 1967 legislation stipulated that 20 per cent of the profits earned by the foreign partner had to be reinvested in Yugoslavia, but this condition was repealed in 1971.

to one-half (the precise rates differing according to the Republic). In Hungary the concessional rates are not explicitly stated in legislation, but tax refunds are allowed on application, each case being considered individually by the Ministry of Finance.[21]

The Role of Western Multinational Corporations

Socialist joint ventures in the capitalist world are, in general, evenly divided between Western and less-developed countries, and in most cases capitalist partners are smaller trading firms without multinational affiliations. Joint ventures which are located in the Socialist countries provide striking contrasts in these respects. The capitalist partners are almost exclusively Western firms, usually of a large size, operating in the industrial field and mostly with affiliates in a number of countries. Of the total number of Eastern-based joint East–West ventures in mid-1974, three-quarters were partnered by Western multinationals. The most prominent multinational corporations which have entered into these partnerships so far include Bayer (FRG), Ciba-Geigy (Swi), Citroën (Fr), Control Data (US), Daimler-Benz (FRG), Dow Chemical (US), Dunlop (UK), Farbwerke Höchst (FRG), Fiat (It), Klöckner-Humboldt-Deutz (FRG), Renault (Fr), Siemens (FRG), St Gobain (Fr), Sumitomo Shoji Kaisha (Ja), Svenska Kullagerfabriken (Swe), Teijin (Ja), Volkswagenwerk (FRG) and Volvo (Swe).

The first joint East–West venture agreement was signed in April 1968 between Fiat and Crvena Zastava (Red Banner Automotive Works) for the manufacture of passenger cars at Kragujevac in Yugoslavia. To the joint foundation capital of $47.5m. the Italian partner contributed 11 per cent, the Yugoslav share being 89 per

[21] For further details of taxation of joint ventures in the three countries available in English, see C. H. McMillan and D. P. St Charles, op. cit., pp. 78-81; M. Manescu, 'Joint Companies in Romania. A Form of International Economic and Technical Co-operation', *Romanian Foreign Trade*, Bucharest, 2/1973, p. 28; T. Nagy, 'The Taxation of Foreign Companies and Foreign Nationals', *Marketing in Hungary*, Budapest, 4/1972, pp. 18-22, and by the same author 'Taxation of Economic Associations with Foreign Participation', *Marketing in Hungary*, 3/1973, pp. 11-15; D. Vukajlovic, ('New Republic Statutes on Taxation of Foreign Nationals Summarized'), *Finansije*, Belgrade, 7-8/1973 (translation in Joint Publications Research Service, US Dept of Commerce, *Translations on Eastern Europe: Economic and Industrial Affairs*, no. 973, 9/10/1973, pp. 16-30); J. Zoubek, op. cit., pp. 83-5, 102, 137-9, 141.

cent; in the following year the joint capital was increased to $112m. and Fiat's share was raised to 19.7 per cent. The largest East–West venture in operation so far is that formed in 1973 by Thyssen Stahlunion-Export (FRG) and Jugometal (Yu) with foundation capital of $147.5m., in which the West German partner's share is 16.8 per cent.[22]

Some ventures may have more than one partner on one side (or both sides). This is illustrated by the Japanese–Romanian venture, 'Roniprot', founded in 1974. To the foundation capital of about $11m. Dai Nippon Ink and Chemical contributed 43 per cent and Sumitomo Shoji Kaisha – 5 per cent, and the majority balance of 52 per cent – the Centre for the Chemical Industry of Romania. The joint enterprise is concerned with the production of proteins from crude oil for animal feeding. The first joint venture established in Hungary, in July 1974, with capital of $1.7m. is owned by Volvo (Swe) – 48 per cent, by Csepel (Hu) – 26 per cent and by Mogürt (Hu) – also 26 per cent. The venture is engaged in the assembly and marketing of four-wheel drive vehicles ('Lapplander'), most components being supplied by the Swedish partner.

Other examples of Western joint ventures located in Hungary, Romania and Yugoslavia can be found in Table 12, pp. 106-7).

[22] A much larger venture was being negotiated at the time of writing (with a letter of intent signed in early 1975). The total capital is envisaged to be in excess of $500m., contributed by Dow Chemical (US) and Industrija Nafte (Yu) in the proportion of 49:51. The partnership is to construct and operate a large petrochemical complex at Rijeka for the production of polyethylene and other plastics to be marketed throughout the world. The complex is to be completed in stages – the first one in 1979 and the last one in 1982. Reported in *Eastwest Markets*, New York, 24/2/1975, p. 11; *Rynki zagraniczne* (Foreign Markets), Warsaw, 18/2/1975, p. 3.

7 Finance

A. THE SOCIALIST PAYMENTS PROBLEM

THE shortage of foreign exchange is a problem which has affected most countries in the capitalist world at one time or another. But this problem has been of a different order under Socialist economic planning where inexorable inherent forces, operating on both import and export sides, generate a tight foreign exchange position. The planned accelerated economic development, based on rapid industrialization requiring foreign equipment, materials and technology, the unsatisfied consumer demand, the non-fulfilment of production targets and the relatively low quality of domestic products place extra demands on imports.

At the same time there are forces militating against a sufficient level of export earnings – developmental programmes are not seriously geared to export production, the prevailing sellers' markets at home reduce the enterprises' inclination to export and moreover Socialist exports are in several ways discriminated against in capitalist markets. The overvaluation of the Socialist currencies at the official exchange rates further tends to induce imports and discourage exports.

Western multinational firms dealing with Eastern countries have been entangled in the Socialist payments problem in several ways. First of all the impressive shopping lists eagerly waved by Socialist political leaders and trade missions usually evoke electrifying interest in Western business circles. In many cases only a fraction of the dazzling offers actually end up in contracts – for which the shortage of foreign exchange and Western discrimination are blamed in the form of prohibitive import quotas, unfair tariff treatment, limitations on currency transferability, restrictions on credit and strategic embargoes. In their disappointment, the large Western companies have often turned into champions of Socialist trading interests and have exerted pressure on their governments in favour of greater and greater liberalization.

Multinational corporations have also co-operated in other ways to alleviate the Socialist foreign exchange problem. Tempted by large deals, in many cases they agree to accept payment in kind even though they usually do not need such goods for their own use and have to resell them. The fact that the corporations have worldwide commercial and financial affiliations makes it easier for them to dispose of such unwanted bargains than would be the case for smaller firms without such connections. Of all the Socialist countries Romania has been most noteworthy for her insistence on such 'counter-purchases' (as they have come to be known), followed by Bulgaria, China, Poland, Hungary, the German DR, the USSR and Czechoslovakia. This order roughly indicates the degree of developmental ambition coupled with a marketing disability in Western countries. When they are accepted, counter-purchases typically cover one-fifth of the total payment to the Western exporter.

The frequency and magnitude of this type of settlement in East–West trade have reached such proportions that some highly specialized firms have entered the field to act as commercial and financial intermediaries. They arrange for the disposal of the bartered goods, usually at a substantial discount, thereby relieving the Western payee of some embarrassment. They may also accommodate Socialist countries by the provision of hard currencies for these countries' unwanted 'clearing credits'. Clearing credits may be earned in countries with inconvertible currencies (e.g. the USSR earning a trade surplus in Egypt) which the Western financial dealer may sell to a prospective importer in need of such otherwise inconvertible (i.e. Egyptian in this case) currency. These operations may involve a complex network of ('multiangular') settlements, and the loss to the Socialist client – in the form of a discount applied by the dealer – may amount to 40 per cent and even more.

The best-developed centres for barter, compensation, switch and clearing operations are found in Switzerland, Austria, the Netherlands and Belgium. Some of this business is carried on by small unit firms, but there is now also a number of companies with multinational affiliations, viz.: [1]

[1] For their multinational affiliations, see the Complete List and Index, pp. 197–232.

Allgemeine Finanz und Waren-Treuhand, A. G., Vienna
Bank Cantrade, A. G., Zurich
Bank für Handel und Effekten, Zurich
Bankhaus Hoffmann, A. G., Zurich
Granax, S. A., Geneva
Handelsverkeer, N. V., Rotterdam
Handelsverkehr, G.m.b.H., Vienna
Interocéan, S. A., Brussels
Tradax, S. A., Geneva
Transmerx Import-Export, A. G., Vienna
Ufitec, S. A., Union Financière, Zurich.[2]

In addition, multinational corporations have facilitated the marketing of Socialist products in capitalist countries through various input–output arrangements involving industrial co-operation and joint ventures (for details, see Chs 5 and 6, pp. 79-114). The remarkable development of these forms of inter-firm collaboration has introduced a new element of far-reaching consequence – enabling an increasing departure from the traditional clumsy barter, and thus contributing to the rationalization of East–West payments. According to some specialists in East–West financial relations, the ratio of barter and similar types of settlements to co-operative transactions in the above sense – which in the past was 9 : 1 – is likely to be reversed, to 1 : 9 by 1980.[3]

B. WESTERN MULTINATIONAL BANKS AND THE EAST

One can hardly imagine more incongruous and unlikely partners in collaboration than capitalist banks and Communist regimes. In

[2] The best-known other, unit firms are André & Cie, Lausanne; Bank K. G. Winter & Co., Vienna; Firma Gebrüder Schöller A. G., Vienna; Hollandsche Bank Unie, Amsterdam; Merban Corporation, New York; Norkompens, Oslo. See J. P. Morgan, 'The Financial Aspect of East–West Trade', *Columbia Journal of World Business*, Winter 1973, pp. 54-6; *Eastern Europe Report*, Geneva, 13/12/1974, pp. 381-2.

[3] e.g., J. Ramsey, 'In East–West Trade "Co-operation" Is In', *Fortune*, 11/1973, p. 182.

the Marxist interpretation of history, industrial capitalism develops into an even more degenerate stage, viz. 'finance capitalism'. This stage is noted for the domination of the economy by large banks which in many cases acquire controlling interests in industrial monopolies. In collusion with the latter and the state apparatus, the 'financial oligarchy' exploits the working class, smaller firms and weaker countries. In his analysis of imperialism, Lenin declared:

> Some three to five of the biggest banks in each of the foremost capitalist countries ... have concentrated thousands upon thousands of millions which form the greater part of the capital and income of entire countries. ... A financial oligarchy, which throws a close network of dependence relationships over all the economic and political institutions ... is the most striking manifestation of this monopoly.[4]

Large international banks have been viewed as arch-manipulators of big business and the state apparatus. Although not contributing to material production they contrive to squeeze out enormous profits, even when the rest of the economy suffers from industrial disputes, unemployment, the fuel crisis, inflation and balance of payments difficulties. Thus it has been recently pointed out in a Polish financial journal that such large British multinational banks as Barclays, Lloyds, Midland and National Wesminster in 1973 (which was a bad year for the British economy) increased their profits by more than 50 per cent (from £400m. in 1972 to £615m. in 1973); in fact the one with the largest number of foreign affiliates, viz. Lloyds, lifted its profits by as much as 75 per cent.[5]

After the Bolshevik Revolution in 1917, Western banking circles were amongst the most bitter critics of Soviet policies and practices. They attempted to apply various forms of discrimination against the USSR, which included a ban on the purchase of Soviet gold. During the Great Depression following the crash on the New York Stock Exchange in 1929 many financial as well as political leaders in Western Europe and the United States believed that Stalin was only waiting for a suitable moment to flood the West with counterfeit currencies and huge quantities of gold – mined at a fraction of its true cost by forced labour in Siberia – in order to destroy

[4] V. I. Lenin, 'Imperialism. The Highest Stage of Capitalism', *Collected Works*, Moscow, Progress Publishers, 1964, vol. 22, p. 299.

[5] *Bank i kredyt* (Bank and Credit), Warsaw, 6/1974, p. 257.

the very foundations of the capitalist monetary and financial system.

That belief was subsequently strengthened by at least two Soviet moves. During 1928-32 attempts were made to circulate Soviet counterfeit dollars in financial centres all over the world, and amongst the Western banks affected were the Continental Illinois Bank & Trust Co. (US), the Deutsche Bank (Germany) and the First National Bank of Chicago (US).[6] Then in 1934 the Soviet Government decided to keep the information on the USSR's foreign exchange, gold reserves as well as current gold production secret, and no figures have been released since.

However, ideological and historical grievances appear to be simply a bad dream if we examine East–West financial relations over the past decade or two. The most spectacular aspect of these relations is the extension of king-size credits to the Socialist countries on surprisingly favourable terms. But close working relationships have been established in other fields, too, involving correspondent dealings, travellers' cheques, credit cards and even the floating of Socialist bonds in Western capital markets. Multinational banks represent a large reservoir of convertible foreign exchange, and moreover have important connections with industrial and commercial interests throughout the capitalist world.

Some of the large Western banks have established special departments for handling transactions with their Socialist clientèle. One of the most active banks in East–West financing is the Dresdner Bank (FRG) which owes 10-15 per cent of its total foreign business to the Socialist countries.[7] Another large multinational bank diligent in this business is the Chase Manhattan Bank, whose Board Chairman and President – Mr David Rockefeller – has travelled extensively in the East in recent years and was received by Mr Chou En-lai, Mr A. Kosygin and other leading Communist Party and government leaders in China, the USSR and Eastern Europe.

For a long time China and the DPR of Korea (in addition to the DR of Vietnam) were most hesitant to enter into financial relations with Western banks. But since the early 1970s these two countries have been gradually departing from their previous orthodox attitudes

[6] For further details, see A. Krammer, 'Russian Counterfeit Dollars: A Case of Early Soviet Espionage', *Slavic Review*, Seattle, Dec 1971, pp. 762-73.

[7] *Eastern Europe Report*, 22/9/1972, p. 81.

and policies. By 1972 the Bank of China (of Peking) had established correspondent relations with 13 banks in Japan alone, including such multinational concerns as the Bank of Tokyo, Daiwa Securities, the Fuji Bank, the Industrial Bank of Japan, the Kyowa Bank, the Sanwa Bank, the Sumitomo Bank and the Tokai Bank. China has also decided to accept credits from Western banks (see the following section of this chapter). Mr David Rockefeller, who in 1971 had criticized Australia's credits to China (for wheat exports), in mid-1973 personally concluded a correspondent agreement in Peking with the Bank of China, hoping to capture some of the other Western banks' business.[8] In 1974 the Foreign Trade Bank of the DPR of Korea was reported to be maintaining correspondent relations with at least 14 Japanese banks, and also with a number of Western European banks. In August 1974 the Union Bank of Switzerland sent a delegation to Pyongyang to explore business opportunities there and was welcomed by both political and financial leaders.

Of the 50 largest multinational banks in the West, 45 have had significant dealings with at least one Socialist country and 10 – with five or more of these countries. Taking into account the geographical spread in, and the volume of business with, the East, the National Westminster Bank (operating in 17 foreign capitalist countries; with 37 affiliates) heads the list, followed by Barclays Bank (33; 46), BankAmerica (56; 97), Banque Nationale de Paris (23; 33), Lloyds Bank (34; 117), Crédit Lyonnais (30; 32), Deutsche Bank (31; 63), Dresdner Bank (25; 42), Chase Manhattan Corporation (44; 56), Bank of Tokyo (9; 13) and the First National City Corporation (32; 74).

The extent of involvement of the 50 large Western multinational banks in East–West banking and other financial services is indicated in Table 13. Only those banks are included which in 1973 had assets in excess of $2,000m. and which had affiliates in three or more countries. The combined assets of these banks in 1973 exceeded $930,000m., which was well over the estimated Gross National Product of the two largest Socialist countries put together – the USSR and China ($850,000m.). In fact the assets of Bank-

[8] *The Age*, Melbourne, 26/3/1971, p. 2; *China Trade Report*, Hong Kong, 7/1973, p. 8.

America alone are larger than the national income of the next largest Socialist country – Poland.

The amount of business handled and the close working relations have led to a number of the leading Western multinational banks being authorized to open permanent offices in some Socialist countries (Bulgaria, China, the German DR, Hungary, Poland, Romania and the USSR), viz.:

Banca Commerciale Italiana (It) – in East Berlin, Moscow, Warsaw
Banco di Napoli (It) – in Moscow, Sofia
Bank of America (US) – in Moscow
Bank of Tokyo (Ja) – in Moscow
Banque de Paris et des Pays Bas (Fr) – in Moscow
Banque Nationale de Paris (Fr) – in Moscow and Warsaw
Barclays Bank (UK) – in Moscow
Chase Manhattan Bank (US) – in Moscow
Commerzbank (FRG) – in Moscow
Crédit Industriel et Commercial (Fr) – in Warsaw
Crédit Lyonnais (Fr) – in East Berlin, Moscow
Creditanstalt Bankverein (Au) – in Budapest
Credito Italiano (It) – in Moscow
Deutsche Bank (FRG) – in Moscow
Dresdner Bank (FRG) – in Moscow
First National Bank of Chicago (US) – in Warsaw
First National City Bank (US) – in Budapest and Moscow
Kansallis-Osake Pankki (Fi) – in Moscow
Lloyds Bank (UK) – in Moscow
Manufacturers Hanover Trust (US) – in Bucharest
Midland Bank (UK) – in Moscow
National Westminster Bank (UK) – in Moscow
Standard & Chartered Banking Group (UK) – in Shanghai
Svenska Handelsbanken (Swe) – in Moscow

More offices are likely to be opened as other multinational banks have lodged applications to this effect, and some of those listed above have been endeavouring to set up additional 'affiliates' in other Socialist countries. The pendulum has certainly swung a long way from Lenin's times, and practically all the swinging has taken place in the last decade.

There is also a number of multinational banks which are either small or have affiliates in less than three foreign countries (and so are not included in Table 13), but nevertheless have been engaging

TABLE 13 LARGE MULTINATIONAL BANKS SIGNIFICANTLY

Name (and Parent Country in brackets*)	Headquarters	Assets in 1973† $m.
Algemene Bank Nederland (Ne)	Amsterdam	10,173
Banca Commerciale Italiana (It)	Milan	18,617
Banco di Napoli (It)	Naples	11,361
Banco di Roma (It)	Rome	19,386
Bank für Gemeinwirtschaft (FRG)	Frankfurt/M	10,158
Bank of Montreal (Ca)	Montreal	14,424
Bank of Nova Scotia (Ca)	Toronto	10,338
Bank of Tokyo (Ja)	Tokyo	23,971
BankAmerica Corporation (US)	San Francisco	49,405
Bankers Trust New York Corporation (US)	New York	18,514
Banque de Bruxelles (Be)	Brussels	7,709
Banque de Paris et des Pays Bas (Fr)	Paris	2,801
Banque Nationale de Paris (Fr)	Paris	32,927
Barclays Bank (UK)	London	30,810
Canadian Imperial Bank of Commerce (Ca)	Toronto	16,118
Chase Manhattan Corporation (US)	New York	36,791
Chemical New York Corporation (US)	New York	18,952
Cie Financière de Suez (Fr)	Paris	14,782
Commerzbank (FRG)	Düsseldorf	14,455
Continental Illinois Corporation (US)	Chicago	16,870
Crédit Commercial de France (Fr)	Paris	4,433
Crédit Lyonnais (Fr)	Paris	24,462
Creditanstalt Bankverein (Au)	Vienna	3,116
Credito Italiano (It)	Milan	13,739
Dai-Ichi Kangyo Bank (Ja)	Tokyo	33,504
Daiwa Bank (Ja)	Osaka	15,935
Deutsche Bank (FRG)	Frankfurt/M	24,538
Dresdner Bank (FRG)	Frankfurt/M	20,921
Fidelity Corporation of Pennsylvania (US)	Rosemont	2,629
First Chicago Corporation (US)	Chicago	15,558
First National City Corporation (US)	New York	44,019
Fuji Bank (Ja)	Tokyo	29,055
Hessische Landesbank-Girozentrale (FRG)	Frankfurt/M	12,918
Industrial Bank of Japan (Ja)	Tokyo	20,937
Kansallis-Osake Pankki (Fi)	Helsinki	2,270

INVOLVED IN FINANCIAL DEALINGS WITH SOCIALIST COUNTRIES

Deposits in 1973† $m.	Foreign Affiliations in Capitalist World ≠	Socialist Partner Countries‡
9,334	14 (19)	Bu, Hu, Po, USSR
16,820	10 (20)	**GDR**, Hu, **Po**, **USSR**
5,434	4 (9)	**Bu**, **USSR**
13,049	12 (14)	Bu, Cu, Hu
8,015	6 (11)	Bu, **GDR**, Hu, Po, USSR
13,304	10 (11)	Bu, Ch, GDR, Hu, Po, Yu
9,370	13 (19)	Bu, Hu, Yu
12,752	9 (13)	Bu, Ch, GDR, Po, **USSR**
41,454	56 (97)	Bu, Hu, **Po**, **USSR**, Yu
14,706	17 (20)	Bu, Hu, Po, USSR, **Yu**
6,947	5 (13)	GDR, Po, Ro, Yu
..	7 (11)	Hu, Po, Ro, **USSR**, Yu
29,835	23 (33)	Bu, **Po**, Ro, **USSR**, Yu
24,717	33 (46)	Bu, Hu, **Po**, **Ro**, USSR, **Yu**
14,816	4 (5)	Bu, Cu, USSR
29,913	44 (56)	Ch, Hu, Po, **USSR**, **Yu**
14,374	5 (7)	Bu, **Hu**, Po, Yu
11,224	11 (14)	Po, **USSR**
13,648	23 (37)	Bu, GDR, **Po**, **USSR**
12,598	27 (35)	Po, Ro
3,718	6 (7)	Bu, Cu, **Po**, Ro
22,672	30 (32)	Bu, **Cu**, **GDR**, **Po**, Ro, **USSR**, Yu
2,327	14 (27)	**Hu**
12,390	4 (7)	USSR
22,192	5 (7)	Bu, GDR, Hu, NK, Yu
11,968	3 (4)	Bu
22,730	31 (63)	GDR, Hu, Po, **USSR**
19,547	25 (42)	**GDR**, Hu, Po, Ro, **USSR**
2,103	18 (22)	Po, Yu
12,042	3 (4)	Bu, **Po**, Yu
34,942	32 (74)	**Hu**, Po, Ro, **USSR**, Yu
19,659	3 (11)	Bu, Ch, GDR
10,859	6 (7)	**Po**, Yu
17,172	9 (10)	Ch, Hu
1,425	3 (3)	**USSR**

TABLE 13 LARGE MULTINATIONAL BANKS SIGNIFICANTLY

Name (and Parent Country in brackets*)	Headquarters	Assets in 1973† $m.
Lloyds Bank (UK)	London	17,619
Manufacturers Hanover Corporation (US)	New York	19,850
Midland Bank (UK)	London	19,080
Mitsubishi Bank (Ja)	Tokyo	27,517
Mitsui Bank (Ja)	Tokyo	20,197
J. P. Morgan & Co. (US)	New York	20,375
National Westminster Bank (UK)	London	27,521
Royal Bank of Canada (Ca)	Montreal	18,382
Sanwa Bank (Ja)	Tokyo	26,597
Société Générale de Banque (Be)	Brussels	8,064
Standard & Chartered Banking Gr. (UK)	London	10,957
Sumitomo Bank (Ja)	Osaka	28,981
Svenska Handelsbanken (Swe)	Stockholm	6,641
Tokai Bank (Ja)	Nagoya	21,129
Westdeutsche Landesbank Girozentrale (FRG)	Düsseldorf	19,890

* For country abbreviations, see footnote 3, Ch. 1, p. 2.

† For qualifications to the figures as given, see *The Banker* and *Fortune* quoted in the *Sources* on the next page.

≠ The number of foreign countries is followed (in brackets) by the number of foreign affiliates – branches, subsidiaries and associates, including sub-affiliates.

in East–West financing: Banque Française du Commerce Extérieur (Fr), Crédit du Nord (Fr), Girard Co. (US), Kjøbenhavns Handelsbank (De), the National and Grindlays Bank (UK), the Republic National Bank of Dallas (US) and several others.[9]

In addition there are several important multinational finance

[9] There is one large bank, Société Générale (Fr), with assets of $24,200m. in 1973, which has carried on a good deal of business in Romania, the USSR and Yugoslavia and which has a permanent office in Moscow, but it has no foreign affiliates.

INVOLVED IN FINANCIAL DEALINGS WITH SOCIALIST COUNTRIES —*cont.*

Deposits in 1973† $m.	Foreign Affiliations in Capitalist World ≠	Socialist Partner Countries‡
16,092	34 (117)	Bu, Hu, **Po**, Ro, **USSR**, **Yu**
17,210	7 (12)	Bu, Po, Ro, Yu
17,256	8 (10)	Bu, Cu, Hu, Ro, **USSR**
18,447	3 (4)	Bu, GDR, Po, USSR
13,040	5 (5)	Bu, Cu, NV, **Po**, USSR
15,367	14 (16)	Hu, **Po**, Ro, **USSR**, Yu
24,771	17 (37)	Bu, **Cu**, Cz, GDR, **Hu**, **Po**, Ro, **USSR**, Yu
16,817	16 (26)	Bu, Ch, Cu, Po
17,064	8 (12)	Bu, Ch, GDR, Yu
8,122	12 (17)	GDR, Hu, Po
9,475	31 (83)	Ch, Po
19,608	4 (4)	**Bu**, Ch, GDR, Yu
3,966	3 (3)	**USSR**
14,010	3 (3)	Bu, Ch, GDR
18,589	7 (16)	Hu, GDR, **USSR**, Yu

‡ These entries should be regarded as minimal, as unreported or unnoticed dealings are not included. Bold type indicates a substantial scale of dealings in terms of value or extent. For country abbreviations, see footnote 3, p. 2.

.. = not available.

Sources. Based on: *The Banker*, 6/1974, pp. 643-85, *Fortune*, 7/1974, pp. 114-15 and 8/1974, p. 183; *Who Owns Whom: Australasia and the Far East 1973*, *Who Owns Whom 1973/74: Continental Edition*, *Who Owns Whom: North America 1973*, *Who Owns Whom 1974: U.K. Edition* – all published in London by Roskill; daily and periodical literature published in Socialist and Western countries.

companies which, together with lending, have been active in providing various fringe banking services – negotiating loans on behalf of the Western and Eastern partners, leasing and facilitating other financial operations. Those which warrant mention here are: the American Express Co. (US), Baring Bros. & Co. (UK), Deutsche Gesellschaft für Wirtschaftliche Zusammenarbeit (FRG), Kleinwort, Benson, Lonsdale (UK), Lazard Bros & Co. (UK), Loeb Rhoades International Inc. (US), Morgan Grenfell & Co. (UK) and N. M. Rothschild & Sons (UK). To this list we must add the finance houses engaging in barter, compensation, switch and clearing operations (see Ch. 7A, pp. 116-17).

Many East–West deals are so large that they are beyond the routine financial capacity of even the largest banks. For this reason credits to the Socialist countries are increasingly extended by national or multinational *ad hoc* syndicates or institutionalized consortia or similar partnerships of multinational banks. This is an interesting development which rather lends support to the views of K. Kautsky who envisaged peaceful 'ultra-imperialism', but contradicts the arguments of V. I. Lenin who insisted that competition amongst international monopolies must necessarily lead to cut-throat rivalry and wars, and not to harmonious co-operation (see Ch. 1B, p. 9). What Lenin once thought to be an unlikely evil has become real and turned to the Socialist advantage. Amongst the institutionalized banking groups participating most in East–West financing are:

(i) 'Abecor' (Associated Banks of Europe Corporation), with its secretariat in Brussels, including the following multinational banks: Algemene Bank Nederland (Ne), Banque de Bruxelles (Be), Banque Nationale de Paris (Fr), Barclays Bank (UK), Bayerische Hypotheken- und Wechsel- Bank (FRG) and Dresdner Bank (FRG).

(ii) 'BTL', London – Barclays Bank (UK), Tozer, Kemsley and Milbourn (UK) and Lazard Bros (UK).

(iii) 'EBIC' (European Banks International Co.), Brussels – Amsterdam–Rotterdam Bank (Ne), Banca Commerciale Italiana (It), Creditanstalt Bankverein (Au), Deutsche Bank (FRG), Midland Bank (UK) and Société Générale de Banque (Be). (In 1973 this group established a new international commerical bank, 'European Banking Co.' in London.)

(iv) 'Intergiro Finanzierungsgesellschaft', Vienna – Bayerische Landesbank Girozentrale (FRG), Girozentrale und Bank der Österreichischen Sparkassen (Au), Norddeutsche Landesbank Girozentrale (FRG) and Westdeutsche Landesbank Girozentrale (FRG).

(v) 'Orion', London – Chase Manhattan Bank (UK), Credito Italiano (It), Mitsubishi Bank (Ja), National Westminster Bank (UK), Royal Bank of Canada (Ca), Westdeutsche Landesbank Girozentrale (FRG).

But what would astound Lenin even more is the fact that some multinational banking partnerships now also include Socialist-owned banks, as is exemplified by the following cases:

(i) The Anglo-Romanian Bank – established in London in 1973 and owned by Barclays Bank International (UK), Manufacturers Hanover Trust (US) and the Romanian Foreign Trade Bank.

(ii) 'Centrofin' – established in 1971, with its head office in Vienna, by Banco di Sicilia (It), Banco Populor Español (Sp), Bank für Wirtschaft und Arbeit (Au), Bank of Tokyo (Ja), Banque Occidentale pour l'Industrie et le Commerce (Fr), Kleinwort, Benson, Lonsdale (UK) and Bank Handlowy (Po).

(iii) 'Gisofra' – set up in Paris in 1971 by Banque Nationale de Paris (Fr), Crédit Lyonnais (Fr), Société Générale (Fr) and (the Soviet-owned bank in Paris) Banque Commerciale pour l'Europe du Nord.

(iv) International Investment Corporation for Yugoslavia – established in 1969, with its headquarters in London, partly moved recently to Zagreb. Amongst its founders are such multinational banks as Amsterdam–Rotterdam Bank (Ne), Banco di Napoli (It), Creditanstalt Bankverein (Au), Commerzbank (FRG), Deutsche Bank (FRG), Dresdner Bank (FRG), Girard Co. (US), Marine Midland Banks (US), Westdeutsche Landesbank Girozentrale (FRG) whilst on the Yugoslav side Stopanska Banka is one of its co-owners.

For other forms of co-operation between Socialist-owned banks and Western banking interests, see the following section, pp. 130-133 and Ch. 8C, pp. 145-51.

C. CREDITS TO SOCIALIST COUNTRIES

From the economic point of view it is natural that credits should flow from the more to the less-developed countries, i.e. in our case from West to East. For several reasons, up to the early 1960s this flow played a minor role. On the one hand, the NATO countries regarded medium and long-term credits, especially if exceeding five years, as a form of economic aid; to varying degrees they withheld government guarantees and applied other restrictions on such credits to the Socialist countries (thereby adhering to the 'Berne Union' convention). On the other, Socialist deals with Western companies had not involved large projects, and these countries were hesitant anyway to incur large foreign debts.

However, since 1963 there has been a remarkable expansion of credits to the East. The growing interest in Western technology and equipment – particularly complete industrial plants and other costly projects – and continued foreign exchange problems have turned the Socialist countries into anxious borrowers. At the same time, owing to keen competition amongst Western industrial and commercial firms and banks, and governments' efforts to promote exports, the Berne Union convention has broken down. According to a Soviet source, Crédit Lyonnais (Fr) and other state-owned banks in France and Italy during 1964-5 were amongst the first to break the 'credit blockade' by granting loans to the USSR for 7-8 years.[10]

The credit policies of the United States Government continued to be more restrictive (with a qualified exception in relation to Yugoslavia, Romania and Poland) than those of any other Western government up to the early 1970s. But even before that the American subsidiaries in Western Europe availed themselves of the local liberal credit facilities; in fact they were also used to finance their affiliates' exports shipped direct from the USA to the European Socialist countries.[11]

The policy of the Japanese Government not to extend government credits to China, in accordance with the 'Yoshida Letter',[12] was quietly dropped in 1972. In the following year the Chinese government abandoned its long-standing aversion to Western credits for financing the import of manufactures,[13] by seeking 'deferred payments' of up to five years in the case of major imports of industrial

[10] A. Vetrov, ('Franco–Soviet Economic Co-operation'), *Mirovaya ekonomika i mezhdunarodnye otnosheniya* (World Economy and International Relations), Moscow, 11/1973, p. 33.

[11] R. S. Kretschmar, Jr, and R. Foor, *The Potential for Joint Ventures in Eastern Europe*, New York, Praeger, 1972, p. 59.

[12] This was a private letter sent in 1964 by Mr Shigeru Yoshida, the Japanese Prime Minister at the time, to Taiwan pledging not to use the funds of the Export–Import Bank of Japan for financing exports to China.

[13] Large short- to medium-term credits have been accepted from Australian, Canadian and other banks to finance massive Chinese imports of grain since the early 1960s.

equipment and plants.[14] A similar reversal of a previous stand has occurred in the DPR of Korea. North Korean foreign trade enterprises have sought Western credits for 2-3 years to finance the import of materials and equipment, and for up to 5 years in the case of larger projects.[15]

All in all, the level of Western lending to the Socialist countries rose sharply in the first half of the 1970s. Eurocurrency credits alone extended to the Socialist countries in 1973 amounted to $1,005m. and in 1974 – to $1,435m.[16] The total amount of credits owed to Western lenders in the mid-1970s stood at about $25,000m. – the FR of Germany, Japan, France, the United Kingdom and the United States being the leading creditors (roughly in that order).

In the case of some countries, notably France and Japan, up to three-quarters of their exports to the East has been credit-financed. As of the mid-1970s, the largest Socialist debtor countries were the USSR – about $9,000m., Poland and Yugoslavia – $5,000m. each. Romania, Hungary, Bulgaria, Czechoslovakia and the German DR (in more or less that order) were also substantial debtors accounting for about one fifth of the total. More than three-quarters of the credits were of a medium or long-term nature.

It is widely agreed in Western financial circles that the capacity of the Socialist countries, with the possible exception of Yugoslavia, has not been exhausted. In the past these countries' borrowing in the West was restrained – in their efforts to balance their resource commitment, to avoid large interest payments and not to become too dependent on the unstable capitalist economies in general. But there is little doubt that Western banks would be willing to lend more. Socialist borrowers have proved to be excellent credit risks, unparalleled in the capitalist world. Although they bargain hard, once the credit contract is signed, they are most meticulous in its observance and repayment is often made ahead of the due dates.

Although a large proportion of Western credits to the East is

[14] Thus in 1974 the Export–Import Bank of Japan granted credits amounting to $26.2m. to finance the construction of an ethylene plant in China. *China Trade Report*, 12/1974, p. 3.

[15] Dick Wilson, 'North Korea Seeks Western Credits', *The Banker*, London, 11/1974, pp. 1305-7.

[16] *East–West*, Brussels, 26/2/1975, p. 9.

extended by government-owned institutions,[17] about one-half now comes from private banking and financial companies – in fact mostly multinational banks. An example of the latter type is provided by the $1.36m. loan granted by the Security Pacific National Bank (US) to Poland in 1974 for the import of $3m. worth of electronic equipment, supplied by the Control Data Corporation (US). The loan, carrying 6 per cent interest, is to be repaid in 10 semi-annual instalments by May 1979.[18]

In the case of larger credits several banks may be involved. Thus in 1971, a $10m. loan, at 5.5 per cent and for 10.5 years, was extended to the USSR by a consortium consisting of Lazard Bros (which arranged the loan), Barclays, Lloyd, Midland and several other British banks. This loan financed the construction of a complete electrolytic tinplate plant by the Head Wrightson Machine Co. (UK).[19] In 1973 the Banque de l'Union Européenne (Fr) led a consortium of 23 Western European and Arab banks to raise a seven-year, $45m. multicurrency loan to the Foreign Trade Bank of the DPR of Korea.[20] Some other cases of medium and long-term credits, involving amounts in excess of $10m., extended by Western banks with multinational affiliations are listed in Table 14.

There have also been instances of Socialist-owned banks collaborating with Western multinational banks in providing credits to Socialist banks and enterprises. Thus in 1970 the Manufacturers Hanover Trust (US) co-operated with the Moscow Narodny Bank in extending a Eurodollar loan of $7.6m. to the Romanian Foreign Trade Bank, to finance the import of equipment and know-how

[17] The main ones being: Commodity Credit Corporation (US), Credito Mobiliare Italiano (It), Export Credits Guarantee Department (UK), Export Development Corporation (Ca), Export–Import Bank (Ja) and Export–Import Bank (US). The largest line of credit granted by any single bank to a Socialist country so far was that of $1,050m. by the Export–Import Bank to the USSR approved in April 1974 for three major development schemes in Siberia – natural gas in Yakutia ($100m.), coal mining in Yakutia ($450m.) and timber exploitation in the Soviet Far East. The total owed by all the Socialist countries (mainly the USSR, Yugoslavia, Poland and Romania) to the Export–Import Bank (US) in the mid-1970s was about $700m. *Bank i kredyt*, 8/1974, p. 350; *Eastern Europe Report*, 11/1/1974, pp. 8-10; *Rynki zagraniczne* (Foreign Markets), Warsaw, 4/7/1974, p. 2 and 19/7/1974, p. 2.

[18] *Eastern Europe Report*, 8/3/1974, p. 78.

[19] C. Levinson, *International Trade Unionism*, London, Macmillan, 1972, p. 174.

[20] Dick Wilson, op. cit.

TABLE 14 SUBSTANTIAL MEDIUM AND LONG-TERM CREDITS EXTENDED BY WESTERN MULTINATIONAL BANKS TO SOCIALIST COUNTRIES IN THE FIRST HALF OF THE 1970S

Western Bank*	Description of the Financed Export to the Socialist Country**	Amount of credit $m.	Period (in years)
Bank of Montreal (Ca)†	Machinery, equipment (Yu)	15	7.5
BankAmerica (US)†	Fertilizer plants (USSR)	180	12
Bankers Trust Co. (UK)†	Industrial equipment (Yu)	28	5.5
Banque Nationale de Paris (Fr)†	Electrical power equipment (Yu)	20	10
Barclays Bank (UK)†	Machinery, equipment (Po)	35	5-8
Chemical Bank (US)†	Industrial equipment, etc. (Hu)	100	8
Citicorp Intern. Bank (US)†	Nuclear power plant (Yu)	216	5-10
Crédit Commercial de France (Fr)†	Industrial equipment (Po)	70	7
Creditanstalt Bankverein (Au)†	Industrial equipment (Hu)	50	8
Dai-Ichi Kangyo Bank (Ja)†	Machinery, equipment (Hu)	50	12
Deutsche Bank (FRG)†	Large-diameter pipes (USSR)	400	11
Dresdner Bank (FRG)†	Heavy trucks (USSR)	300	5
Fuji Bank (Ja)†	Industrial equipment (GDR)	20	7
Industrial Bank of Japan (Ja)†	Machinery, equipment (Yu)	22	12
Kjøbenhavn Handelsbank (De)†	Cement plants (Po)	60	10
Lloyds Bank (UK)†	Industrial plants (Yu)	64	10
Manufacturers Hanover Trust (US)†	Metallurgical equipment (Yu)	18	12
Midland Bank (UK)†	Chemical equipment (Hu)	12	8.5
Mitsui Bank (Ja)†	Container port facilities (USSR)	80	7
Morgan Guaranty Trust Co. (US)†	Copper mining development (Po)	100	7
National Westminster Bank (UK)	Electronic equipment, etc. (Po)	18	5-8
N. M. Rothschild & Son (UK)	Machinery, equipment (Ro)	12	2-5
Royal Bank of Scotland (UK)†	Miscellaneous items (USSR)	60	5-8.5
Sanwa Bank (Ja)†	Industrial equipment (GDR)	15	7
Sumitomo Bank (Ja)†	Machinery, equipment (Bu)	30	10

* For their multinational affiliations, see the Complete List and Index, pp. 197-232 and for further details of parent banks, Tables 13, pp. 122-5. The symbol † indicates that other banks also participated.

** For country abbreviations, see footnote 3, Ch. 1, p. 2.

Sources. Based on daily and periodical literature published in Socialist and Western countries.

to be supplied by American Metal Climax (US) for the production of aluminium.[21] In 1974 the Union de Banques Arabes et Françaises (Fr) arranged a $4.4m. loan to a Yugoslav enterprise (Sumsko Poljoprivredno Industrijski Kombinat, Ivanjica) in which, in addition to other capitalist multinational banks, the Banque Commerciale pour l'Europe du Nord and the Moscow Narodny Bank participated.[22]

For a variety of reasons, credit terms conceded by Western banks to the Socialist countries are most favourable, and it is widely believed that the interest rates are below those normally accorded to capitalist borrowers.[23] The impeccable Socialist payment record, the typically large size of the loans involved, the keen competition amongst Western lenders, the pressure from industrial and commercial affiliates of the banks concerned, and the Socialist skill and patience in negotiations are the main forces operating in this direction.

This privileged treatment became most obvious during 1973-4 when the rates of discount of the central banks in the leading Western countries reached up to 13 per cent.[24] Thus complaints were made in the FR of Germany that whilst the interest rates charged to domestic borrowers were up to 14 per cent, credits extended to the Socialist countries (such as Poland, the USSR and Yugoslavia) for up to 20 years carried only 2-7 per cent;[25] such cheap credits, it was further argued, in effect mean a free gift to the East amounting to 200m.–500m. DM ($75m.–$190m.) annually.[26] Moreover, complaints were also levelled against other Western lenders who were charging even lower rates, thereby

[21] *East–West*, 20/11/1970, p. 5.

[22] *Eastern Europe Report*, 29/11/1974, p. 370.

[23] See, e.g., R. S. Kretschmar, Jr, and R. Foor, op. cit., p. 94; H. J. Mahnke, ('Critical View of West German Credits to the East Bloc Countries'), *Die Welt* (The World), Hamburg, 14/9/1973, p. 9; *The Oriental Economist*, Tokyo, 4/1967, p. 242.

[24] Peak discount rates prevailed at the end of 1973 and beginning of 1974; Austria – 6.50, Belgium – 8.75, Canada – 9.25, Denmark – 10,00, France – 13.00, FR of Germany – 7.00, Italy – 9.00, Japan – 9.00, Netherlands – 8.00, Sweden – 7.00, United Kingdom – 13.00 and United States – 7.50. United Nations *Monthly Bulletin of Statistics*, 9/1974, p. 241, and 11/1974, p. 241.

[25] *Handelsblatt* (Commercial News), Düsseldorf, 21/2/1974, p. 13 and 25/6/1974, p. 4.

[26] Quoted from R. Hacker, ('From the "Cold War" to Détente'), *Die Wirtschaft* (The Economy), East Berlin, 10/1974, p. 31.

threatening the competitive position of West German exports to the East; the Americans were accused of charging only 6.25 per cent, the British and French – 6 per cent, the Italians – 5.8 per cent and the Japanese – as low as 4 per cent.[27]

The pace for the depressed level of these interest rates is often set by government-owned credit institutions. Examining the Western European practice, two American specialists in the field explained:

> These loans [to the Socialist countries] are often at 'subsidized' interest rates. By granting special rediscount privileges at the Bank of England, for example, the United Kingdom's ECGD persuades (one banker uses the word 'bludgeons') the large clearing banks to extend credit at below-market rates. Coface in France and Hermes in West Germany achieve the same result.[28]

Government-owned or government-controlled financial institutions in many Western countries also provide credit guarantees and insurance against risks of not only a commercial but also a political nature. The leading Western agencies in the field are:

Compagnie Française d'Assurance pour le Commerce Extérieur (Coface) (Fr)
Export Credits Guarantee Department (UK)
Export Development Corporation (Ca)
Export Finance and Insurance Corporation (Australia)
Export-Import Bank (Ja)
Export-Import Bank (US)
Export Kreditnämnden (Swe)
Hermes Versicherungs (FRG)
Istituto Mobiliare Italiano (It)
Nederlandse Credietverzekering (Ne)
Office Nationale du Ducroire (Be)

To some extent, insurance cover is also provided by the Overseas Private Investment Corporation for American investors in joint ventures in Romania and Yugoslavia, and by the International Investment Corporation for Yugoslavia – for Western partners in joint ventures in Yugoslavia.

There are also two Soviet-owned insurance companies in the

[27] *Die Welt*, 18/1/1974, p. 9; *Handelsblatt*, 28/2/1974, p. 4.
[28] R. S. Kretschmar, Jr, and R. Foor, op. cit., p. 94.

West – the Garant Versicherungs, in Vienna, and the Black Sea and Baltic General Insurance Co., in London – which offer commercial and non-commercial cover to Western customers dealing not only with the USSR but also other European Socialist countries.

The various forms of insurance cover were regarded for a long time as indispensable, particularly during the Cold War. However, owing to the excellent credit risk rating established by the Socialist countries there has been a tendency in recent years for Western banks and financial companies to extend credits outside the governmental framework of security.

8 Socialist-owned Multinationals

A. THE QUESTION OF SOCIALIST FOREIGN PROPERTY

THE designation 'multinational' usually brings to mind multinational corporations – large, private companies owned by Western capitalists. But it is not generally realized that the Socialist countries now also have multinational enterprises. Some of them carry on their activities in more than one Socialist country, but in addition there is a surprisingly large number operating in the capitalist world – with subsidiaries and associates in Western and less-developed countries. In this chapter we shall examine the question of the Socialist ownership of the means of production in foreign countries from the ideological point of view, then the nature and operation of multinationally-owned enterprises in Comecon,[1] Socialist banking and financial institutions in the West and finally the Socialist enterprises engaging in production and marketing in capitalist countries.

In the ultimate analysis, socialism – and particularly its higher phase, communism – claims to be international, or at least it was envisaged so by the founding fathers of the communist ideology. Marx and Engels spoke of the international solidarity of the proletariat.[2] Lenin in his writings went further and explained:

[1] The Council for Mutual Economic Assistance, established in 1949, with its headquarters in Moscow. Its members are: Bulgaria, Cuba, Czechoslovakia, the German DR, Hungary, Mongolia, Poland, Romania and the USSR; Yugoslavia is an associate member and Finland has also been accorded a sort of associate status. The bloc of the nine full member countries constitutes one-tenth of world population and one-fifth of world area, and it contributes one-fifth of the world's national income and as much as one-third of the world's industrial output. In contrast to economic groupings in capitalist market economies, economic integration in Comecon is essentially based on direct inter-governmental agreements and economic planning.

[2] K. Marx and F. Engels, *Manifesto of the Communist Party*, Moscow, Progress Publishers, 1952, pp. 56-7, 94.

> ... already under capitalism all economic, political and spiritual life is becoming more and more international. Socialism will make it completely international.[3] ... the aim of socialism is not only to end the division of mankind into tiny states and the isolation of nations in any form; it is not only to bring the nations closer together but to integrate them.[4]

Applying Leninist ideas, N. S. Khrushchev (when he visited Leipzig in 1959) outlined his vision of the integration of the Socialist countries belonging to Comecon:

> As to the future, it appears to me that further progress in the Socialist countries will lead to the formation of a single Socialist economic system. The barriers which separated our economies under capitalism will gradually disappear ... making national frontiers pointless.[5]

It is agreed amongst Socialist ideologists that the trend towards the internationalization of production is inevitable and the scientific and technical revolution has added new impetus to this development in both capitalist and socialist economies. But Socialist observers are quick to point out that there are significant differences in this development under each system. They view it essentially from the standpoint of class struggle, and they see the process under socialism as being superior to that under capitalism. H. Sindermann, a member of the Central Committee of the Socialist Unity Party of Germany (the East German Communist Party), recently emphasized:

> In the developed capitalist countries internationalization of production has resulted in more intensive exploitation of workers at home and in countries economically, and in varying degrees politically, dependent on imperialist monopolies and states. And since the principal powers in the capitalist world pursue their egoistic interests in the drive for maximum profit, the contradictions between countries and groups of countries are growing more acute. This results in inequality and discrimination. In contrast, the content of international relations within the Socialist world is distinctly internationalist, for internationalism is an essential feature of the working class whose social nature is opposite to that of bourgeoisie.[6]

[3] V. I. Lenin, *Collected Works*, Moscow, Progress Publishers, 1968, vol. 19, p. 246.

[4] Ibid. (1964 ed.), vol. 22, p. 146.

[5] *Pravda*, Moscow, 27/3/1959, p. 2.

[6] H. Sindermann, 'Economic Integration of Sovereign States', *World Marxist Review*, June 1974, p. 17.

Although there is general agreement amongst Socialist leaders and theoreticians on the inevitability of the internationalization of economic relations and the superiority of the Socialist practice, views differ widely on the precise nature of the Socialist property involved. The question of the ownership of the means of production in a Socialist country has always been a sensitive affair, and how one sovereign Marxist state can permit another to own property within its borders poses a new complex problem. These matters have aroused considerable interest in recent years and the extent of the controversy was reflected in a conference of Polish and Soviet theoreticians on 'International Socialist Property', held in Warsaw in 1974.[7]

Some participants in that conference, such as Z. Bombera of Poland, believed that the internationalization of production in the form of Socialist multinational enterprises does not lead to international socialist property – only an act at the top political level can establish that.[8] On the other hand the Soviet delegate, O. T. Bogomolov (Director of the Institute of Economics of the Socialist World System, in Moscow), maintained that such joint projects are not only indivisible technologically and in terms of management but they also amount to, or certainly lead to, the international socialization of property. Bogomolov sees three stages in this process – the highest (third) stage still belonging to the future.

(a) *The joint use of resources* – by several national Socialist enterprises, each retaining its financial identity.

(b) *The pooling of financial resources into a common fund* – the International Bank for Economic Co-operation, the Common Rail Freight Car Pool in Comecon being given as existing examples.

(c) *International economic organization* – undertaking production, marketing, and research and development (R & D) in a particular industry, going beyond co-operative or partnership arrangements. This will amount to international Socialist property serving all member countries. Profit will not be distributed according to the original capital contribution but will be based on equivalent exchange and the need to even out economic levels between less-

[7] Its proceedings were reported in *World Marxist Review*, June 1974, pp. 66-74.

[8] Ibid., p. 68.

developed and more-developed member countries. In fact, profits may not be distributed at all but retained by the organization to form a large international fund for financing schemes of common social and political concern (such as regional developmental projects, the development of new power resources).[9]

There are still many problems besetting the development of multinational enterprises in the Socialist countries. Although in some of them foreign ownership is legally sanctioned or at least not prohibited (Hungary, Poland, Romania and Yugoslavia), in others – notably in the USSR – it is not permitted. The cumbersome currency regulations and the clumsy and widely differing price-setting procedures also impede the development of the Socialist multinationals. But work is being carried on in Comecon to resolve these problems.

Although the zealous Communist regimes soon after their seizure of power socialized the assets belonging to owners from capitalist countries, they have no qualms about acquiring property and establishing enterprises in the very same countries. Socialist legislation allows the state to acquire foreign assets as long as there is no local prohibition to this effect.

B. MULTINATIONAL ENTERPRISES IN COMECON

Comecon is an economic grouping where multinational enterprises have been developed better than in other Socialist countries. The first enterprise of this nature was established in 1959 ('Haldex', Hungarian–Polish). Then a number was formed in the early 1960s and the late 1960s, mostly concerned with the joint exploitation of resources (such as bauxite, coal, copper, iron ore, potash and timber) or the co-ordination of production of certain basic manufactures (iron and steel, bearings, selected types of machinery and equipment, computers and chemicals); several partnerships in transport were also created (in shipping, pipelines, electricity transmission and rail freight cars).

But a new stimulus to multinational undertakings was given by the 'Complex Programme of Further Intensification and Perfection

[9] Ibid., pp. 69-72.

of Co-operation and the Development of Socialist Economic Integration amongst the Comecon Countries', adopted in Bucharest at the 25th Comecon Session in July 1971. The Programme postulated the creation of 'international economic organisations' covering R & D, production and trade – especially in the technologically most dynamic branches affecting the grouping as a whole. More than a dozen such organizations have since been established involving chemicals, communications, electrical equipment, measurement apparatus, nuclear power and textiles.

By the mid-1970s there were about 50 enterprises in Comecon which could be classed as multinational. These enterprises differ in several important respects from Western multinational corporations. In contrast to the latter they are, of course, state-owned and are more like permanent consortia than networks of affiliates owned and controlled by the parent company. They are formed on the basis of inter-governmental agreements, with practical problems subsequently resolved at lower levels. They can be either international economic associations – consisting of essentially independent and separate member enterprises, or joint enterprises – with jointly-owned capital and more integrated management.

From the point of view of state control and financing, they fall into two types. The first type includes those multinationals which have a 'Governing Council' consisting of the ministers of the member countries responsible for the branch of economic activity concerned and it is financed directly by the state budgets of the member countries (and their income also forms part of the state budgets). The other type embraces entities directly controlled by the member enterprises, run on a more or less commercial accounting basis. Accordingly, the freedom of operation of the different categories of these multinationals varies widely. Some are little more than agencies making recommendations to the government departments concerned or the affiliated entities, whilst others are largely independent and integrated enterprises primarily (but not exclusively) guided by profit. There is a clear trend in favour of the latter type.

Multinational enterprises, especially of the integrated type, are regarded in Comecon as a progressive step – from economic co-operation to more advanced integration. In addition to their intra-

TABLE 15 MULTINATIONALLY-OWNED ENTERPRISES IN COMECON

Name (with Headquarters and Year of Foundation in brackets*)	Field of Operation	Member Countries*
Adriatika Oil Pipeline (Rijeka, Yu, 1974)	Oil transport by pipes	Cz, Hu, Yu
Agromash (Budapest, 1965)	Horticultural machinery	Bu, GDR, Hu, USSR
Assofoto (Moscow, 1973)	Photochemical products	GDR, USSR
'Friendship' Cotton Spinning Mill (Zawiercie, Po, 1973)	Spinning	GDR, Po
Haldex (Katowice, Po, 1959)	Coal waste extraction	Hu, Po
Interatomenergo (Moscow, 1973)	Nuclear power equipment	Bu, Cz, GDR, Hu, Po, Ro, USSR, Yu
Interatominstrument (Warsaw, 1972)	Atomic appliances, apparatus	Bu, Cz, GDR, Hu, Po, USSR
Interchim (Halle, GDR, 1969)	Light chemicals	Bu, Cz, GDR, Hu, Po, Ro, USSR
Interchimvolokno (Bucharest, 1974)	Chemical fibres	Bu, Cz, GDR, Hu, Po, Ro, USSR
Interelektro (Moscow, 1973)	Electrical equipment	Bu, Cz, GDR, Hu, Po, Ro, USSR
Intermetal (Budapest, 1964)	Iron and steel	Bu, Cz, GDR, Hu, Po, Ro, USSR, Yu
International Bank for Economic Co-operation (Moscow, 1964)	Clearing and short-term credits	Bu, Cu, Cz, GDR, Hu, Po, Ro, USSR, Yu
International Investment Bank (Moscow, 1970)	Long-term financing	Bu, Cu, Cz, GDR, Hu, Po, Ro, USSR
Interpodshypnik (Warsaw, 1964)	Bearings	Bu, Cz, GDR, Hu, Po, Ro, USSR
Interport (Szczecin, 1974)	Major seaports	GDR, Po
Intersputnik (Moscow, 1972)	Satellite telecommunications	All Comecon members
Intertextilmash (Moscow, 1973)	Textile machinery	Bu, Cz, GDR, Hu, Po, Ro, USSR
Intransmash (Sofia, 1965)	Intra-factory transport	Bu, Hu
Kingisep Potash Mining (Kingisep, USSR, 1963)	Potash exploitation	Bu, Cz, GDR, Hu, Po, USSR
Kiyembayev Asbestos Concentration Plant (Kiyembayev, USSR, 1973)	Asbestos extraction	Bu, Cz, GDR, Hu, Po, Ro, USSR
Komi Timber Cutting (Komi, USSR, 1969)	Timber exploitation	Bu, USSR
'Peace' Power Grid (Prague, 1962)	Central electricity transmission	Bu, Cz, GDR, Hu, Po, Ro, USSR, Yu
Rail Freight Car Pool (Prague, 1962)	Rail freight transport	Bu, Cz, GDR, Hu, Po, Ro, USSR
Uniafrika (Szczecin, 1961)	Baltic-West Africa shipping	GDR, Po, USSR
Ust-Ilim Pulp Plant (Ust-Ilim, USSR, 1973)	Pulp and cellulose	Bu, GDR, Hu, Po, Ro, USSR

* For country abbreviations, see footnote 3, Ch. 1, p. 2.
Sources. Based on daily and periodical literature published in Socialist countries.

Comecon activities, they are meant to appear in capitalist markets as strong partners and deal with Western multinational corporations on a reasonably equal footing. It is likely that in the future lasting working associations may be developed between these Socialist-capitalist multinationals, in the form of licensing agreements, industrial co-operation and even joint ventures.

Table 15 provides details of the 25 more interesting cases of multinational enterprises in Comecon, about one-half of the total number in existence in 1975. Further comments on some of them may be of additional interest.

The task of the 'Adriatika Oil Pipeline' is to construct a 1,000 km pipeline from the Adriatic coast in Yugoslavia (Rijeka) to Czechoslovakia (Bratislava) and Hungary, with a possible extension to Romania, linking it with the Comecon 'Friendship Oil Pipeline'. The main shareholders are three Yugoslav enterprises (Energoinvest, INA, and Naftagas) which are to provide 150m. dinars (nearly $10m.) whilst the Czechoslovak and Hungarian entities are to contribute $25m. each in the form of credits (Kuwait is also to provide some finance). The pipeline, which is to be completed in 1977, is to carry up to 34m. tons of crude oil annually, to be obtained mainly from Arab countries of the Middle East and North Africa. The three countries are also building an oil port near Rijeka – the largest in South-Eastern Europe (to be completed in 1976).[10] 'Haldex' is an example of a fully integrated joint-stock company. It is owned by Tatabánya Coal Mines (Hu) and Katowice Coal Mines (Po) on a 50:50 basis and profits are shared accordingly.[11] It is concerned with the processing of the refuse dumps produced by coal mines in Polish Silesia and protecting the environment against pollution, using a unique Hungarian invention.[12]

'Interatominstrument', the first multinational economic associa-

[10] *International Affairs*, Moscow, 6/1974, p. 112; *Seewirtschaft* (Marine Economy), East Berlin, July 1974, p. 441; *Życie gospodarcze* (Economic Life), 10/2/1975, p. 13.

[11] The Hungarian legislation of 1970-72, applicable to joint East–West ventures in Hungary, specifies that the Hungarian side must own at least 51 per cent of the joint capital. Thus the majority ownership does not apply to partnerships with Socialist countries. Similarly, the 'Friendship Cotton Spinning Mill' of Zawiercie in Poland is owned by the German DR and Poland on a 50:50 basis.

[12] *Hungarian Exporter*, Budapest, 4/1974, p. 4.

tion of a scientific-production nature, co-ordinates the production of apparatus and appliances for nuclear medicine and physics as well as for nuclear R & D in general. It itself engages in R & D and arranges specialization amongst its 14 essentially independent member organizations. Its task is to ensure sufficient output for the member countries' needs, and in the long run for export. 'Interatomenergo' on the other hand is responsible for the co-ordination of the production of nuclear power equipment and the construction of nuclear power stations. Its foundation capital of 8m. transferable roubles has been contributed on an equal basis by each of the eight member countries (and it is to be further increased in the same proportions); by the end of the century one-half of total electricity in Comecon is expected to be generated in nuclear power stations.[13]

'Interelektro' best illustrates an inter-governmental corporation controlled by a ministerial Governing Council and operating as a budgetary entity (in which respects it is similar to 'Interchim' and 'Intermetal'). The decisions of the Council (composed of the ministers responsible for the electrical industry in the member countries) must be unanimous and the expenditure of the corporation is met in equal shares out of the state budgets of these countries. It is to be responsible for the production of about 70 per cent of the items of electrical machinery and apparatus produced in Comecon.[14]

The two Comecon banks, the IBEC and the IIB, provide examples of fully integrated enterprises with differing capital shares contributed by the member countries. The foundation capital of the IBEC, of 300m. transferable roubles, was contributed in the following percentage ratios (determined by the volume of exports in their mutual trade): the USSR – 38.7, the German DR – 18.3, Czechoslovakia – 15.0, Poland – 9.0, Hungary – 7.0, Bulgaria – 5.7, Romania – 5.3 and Mongolia – 1.0. The foundation capital of the IIB is 1,052m. transferable roubles contributed in the same proportions. Each Bank is governed by a Council consisting of representatives appointed by the member governments.[15]

'Intertextilmash' illustrates a complex approach to Socialist international ownership. Its foundation capital of 5m. transferable roubles

[13] *Bulgarian Foreign Trade*, Sofia, 1/1973, p. 21; *Gospodarka planowa* (Planned Economy), Warsaw, 8/1974, p. 564.

[14] *Gospodarka planowa*, 8/1974, pp. 563-4.

[15] *Hospodářské noviny* (Economic News), Prague, 38/1974, p. 10.

has been contributed by the participating countries out of the state budgets. It will be similarly subsidized in the early stages, but it is to become a self-supporting business association carrying out joint production on its own account. All the national enterprises affiliated with it, 26 at the end of 1974, remain the property of the respective countries. It is to establish branches and agencies in the member countries; however, these will not be owned by the host countries but will become the international property of Intertextilmash.[16]

The 'Ust-Ilim Cellulose Combine' represents a case of joint investment, construction and operation of a project which is to become fully owned by the host country (the USSR) after an agreed period of joint exploitation. To the total investment outlay, the Soviet contribution is 60 per cent while the balance of 40 per cent is shared by Bulgaria, the German DR, Hungary, Poland and Romania – mostly in the form of deliveries of machinery and equipment. Thus the USSR is supplying raw materials, power, basic machinery and equipment; the German DR – metal structures, electric and laboratory equipment and air-conditioning installations; Romania – a cellulose plant, certain steel structures, pipes, cables and cement; other participating countries are contributing certain other machines, equipment and materials (some advanced machinery and equipment are also being supplied by French and Swedish multinational corporations). It is a huge undertaking designed to produce 500,000 tons of pulp annually (more than the output in all the existing Hungarian and Polish plants combined). Once the project is completed the USSR will be delivering sulphate pulp to the participating countries, in proportion to the contributed investment, for 12 years in repayment. Thereafter deliveries may continue on a conventional sale basis.[17]

In addition to the multinational enterprises, the Comecon countries have also established several collusive associations resembling capitalist cartels (see Ch. 10A, pp. 184-5).

The trend towards the internationalization of economic processes in Comecon has two significant implications. First, in spite of the

[16] *Gospodarka planowa*, 8/1974, p. 563; *Rynki zagraniczne* (Foreign Markets), Warsaw, 14/12/1974, p. 1.

[17] *Izvestiya*, Moscow, 1/5/1974, p. 2; *Stroitelnaya gazeta* (Construction Gazette), Moscow, 8/3/1974, p. 3.

different social system, the rise of multinational enterprises under developed socialism in essence parallels a similar development initiated much earlier under capitalism. Second, although in the past the Comecon multinationals were of little relevance to capitalist markets, in the future they may very well become a powerful factor to reckon with.

C. SOCIALIST BANKING AND FINANCE IN THE WEST

Socialist interest in Western finance goes back to the early years of the first Socialist state. In 1919 the Soviets established the Moscow Narodny Bank in London – the very centre of *haute finance* in the capitalist world. In 1925 they established the Black Sea and Baltic General Insurance Co., also in London (which now operates as a member of the British Insurance Association). In the same year the USSR bought out the Banque Commerciale pour l'Europe du Nord in Paris, from the White Russian emigrés (who had established it in 1921). China, Czechoslovakia, Hungary and Poland have continued to operate their four Western-based banks, originally established under capitalist regimes between the two World Wars – the Bank of China in London, Zivnostenska Banka in London, Central Wechsel und Credit Bank in Vienna and Bank PKO in Paris, respectively. The greatest wave of new Socialist banks came in the first half of the 1970s when 11 banks were established in Western Europe by Cuba, Hungary, Poland, Romania, the USSR and Yugoslavia in Frankfurt/M, London, Luxemburg, Paris and Vienna. All these institutions have been set up in conformity with the local capitalist law and they adhere to the Uniform Rules and Usages for Documentary Credits of the Paris-based International Chamber of Commerce. Some of them are fully Socialist-owned, whilst others constitute joint ventures with capitalist banks.

All in all, as of the mid-1970s, there were 18 wholly or partly Socialist-owned banks plus three financial enterprises located in the West – and more were in the offing. The details concerning the 21 entities can be found in Table 16.

Of these the largest and most dynamic are the two Soviet banks –

TABLE 16 SOCIALIST BANKS AND OTHER FINANCIAL ENTERPRISES LOCATED IN THE WEST

Name	Location	Year of Foundation	Ownership[1]
Anglo-Romanian Bank	London	1973	Ro; UK, USA[2]
Bank of China	London	1929	Ch
Bank PKO	Paris	1930	Po
Banque Commerciale pour l'Europe du Nord	Paris	1925	USSR; Fr[3]
Banque Franco-Roumaine	Paris	1971	Ro; Fr[4]
Banque Franco-Yougoslave	Paris	1975	Yu; Fr[5]
Banque Unie Est-Ouest	Luxemburg	1974	USSR
Black Sea and Baltic General Insurance	London	1925	USSR
Central Wechsel und Credit Bank	Vienna	1922	Hu
Centro Internationale Handelsbank	Vienna	1974[6]	Po[7]
Donau Bank	Vienna	1974	USSR
Garant Versicherungs	Vienna	1958	USSR
Havana International Bank	London	1973	Cu
Hungarian International Bank	London	1973	Hu
Intern'l Inv. Corp. for Yugoslavia	London, Zagreb[8]	1969	Yu[9]
LHB Internationale Handelsbank	Frankfurt/M	1973	Yu; FRG[10]
Mitteleuropäische Handelsbank	Frankfurt/M	1973	Po; FRG[11]
Moscow Narodny Bank	London	1919	USSR
Ost-West Handelsbank	Frankfurt/M	1971	USSR
Wozchod Handelsbank	Zurich	1966	USSR
Živnostenska Banka	London	1922	Cz

1 For country abbreviations, see footnote 3, p. 2.

2 Barclays Bank International (UK) owns 30 per cent and Manufacturers Hanover Trust (US) – 20 per cent of the share capital.

3 The French Communist Party reportedly owns a small share.

4 50 per cent of the share capital is owned by 8 French banks including (those with multinational affiliations) Banque de Paris et des Pays Bas, Banque Nationale de Paris, Crédit Commercial de France, Crédit du Nord, Crédit Industriel el Commercial, and Crédit Lyonnais.

5 Also owned by 5 French banks, including Banque de Paris et des Pays Bas, Banque Française du Commerce Extérieur, Banque Nationale de Paris, and Crédit Lyonnais.

6 Originally established in 1971 as an *ad hoc* banking consortium ('Centropa'), transformed into a bank in 1974.

7 Poland owns 14 per cent of the share capital, the rest being held by 6 Western banks, including Banco di Sicilia (It), Banco Populor Español (Sp), Bank of Tokyo (Ja), and Kleinwort, Benson, Lonsdale (UK).

8 In 1974 its headquarters were partly moved from London to Zagreb.

9 Also owned by 42 banks and financial institutions in capitalist countries, including Amsterdam–Rotterdam Bank (Ne), Banco di Napoli (It), Creditanstalt Bankverein (Au), and Deutsche Bank (FRG).

10 Hessische Landesbank-Girozentrale is a part-owner.

11 Hessische Landesbank-Girozentrale holds 30 per cent of the share capital.

Source: Based on daily and periodical literature published in Western and Socialist countries.

the Banque Commerciale pour l'Europe du Nord and the Moscow Narodny Bank. At the end of 1973 their respective total assets stood at \$2,362m. and \$1,944m., their total deposits – \$2,196m. and \$1,669m. and their capital and reserves – \$46m. and \$32m. Of the 300 largest banks located in the capitalist world in 1973, listed by *The Banker*, the former (also known as the 'Eurobank') was ranked 202nd and the latter – 240th.[18] The Eurobank is the largest foreign bank in Paris – two and a half times larger than the next largest, the Bank of America! The two Soviet banks are efficiently run along orthodox businesslike lines in the best bourgeois tradition. They have won respect and co-operation from capitalist banks and firms. They have risen to the position of the foremost East–West financial institutions symbolizing reputable, no-nonsense transideological relations. Of the two, the Moscow Narodny has a more expansive and international outlook. Over the decade 1963-73 its assets grew at the average annual rate of 35 per cent, and in 1973 it made a profit of £1.3m. (representing a 15 per cent return on its paid-up capital). Since the mid-1960s it has established two wholly-owned subsidiaries in Beirut and Singapore and an associate (Banque Unie Est–Ouest) in Luxemburg.

In addition, a number of Socialist banks have established branches or representative offices in the leading financial centres of the West, such as:

Bank Handlowy (Po) – in London and New York
Beogradska Bank (Yu) – in Frankfurt/M, London and Paris
Bulgarian Foreign Trade Bank – in London
Jugobanka (Yu) – in Frankfurt/M, London, Milan, New York, Paris (and Tripoli)
Ljubljanska Bank (Yu) – Munich, New York, Paris, Trieste and Vienna
National Bank of Cuba – in Tokyo
National Bank of Hungary – in Frankfurt/M, Paris, San Francisco and Zurich
Romanian Foreign Trade Bank – in Frankfurt/M
Yugoslav Investment Bank – in London and Paris.

The central banks of Albania, Bulgaria, Czechoslovakia, Hungary, Poland, Romania and Yugoslavia are members of the Bank for International Settlements in Basle.

[18] *The Banker*, London, 6/1974, pp. 643-85.

Most other Socialist banks, especially those concerned with foreign trade, have established worldwide correspondent relations. Amongst these the Foreign Trade Bank of the USSR (Vneshtorgbank) is most conspicuous for its multinational dealings – with correspondent links with at least 1,520 banks in more than 100 foreign countries.[19] But even the Bulgarian Foreign Trade Bank now maintains correspondent relations with 1,000 foreign banks.[20]

Socialist Western-based banks now often participate with capitalist banks in the extension of credits not only to Socialist countries but also to customers in Western and less-developed countries. Amongst the Western co-operating partners are banks which were once blacklisted by Lenin as arch-manipulators of imperialism, viz. the Banque de Paris et des Pays Bas (Fr), the Chase Manhattan Bank (US, owned by the Rockefellers), Crédit Lyonnais (Fr), the Deutsche Bank (FRG) and the Morgan Guaranty Trust (US).[21]

In 1973 the Banque Commerciale pour l'Europe du Nord participated with the Bank of America (US), the Bank für Gemeinwirtschaft (FRG), the Canadian Imperial Bank of Commerce, Crédit Lyonnais, the National Westminster Bank (UK), the Swiss Bank Corporation and other Western banks in lending $50m. to the Bulgarian Foreign Trade Bank; it also took part in a $30m. loan extended to the Bank Handlowy (Po), in co-operation with such multinational banks as the Bank of Montreal (Ca), the Banque de Suez et de l'Union des Mines (Fr) and the Banque Européenne de Tokyo (Ja).[22] In the same year the Moscow Narodny Bank partnered a $60m. line of credit to the Foreign Trade Bank of the USSR arranged by Morgan Grenfell & Co. (UK), on behalf of the Royal Bank of Scotland, and the Bank of Scotland; in the following year, it joined a syndicate including such American banks as the Citicorp International Bank, the First National Bank of Chicago and the Morgan Guaranty Trust in providing $216m. credits to Yugoslavia for the construction of a nuclear power station.[23] The Banque Commerciale pour l'Europe du Nord also took part recently in the

[19] *Rynki zagraniczne*, 20/6/1974, p. 2.

[20] *Bank i kredyt* (Bank and Credit), Warsaw, 9/1974, p. 387.

[21] V. I. Lenin, op. cit., vol. 22, pp. 211-14, 219, 222, 232, 237, 249-51.

[22] *East–West*, Brussels, 10/9/1973, p. 4; *Eastern Europe Report*, Geneva, 15/6/1973, p. 164.

[23] *Eastern Europe Report*, 9/3/1973, p. 68 and 26/7/1974, pp. 237-8.

$500m. credit granted to the Greater London Council, and together with the Moscow Narodny – in a $60m. loan to the Istituto Mobiliare Italiano (It). The Hungarian International Bank co-operated in a credit line extended to the Quebec Hydroelectric Commission.[24]

Loans to less-developed countries have also become an object of this strange bedfellowship. In 1974 the Moscow Narodny participated with a number of Western leading banks in a loan to the Dubai Dry Dock Co. (in the Middle East).[25] Two years earlier an East–West banking consortium headed by the Foreign Trade Bank of the USSR and the Bank of London and South America (UK) extended a $20m. loan to an electricity authority in Brazil (CESP) to finance a large hydroelectric project at Capivara constructed by the USSR.[26]

Socialist Western, and even Eastern-based banks have become significant operators in the Eurocurrency market – at first as depositors and in recent years also as borrowers. In fact, it is not generally realized that the Socialist countries have largely contributed to the appearance of this largest and most dynamic financial empire in the capitalist world. As early as the late 1940s Socialist banks had begun to deposit their dollar earnings in Western European banks – rather than in the USA where it was feared that dollar accounts might be blocked by the government as a matter of political intimidation or retaliation. By the late 1950s these deposits had become quite large, and the Western European banks accepting such moneys found it profitable to use them as short-term advances to customers who for a variety of reasons did not want to turn to the US-based banks. Indeed, it appears that the original name of 'Eurodollars' was derived from the dollars deposited in the 'Eurobank', the latter being the telegraphic address of the Banque Commerciale pour l'Europe du Nord.[27]

The term 'Eurocurrency' has come to denote those dollars which are acquired by banks in Western Europe (including branches of US banks) and extended as short-term or medium-term (up to five years) loans to various borrowers – either in dollars or in another

[24] *Bank i kredyt*, 8/1974, p. 348.
[25] Ibid.
[26] *East–West*, 8/10/1972, p. 6.
[27] S. W. Robinson, Jr, *Multinational Banking*, Leiden, Sijthoff, 1972, pp. 164, 277.

convertible currency. The size of these deposits has increased in a most spectacular way – from less than $10,000m. in the mid-1960s to more than $200,000m. by the mid-1970s. The two Soviet banks in London and Paris are now recognized as some of the largest operators in the Eurocurrency market. But other Socialist banks have also joined in the game. In addition to the short-term and medium-term market, a Eurobond market has also developed in which some Socialist banks have appeared as customers.

Yugoslavia was the first Socialist country to venture into the Eurocurrency market as a borrower. More recently, in 1972 – aided by a sympathetic syndicate consisting of the Bankers Trust Co. (US), the Chase Manhattan Bank (US), the First National City Bank (US) and 16 other Western banks – she managed to raise a large loan of $100m.[28] The National Bank of Hungary raised its first loan in 1968 with the aid of a consortium led by the Bank of London and South America (UK). Larger raisings were made in 1970 ($30m.), 1972 ($50m.) and 1974 ($100m.). In 1975 the East German Bank of Foreign Trade benefited from a loan of $50m. arranged by Loeb, Rhoades & Co. (Swi) on behalf of a banking syndicate.[29] Loan raising by the European Socialist countries in the Eurocurrency market has now become a common feature.

The National Bank of Hungary has earned the distinction of being the first Socialist bank to float bonds in the Eurobond market. This was done in 1971 to the tune of $25m. (for 10 years at 8.75 per cent); it was underwritten by the National Westminster Bank (UK), Morgan Grenfell & Co. (UK) and the Moscow Narodny Bank, and 80 other Western banks participated. The issue, which caused quite a sensation in the Western capital markets, was a great success and in fact it was oversubscribed. The second bond issue followed in 1972 – for $50m. at 8.75 per cent with a currency of 15 years – and was underwritten by the Bank für Gemeinwirtschaft, the Bank of America, the Japan International Bank and the Moscow Narodny Bank; in 1974 another issue was launched, this time underwritten by the Kuwait International Investment Co.[30]

Another interesting development worth noting is the recent appearance of the Comecon twin banks – the International Bank for

[28] *East–West*, 8/3/1972, p. 5.
[29] *East–West*, 26/2/1975, p. 9.
[30] *Hungarian Exporter*, 7/1972, p. 11; *Rynki zagraniczne*, 7/12/1974, p. 2.

Economic Co-operation and the International Investment Bank – in the Euromoney market. In 1972 the IBEC raised three loans in the Eurocurrency market – for $20m., managed by a French–Belgian banking group, for $60m., underwritten by Crédit Lyonnais, and for another $60m. arranged by Morgan Grenfell & Co., the National Westminster Bank and the Moscow Narodny. Another impending raising, of $50m. with the aid of Crédit Lyonnais, was reported in 1974.[31] The IIB raised a $50m. loan in 1973, and it was underwritten by the National Westminster Bank as the leader of a syndicate comprising the Banque Commerciale pour l'Europe du Nord, the Moscow Narodny, plus the Bank of America, the Banca Commerciale Italiana (It), the Bankers Trust Co. (UK), Crédit Lyonnais, the Midland Bank, the Royal Bank of Canada, the Union Bank of Switzerland and two other (non-multinational) banks.[32]

These are only beginnings. The two Comecon banks are likely to become larger and more regular borrowers in the future, as through these channels the member countries can secure better credit terms than by individual action. More ambitious tasks are envisaged particularly for the IIB, judging by the member countries' decision in 1973 to establish a special fund of 1,000m. roubles partly in convertible currencies for financing investment projects in less-developed countries.

It is significant that the charters of each of the two banks stress that their membership is open to other (than Comecon) countries as well, including banks from the capitalist world. It has been rumoured that the Export–Import Bank of Japan, which has recently opened a representative office in Moscow, may join the IBEC. This bank, incidentally, has an impressive record of achievement. The value of settlements it carried out in 1973 amounted to 47,400m. transferable roubles (about $63,700m.) and its profit in that year increased by 25 per cent to 17.4m. tr. r. ($23m.).[33] It has established business relations with more than 300 banking institutions all over the world, of which one-half are Western banks.[34] In January 1974

[31] *Eastern Europe Report*, 19/7/1972, p. 10 and 14/6/1974, p. 192.
[32] *Eastern Europe Report*, 6/4/1973, p. 98.
[33] *Bank i kredyt*, 8/1974, p. 332.
[34] *Sozialistische Finanzwirtschaft* (Socialist Financial Management), East Berlin, 1/1974, p. 6.

the IBEC celebrated its 10th anniversary, to which 200 representatives of the largest Socialist and capitalist banks were invited. Vodka and champagne were drunk in the best Orwellian image, and from the shop-talk it was difficult in fact to know who was who or what.

In the banking and financial developments discussed so far, virtually no reference has been made to one large Socialist country – China. In the past she showed little interest in participating in these developments in the West, apart from maintaining a branch of the Bank of China in London. Instead she was more active in South-East Asia. In Hong Kong she established 12 banks, which now have 80 branches – all headed by two local branches of the Bank of China (Peking-controlled); these banks hold 17 per cent of Hong Kong's total bank deposits and are responsible for 10 per cent of total lending in the colony.[35] The Bank of China also has a branch in Macao and Singapore and is likely to establish more – in the Middle East, France, the FR of Germany, Switzerland, the USA and Japan.[36] The Chinese Government was also anxious to take over the (Taiwan-controlled) Bank of China in the USA, but the latter was transformed in 1972 into a private bank ('the International Commercial Bank of China') before the normalization of Sino–American relations.

In line with her new attitude to foreign credits (see Ch. 7C, p. 128), China appears to be inclined towards greater participation in Western financial operations. In late 1973 the Bank of China and the Foreign Exchange Bank of Japan agreed on the mutual depositing of third countries' currencies, in particular convertible Western currencies – a sort of mini-Eurocurrency arrangement in an oriental setting. The London branches of Japanese banks have also opened time deposit accounts at the London branch of the Bank of China, but apparently such depositing is moving to Hong Kong.[37] It may be noted here that this London branch now carries on business with more than 75 British and other Western banks in London and in recent years it has actively engaged in foreign exchange operations in Western Europe.

[35] A. A. Stahnke (ed.), *China's Trade with the West*, New York, Praeger, 1972, pp. 201-2; *The Banker*, 7/1974, p. 793.

[36] Dick Wilson, 'The Bank of China Steps Out', *The Banker*, 2/1974, p. 105.

[37] C. Lewis, 'China's Special Relationship', *The Banker*, 7/1974, pp. 798-9.

In reassessing the developments in the last decade and attempting to anticipate future tendencies one wonders if one day the Socialist banks may not challenge the traditional supremacy of the Western banks in the world financial scene. More than 20 Socialist financial institutions have already established a solid foothold in the leading financial centres of the capitalist world and, no doubt, more will join. In several respects they are in a better position than Western banks. They have the support and backing of the state and they have a better knowledge and links with the Socialist countries. They certainly have greater freedom of movement and operation than their Western counterparts in the Socialist countries (see Ch. 7B, p. 121). The Western monetary and financial system has suffered in recent years from disruptive balance of payments problems, inflation and devaluation. But the Socialist countries have enjoyed greater stability and orderliness. Whilst the American dollar and British pound have been on the decline, the Soviet rouble has been constantly gaining in strength and importance and is on the way towards convertibility.

In the past the world monetary system was essentially dominated by a dozen industrial Western nations led by the USA, to the exclusion of the Socialist countries. But the monetary upheavals since the late 1960s together with the radically changing political and economic role of other nations indicate that that set-up is no longer viable. In the new system that is likely to emerge in the future the Socialist monetary, banking and financial institutions are certain to play an important role.

D. PRODUCTION AND MARKETING IN CAPITALIST COUNTRIES

Up to about the early 1960s the Socialist countries were not much interested in establishing enterprises in the capitalist world. This had been conditioned by their mistrust of capitalist nations, autarkic ambitions, timid commercial policies and the preoccupation with domestic problems. That traditional picture still seems to be retained by many observers in capitalist countries, and if it is seriously viewed it must be consigned to history. The willingness and capacity of most Socialist countries to expand their economic presence beyond the Eastern bloc in this way is one of the intriguing features of international economic relations over the past decade. By 1976 these countries had over 700 enterprises (compared with 50 in 1962) in the capitalist world – of which two-thirds were located in the West and the rest in less-developed areas. To the total number Yugoslavia contributed about 400, the USSR – 100, Hungary – 60, Poland – 50, Romania – 40, Bulgaria – 20 and the balance by some of the remaining Socialist countries (such as China, Cuba, Czechoslovakia and the German DR). The total number of sub-affiliates and agencies established outside the Socialist bloc is estimated to be 10,000, the USSR being the most active country in this new-style empire-building.

Most of these firms are joint ventures with capitalist partners in which Socialist enterprises hold minority or majority shares, whilst the rest are wholly-owned subsidiaries.[38] Some of them are found in all major spheres of production, especially in fishing, mining, construction and manufacturing, but more than one-half are concerned with the marketing of Socialist products. We shall now outline the extent of foreign affiliations of some (owing to space limitations, 10) of the most dynamic Socialist multinational enterprises.

(a) Avtoexport. This is a large Soviet enterprise engaging in foreign trade in motor vehicles. It resembles a national monopolistic-monopsonistic cartel in that it enjoys the exclusive right to export and import motor cycles, passenger cars, buses, trucks, specialized commercial vehicles, garage equipment, and spare parts. As in the case of Western multinational corporations, the volume of its business has been growing faster than that of other enterprises without foreign affiliates – over the last decade twice as fast as Soviet foreign trade as a whole. In 1972 its total trade turnover reached 800m. roubles, and the anticipated figure for 1975 is 1,000m. roubles (about $1,300m.).[39] On the export side, it handles over 50 types of vehicles (including such well-known passenger cars as Chaika,

[38] There are also firms operated by the local Communist Parties or trade unions, in some cases in partnership with Socialist enterprises, with which the Communist Parties of the Socialist countries (especially of the USSR) co-operate to varying degrees.

[39] *Foreign Trade*, Moscow, 9/1973, p. 30.

Lada,[40] Moskvich, Volga and Zaporozhets) and more than 450 related items supplied by more than 100 Soviet factories. It exports vehicles to more than 60 capitalist (plus 13 Socialist) countries, including such traditional Western car makers as Britain, France, the FR of Germany, Italy, Sweden and the USA. Its best-developed networks of affiliates are found in the Benelux and Scandinavian countries. Its Brussels-based joint stock company is Scaldia-Volga which is owned in addition to Avtoexport by Mashinoexport, Stankoimport, Traktorexport – all of the USSR – and by several Belgian firms and individual stockholders. It has at least five major branches – in Antwerp, Charleroi, Ghent, Liège and Namur – with 115 sub-affiliates throughout Belgium and Luxemburg. In the Netherlands Scaldia-Volga has a subsidiary, Gremi Co., and 156 dealers and workshops.[41] Another joint stock company – Konela, in Finland – is one of the largest in that country, operating over 400 service stations and workshops. Konela Norge Bil operates from Oslo (with 40 dealers in Norway), Matreco Bil – from Stockholm (with more than 30 dealers in Sweden) whilst in Denmark Avtoexport uses the channels of the Fredericia Motor Kompagni and Darlov Motor Co.[42] Avtoexport is also busy in establishing subsidiaries or agencies in other Western countries, especially Britain, France, the FR of Germany, Italy and the USA. An example of a large subsidiary in a less-developed country is WATECO (the West African Automobile and Engineering Joint-Stock Co.), based in Lagos, with a growing network of modern servicing and repair workshops. Kateco Stock Co., operating in Cameroon is another example of a joint venture for the purpose. All in all Avtoexport has established more than 2,700 servicing stations and spare parts depots outside the USSR.[43]

(b) Dal. This Polish foreign trade enterprise wholly or partly owns 23 subsidiaries in at least 15 capitalist countries and it handles

[40] 'Lada' is in fact what in the USSR is called 'Zhiguli'. But owing to the difficulty of the latter term and its uncomplimentary meanings in several foreign languages a simpler name was coined to facilitate marketing in capitalist countries. It is manufactured at Togliattigrad, the largest industrial plant in operation in the USSR, constructed by Fiat, producing 800,000 cars annually.

[41] *Foreign Trade*, 7/1974, pp. 18-21.

[42] *Foreign Trade*, 1/1972, pp. 46-7.

[43] *Ekonomicheskaya gazeta* (Economic Gazette), Moscow, 47/1973, p. 21; *Foreign Trade*, 9/1973, p. 30.

business in excess of $300m. annually. Most of its affiliates engage in trading activities (especially promoting Polish exports), such as Agra-Polcommerce in Vienna, Anglo-Dal in London, Beldal in Brussels, Calanda in Amsterdam, Dal International Trading Co. in Beirut, Dalco in Hamburg, Dalimpex in Montreal, Dalinco in Zurich, Daltrade in Lagos, Falconda Venezolana in Altamira (Venezuela), Indopol in Bombay, Italmex in Milan and Metalex-france in Paris. It also engages in industrial pursuits through such subsidiaries as the Ethiopian Metal Tools Private Co. in Addis Ababa, Kenya Engineering Industries in Nairobi and Polfa (Nigeria) in Lagos.[44]

(c) Energomashexport. This Soviet enterprise engages in the export of power-generating equipment and also carries on extensive works involving the construction, servicing and repair of such projects and related installations. The annual value of its exports in the mid-1970s approached $500m. It operates in at least 43 foreign (including 10 Socialist) countries, enlisting the co-operation of 66 Soviet enterprises and organizations. Thus in Finland it partly owns Koneisto Co. (in partnership with six other Soviet foreign trade enterprises) based in Hanko. This affiliate is manned by Soviet engineers and technicians (in addition to local employees) and it operates repair workshops, a spare parts depot and its own rail terminal and it deals with 3,200 Finnish firms. In Ethiopia it has a partly-owned subsidiary (jointly with local shareholders) with its headquarters in Addis Ababa, employing 50 men under the guidance of Soviet specialists; its operations have been expanding most successfully and it is to establish sub-affiliates in the neighbouring countries. Energomashexport has been co-operating, as well as competing, with several Western multinational corporations. It has supplied diesel locomotives to the Metallurgical Complex at Fos-sur-Mer in France, co-operating with Creusot Loire; it has participated in the construction of the Sigalda hydroelectric power station in Iceland in co-operation with Brown, Boveri (FRG); it has supplied Svenska Kullagerfabriken (Swe) with an electric melting plant and it has delivered power equipment to Jenpeg hydroelectric power station in Canada and to Rock Island hydroelectric power station in

[44] *Polish Foreign Trade*, Warsaw, 5/1973, p. 32; *Rynki zagraniczne*, 1/9/1973, p. 3; *Życie Warszawy* (Life in Warsaw), Warsaw, 20/8/1974, pp. 1, 2.

the USA. Recently it has submitted tenders as far as Australia (on two occasions, unsuccessfully) in competition with Brown, Boveri, Mitsubishi, Siemens and other Western multinationals. Energomashexport maintains permanent showrooms in at least 10 capitalist countries and is a frequent participant in international trade fairs and specialized exhibitions.[45]

(d) Hungarhotels. This Hungarian enterprise, which owns over 25 hotels in Hungary, has expanded its operations to capitalist countries where it has established a number of restaurants. The largest are those in Rotterdam ('Tokaj') and in Munich ('Piroshka'), but there are others in West Berlin, Denmark, France, Canada, the USA, Japan (and several in the Socialist countries). It also operates more than two dozen so-called 'seasonal' restaurants – in such cities as Amsterdam, Brussels, Graz, London, Lucerne, Lugano, Manchester, Milan, St Moritz and Teheran.[46]

(e) Hungarotex. This is a monopolistic-monopsonistic Hungarian enterprise for exporting and importing textiles, handling some 7 per cent of total Hungarian foreign trade. In the mid-1970s the annual value of its trade turnover was close to $500m. It markets products supplied by nearly 50 large textile and clothing factories and several hundred co-operatives. It has established subsidiaries in partnership with local firms in at least seven countries – Al-Asfoor in Kuwait, Goldsoie in France, Hungarotex Espagñola in Spain, Hungarotex-Faulkner in Britain, Hungarotex Italiana in Italy, Neho in the Netherlands and Tago in the FR of Germany (and another was in the process of formation in Canada at the end of 1974). In all, Hungarotex operates in 100 foreign (including Socialist) countries where, in addition to the subsidiaries listed, it has 10 independent offices and 240 representatives.[47]

(f) Iskra Commerc. This is a Yugoslav foreign trade enterprise handling the export and import of a large variety of electrical and electronic goods and equipment. It has subsidiaries, jointly owned with local firms, in Britain, Brazil, the FR of Germany, Italy, Switzerland, the USA and Venezuela, plus 510 service shops and

[45] *Ekonomicheskaya gazeta*, 13/1974, p. 21; *Foreign Trade*, 1/1973, pp. 32-3; *Rynki zagraniczne*, 13-15/6/1974, p. 6.

[46] *Hungarian Exporter*, 7/1973, p. 15.

[47] *Hungarian Exporter*, 8/1973, p. 14 and 10/1974, p. 28. *Rynki zagraniczne*, 3/7/1971, p. 2 and 13/1/1972, p. 5.

agencies all over the world. Its annual trade turnover in the past exceeded $150m. Iskra Commerc is a division of 'Iskra', the largest manufacturer of electronic equipment in Yugoslavia and a product of a number of mergers and takeovers. In 1974 it merged with another large Yugoslav enterprise, 'Gorenje', producing electrical goods and equipment, which will provide a further boost to its foreign expansion.[48]

(g) *Jugometal.* This largest Yugoslav foreign trade enterprise is concerned with the export and import of ferrous and non-ferrous metals, certain minerals and solid fuels as well as related equipment and complete plants. It has subsidiaries in Austria – Metall und Stahl Handelsgesellschaft, Vienna, in Britain – Metalchem International, London, in the FR of Germany – Metalia, Düsseldorf, in Italy – Ferrochimetal, Milan and in the USA – Metalchemical Commercial Corporation, New York. It also has representative offices in Ankara and Teheran, not to mention those in several Socialist countries (especially in East Berlin, Katowice, Moscow, Prague and Sofia).[49]

(h) *Medicor.* This enterprise produces 90 per cent of medico-technical equipment in Hungary, and in fact it is the seventh largest establishment in this field in the world. Nine-tenths of its output is directed to foreign markets and since the mid-1960s its exports have been rising at 13 per cent annually. These exports include a wide range of medical instruments and apparatus, complete medical laboratories and even complete hospitals. It also engages in leasing such equipment. It has a number of subsidiaries in foreign countries, owned jointly with other Hungarian and local capitalist partners. The most active appears to be that in Britain, 'Medicharge', situated in London engaging in both local production and in marketing in Western Europe, and as far as South Africa.[50]

(i) *Škoda.* This is a well-known Czechoslovak enterprise with a long tradition of operations in world markets. Through its foreign trade division, Škodaexport, it exports not only cars (as is generally known) but also buses, trucks, tractors, electric locomotives, metal-

[48] *Delo* (Work), Ljubljana, 5/8/1973, p. 4; *Privredni pregled* (Economic Review), Belgrade, 16/8/1974, p. 4; *Yugoslav Survey*, Belgrade, 3/1973, pp. 169-72.

[49] *Yugoslav Survey*, 2/1972, p. 141.

[50] *Hungarian Exporter*, 11/1972, p. 11, 4/1973, p. 10 and 7/1973, p. 11; *Marketing in Hungary*, Budapest, 2/1973, pp. 10-11.

lurgical equipment and plants, power plants, a variety of food-processing plants (especially breweries and sugar refineries) and various chemical plants. It operates subsidiaries and agencies – including servicing stations, workshops and spare parts depots – in 100 countries. In Britain, it partly owns Škoda-Britain, and it has recently built assembly plants in at least India, Iran, Mexico and Turkey.[51]

(j) *Soyuznefteexport*. This is another monopolistic-monopsonistic foreign trade enterprise in the USSR concerned with the export and import of crude oil, lubricants, kerosene, motor and aviation fuels and other oil products. Its annual turnover in the mid-1970s exceeded $4,000m. It markets oil and products in 50 capitalist countries, in some of which it has subsidiaries with very well-developed networks of depots, road tankers and filling stations. In Belgium it owns 'Nafta (Be)', in partnership with several Soviet and Belgian enterprises, with its headquarters in Antwerp. Another subsidiary, 'Nafta', operates in Britain, with about 400 filling stations mostly in South-East England (including the London area). In Finland the Soviets acquired large proportions of shares in Suomen Petrooli and in Teboil. These two companies have 20 depots, 150 road and rail tankers and 400 filling stations controlling more than one-fifth of the Finnish market. Another subsidiary operates in Iran under the name 'Iransovneft'. The Soviets want to build an oil refinery near Kassel in the FR of Germany but the West German partners insist that Soyuznefteexport undertakes to supply larger quantities of crude oil.[52]

Thus it can be concluded that the size and extent of the operations of some of the Socialist multinationals are sufficient to impress even the largest Western multinational corporations (cf. Tables 2, 3 and 4, pp. 36-47). The Socialist multinationals have the advantage of the support of their state, the Communist Parties in the host countries as well as of various left-wing elements opposed to Western monopolies and ex-colonial powers. The Socialist strategy also benefits from a careful study of the successes and mistakes of the Western multinational companies. Although there is a good deal of published evidence of the expansion of Socialist capital in the capitalist world, it is certain to be incomplete. It is believed that the actual scale

[51] *Czechoslovak Foreign Trade*, Prague, 4/1974, pp. 14-19.

[52] *Foreign Trade*, 5/1974, p. 29; *Handelsblatt* (Commercial News), Düsseldorf, 5/9/1974, p. 3.

is much larger as in many cases the Socialist shareholding, for a variety of reasons, is carefully camouflaged.

The growing expansion of the Socialist enterprises into capitalist countries, although following economic common sense, is surprising on ideological grounds. The traditional Socialist views of imperialism and neo-colonialism and continued diatribes against 'international monopolies' penetrating less-developed countries are well known (see Ch. 1, pp. 6-14). India, noted for her sympathetic attitude to socialism and the European Socialist countries, is an interesting case study. All the European Comecon countries have established subsidiaries or close co-operation links with local firms in one form or another, and it is evident that many Indians have been mystified by this new historical development. Soviet enterprises have built the largest metallurgical plants (at Bhilai and Bokaro) and the largest oil refineries (at Barauni, Koiali and Mathura) while every third tractor used in India is of Soviet make, not to mention the large quantities of military equipment supplied by the USSR. Reflecting on this brave new world an Indian writer recently stated:

> India's economic relations with the USSR and other communist countries have virtually converted this country in[to] a captive colonial economy. ... But to mortgage our national interests in the name of socialist ideology is to invite a new form of slavery after having won our political independence.[53]

[53] M. R. Pai, 'Is India a New Economic Colony?', *East–West Relations*, The Hague, vol. VII, no. 1, 1973, pp. 34, 37.

9 Conflicts and Safeguards

A. SOURCES OF CONFLICT

As is well known, multinational corporations encounter a good deal of criticism and even hostility in their own parent countries, and more so in other capitalist host countries. But when the dealings of the Western and Socialist multinationals take them across the East–West demarcation line, the potential for conflict is virtually unlimited. The sources of conflict are compounded by the political, economic and legal differences between these basically opposing social systems. A particular decision under one system may be hastily interpreted by the unsympathetic affected party on the other side as a calculated, sinister act, although such a decision may be a logical and legitimate consequence of the social system in force. The memories of past grievances (real or imagined), the legacy of the Cold War and the difficulty of communication are even more likely to contribute to suspicion and mistrust.

The fundamental features of the economic system in the West include the operation of the market mechanism, the basically private ownership of property and the freedom of enterprise. This contrasts with central economic planning, the social ownership of the means of production and the more or less bureaucratic controls over enterprises prevalent in the East. Consequently, the determination and role of interest, rent, prices and profit are different under each system.

Complaints on the part of multinational corporations revolve around the peculiarity of Socialist thinking and practices, especially bureaucratic procedures. They find the Socialist economies unwieldy and inflexible, with a poor capacity for adaptation to changing conditions, and their foreign economic relations are even more dominated by red tape than is the case domestically. Western firms have much less freedom of operation in the East than Socialist enterprises in the West. To start with, negotiations may be most exasperating, especially in the case of larger deals. In most Socialist countries there is no direct access to the producing or using enterprises, except through a foreign trade enterprise, ministry or branch association.

A Western negotiator is typically confronted with a formidable team of technical, commercial, legal and other specialists, each preoccupied with his own responsibilities and to whom time is of little concern. One Western firm negotiating the sale of a licence had to supply 200 lb of technical documentation.[1] Yet many Western negotiators are not willing to provide too much information, fearing that if negotiations break down the Socialist side may utilize the technology incidentally acquired without payment.

Socialist partners are noted for being more proficient as negotiators than producers. A journal published by Business International in Geneva, reviewing the experience of International Telephone and Telegraph (US) noted: 'ITT finds that East Europeans are more skilful at buying than they are at manufacturing and selling.'[2] The successive stages of approvals up the hierarchical ladder through which the Eastern enterprise has to go, further add to delays. Agreements involving a licence, industrial co-operation or a joint venture usually take two years to negotiate. In one case, a joint venture contract (between Control Data and Romania) took five years to conclude.[3]

The fulfilment of the contract is then studded with further pitfalls. Failure to maintain delivery schedules, poor quality and misunderstanding arising from different Socialist specification, costing and pricing practices have caused headaches to many a Western partner. Another complaint is the inflexible Socialist attitude to rising costs and interest rates in the West, even though such increases are beyond the control of their partners. At the same time the Socialist countries – although, by their assertions, they have no inflation – are quick to take advantage of rising prices in the West and charge unjustifiably high prices to their Western partners.

The power of the Socialist state to change prices and consequently costs (by manipulating turnover taxes and other imposts) at short

[1] R. S. Kretschmar, Jr, and R. Foor, *The Potential for Joint Ventures in Eastern Europe*, New York, Praeger, 1972, p. 102.

[2] *Eastern Europe Report*, Geneva, 14/6/1974, p. 179.

[3] *International Commerce*, London, 9/1974, p. 20.

notice has also caused concern – particularly when the same state is, however indirectly, a party to contracts with capitalist partners. In the case of industrial co-operation or joint ventures, cumbersome import formalities in the East can delay the procurement of vital parts or equipment urgently needed to rectify breakdowns. In Yugoslavia, where a joint venture is formally considered as an integral part of a Yugoslav enterprise, the problem may arise as to how to disentangle the profit of the former from the rest of the enterprise.

Then arguments may crop up as to the Western partner's amount of profit, considering that under Yugoslav self-management conditions workers are residual claimants to net income (gross receipts minus extra-enterprise expenses and taxes), and the Worker's Council is vested with the right to determine its distribution (including its apportionment between wages and profits). Furthermore, the management which concluded the joint venture contract may be replaced by the government or not re-elected by the Worker's Council and the new executives may interpret the joint venture contract in a different way. In Romania, joint ventures have to sell in other Socialist markets for hard currencies, whilst Romanian enterprises are allowed to do it for soft currencies or on a barter basis.

Many a potential Western partner to industrial co-operation or joint ventures is put off by the prospect of close association with persons on the Eastern side, being convinced of their hostility to private enterprise and to big business in particular. It is worth pointing out here that no Western firm has a wholly or even majority-owned subsidiary anywhere in the East, but the Socialist countries have more than 200 such subsidiaries in the West. Whilst there are over 30 Socialist banks or fully-fledged branches (in addition to at least a dozen representative offices) in the West, there is only one Western bank which has been permitted to open a branch (as distinct from representative offices) in the East (Manufacturers Hanover Trust in Bucharest). Some Western specialists are convinced that the share of the gains from East–West economic and technological relations secured by the East is much greater than that falling to the West.[4]

[4] e.g. see Marshall I. Goldman, 'Who Profits More from US–Soviet Trade?', *Harvard Business Review*, Nov-Dec 1973, pp. 79-87.

The Socialist accusations levelled against multinational corporations dwell mainly on the outdated technology that is passed on, attempts at domination, instability and exorbitant prices and interest rates. The denial of up-to-date technology to the Eastern licencees or partners in industrial co-operation or joint ventures is effected firstly, by the provision of relatively dated inventions and secondly, by withholding any subsequent improvements to the technology in question.[5]

In general, Socialist enterprises are in a weaker bargaining position when confronted with large Western companies. Complaints have been made of intolerant and domineering attitudes where the multinationals try to reduce Socialist partners to less profitable and less sophisticated forms of production, and a subordinate position in general.[6] A good deal of publicity was recently given in Yugoslavia to the fact that in a joint venture with Unis of Sarajevo, for the production of bearings, its Swedish partner (Svenska Kullagerfabriken) – although holding only 22 per cent of the capital – in fact managed the venture in the way it pleased, disregarding the Yugoslav partner. The corporations have also been criticized for taking advantage of the traditional Socialist predilection for import-replacement production, and they insist on a protected local market without competition.[7]

Socialist partners to industrial co-operation and joint ventures often complain of the exacting demands placed on them by the Western partners as to the schedules of delivery, quality and assortment. In many cases they consider them as petty and unreasonable, and see themselves as bearing the brunt of the whims and fluctuations of the unstable capitalist markets. The Socialist countries are also against casual, short-term inter-enterprise associations involving small commitments – which may be convenient to Western

[5] For evidence, see e.g., V. Aldea, ('Industrial Co-operation between Eastern and Western Europe'), *Probleme economice* (Economic Problems), Bucharest, 11/1973, p. 131; J. Olszyński, ('Trade and Industrial Co-operation between Poland and the FR of Germany'), *Sprawy międzynarodowe* (International Affairs), Warsaw, 5/1974, p. 33; M. Siami, 'International Interfirm Co-operation in East–West Relations', *Marketing in Hungary*, Budapest, 1/1973, p. 9.

[6] J. Olszyński, op. cit., p. 33.

[7] W. Mostowicz, ('The Problem of Prices in Co-operation Agreements') *Rynki zagraniczne* (Foreign Markets), Warsaw, 15/12/1973, p. 4.

partners to meet their passing needs but which cause disruption to the Socialist planned economies.[8]

That the Socialist importers are often charged higher prices in the case of capital equipment than is otherwise normal, is generally known. Western exporters in many cases add what has become known as the 'East European (or 'Socialist') cost factor' – commonly 25-35 per cent above the normal price. This mark-up represents compensation for longer negotiations, higher travel costs, more detailed bids, translation fees, sets of spare parts demanded, inflation and other incidentals. The mark-up may reach 60 per cent if allowance is made for counter-purchases and financing.[9] But the Socialist countries do not usually see these loadings as fully justified, but rather as evidence of greed by unscrupulous monopolies taking advantage of their superior bargaining power.

The Socialist objection to paying high interest rates is based on two grounds. Firstly, in Marxist ideology interest – especially above 3-4 per cent (covering the reasonable cost of credit administration) – is regarded as part of 'surplus value', and as such a form of capitalist exploitation. Secondly, in recent years the Socialist countries have greatly extended their indebtedness to the West (now at the level of about $25,000m.). Consequently, their burden of interest payments – in hard currencies at that – has increased alarmingly. The recent steep increases in interest rates in most Western countries as an anti-inflationary measure[10] have further enhanced this cause of conflict as the Socialist countries have been faced with paying more than 7 per cent.

However, it must be pointed out that although the sources of conflict still exist, the extent and incidence of disputes have tended to decrease. Political relations between Western and Socialist countries have been improving (see Ch. 10B, pp. 186-91) and East–West rapport and travel have become easier – affording better opportunities for closer personal contacts and evolving reasonable solutions

[8] Thus in the past, as illustrated by Polish experience, the average value of co-operation contracts with Western partners was only $400,000 (which was six times smaller than in intra-Comecon co-operation) and lasted on the average only 1.4 years (compared with 5.25 years in intra-Comecon co-operation agreements). J. Likowski, ('Congress of Industrial Co-operation'), *Rynki zagraniczne*, 2/4/1974, p. 1.

[9] *Eastern Europe Report*, 20/9/1974, pp. 288-90.

[10] See footnote 24, Ch. 7C, p. 132.

to common problems. Both multinational corporations and the Socialist states are large entities accustomed to thinking in long-run cost-benefit terms and acting in a responsible manner. In contrast to the bitter recriminations common during the Cold War, it appears that the two sides have made genuine attempts to appreciate each other's special problems and devise safeguards for mutual protection.

Before we consider these safeguards in the following two sections of this chapter, it may be pointed out here that multinational corporations and the Socialist countries are not strikingly unequal partners, and thus each is capable in its own way of protecting itself. The multinationals are large enterprises with large financial and technological resources by virtue of their international operations, with many options open to them. At the same time, the Socialist partners are usually large enterprises, too, and they have the full backing of the state, and in some cases of several states (especially those co-operating under the auspices of Comecon).

B. THE WESTERN MULTINATIONALS' PRECAUTIONS

In endeavouring to protect the interests of multinational corporations, of crucial importance is the formulation of the agreement contract – whether it applies to the sale or purchase of goods, or licences or services, or to industrial co-operation or joint ventures. Socialist enterprises and authorities have great respect for written contracts and they are noted for their meticulous adherence to the terms to the letter. The Socialist countries are most anxious to protect their commercial reputation – and even where the Socialist enterprise has not, the Socialist state has sufficient power and resources to honour the contract.

Multinational corporations, by virtue of their international operations, have accumulated a good deal of experience in dealing with foreign enterprises and governments. Although it may be argued that this may be of little specific use in dealing with partners representing a different social system, there is now in the West a sizeable reservoir of legal experts and specialized consultants to draw upon. Many multinationals in fact have built up their own pools of specialists in required fields. Experienced Western companies are careful not to concede too much in the original contract, especially in the case of industrial co-operation and joint ventures. Instead, they prefer to hold their trump cards (such as extra technology, markets, trade-marks, credits) and use them on an on-going basis – in order to maintain their bargaining power, secure additional quid pro quo concessions and ensure compliance with previously negotiated conditions.[11]

On the whole, the Socialist countries appear to be increasingly accommodating to Western partners, and they may even agree to the alteration or breach of the contract provided that the circumstances are reasonable and covered in the contract agreement. Most Socialist countries are now prepared to base trade or industrial co-operation contracts on foreign (including capitalist) legal systems. We shall now outline common safeguards in certain specific fields.

(a) Bureaucratic Controls. The scope of these controls has been substantially reduced in the European Socialist countries (except Albania) since the economic reforms of the early 1960s (begun in Yugoslavia some 10 years earlier). But in addition special exemptions have been enacted in some of these countries in deference to Western partners. In Hungary, Romania and Yugoslavia dealings with partners in joint ventures and industrial co-operation can be completely or almost completely direct, without having to go through the foreign trade enterprises. In Hungary and Yugoslavia the directive powers of central planners have been virtually discontinued, whilst in Romania (where they have not been) joint ventures are specifically exempt from them. Penalty clauses, compensating the Western partner for losses caused by bureaucratic delays on the Eastern side are now commonly embodied in contracts. In joint venture contracts with Yugoslav enterprises the Western partner may now insist that certain powers of the Worker's Councils (vested with almost absolute powers in enterprises) be transferred to the venture's 'Management Board'. Although in joint ventures (in Hungary, Romania and Yugoslavia) Western partners are limited to minority ownership, in management they usually have an equal voice, i.e. they have the power of veto in all major decisions.

[11] J. B. Holt, 'New Roles for Western Multinationals in Eastern Europe', *Columbia Journal of World Business*, Fall 1973, p. 134.

(*b*) *Technology*. The Socialist countries which are most interested in Western technology (the European Socialist countries, except Albania) now belong to the International Union for the Protection of Industrial Property. In licensing agreements the Western corporation usually specifies who is entitled to utilize the licence and in which market the article so produced can be sold. It now generally insists on regular royalty payments, according to the size of the output produced by the Socialist licensee, instead of the previously common but less advantageous lump-sum (once-for-all) payment. Socialist countries now accept these conditions as not unreasonable. The fear of illegal utilization of information provided to Socialist negotiators, in case the contract is not concluded, is not justified according to Socialist assertions. But if the Western firm wants explicit protection, it can – as suggested by a Polish economist on the basis of the practice already established – conclude a conditional preliminary contract restraining the Socialist party from using such information in the case of a breakdown of negotiations.[12]

(*c*) *Trade-marks*. The well-established Western firms are usually most anxious to protect their trade-marks, and this can be done by inserting an appropriate clause in the licensing, industrial co-operation or joint venture contract. Thus the Socialist partner may be either barred from using the trade-mark, or be required to submit the products concerned for rigorous inspection and pay a suitable margin to the Western firm. For example, it is reported that Philips (Ne) insists on a 40 per cent proprietary mark-up if the product involved is marketed under its brand by the Eastern enterprise.[13] Alternatively, a compromise may be agreed upon, whereby the article is marketed under a new joint trade-mark – such as the automation equipment produced by Pnefal (Po) in co-operation with Honeywell (US) and marketed under the brand name 'Honeywell-Pnefal'.

(*d*) *Prices and Interest Rates*. As a safeguard against inflation, the so-called 'escalation clauses' are commonly included in contracts,

[12] M. Mazur, ('Foreign Licences in Economic Development'), *Gospodarka planowa* (Planned Economy), Warsaw, 3/1973, p. 269.

[13] W. Mostowicz, op. cit., p. 4. For the extent of the multinational affiliations of the Western firms mentioned in this book see the Complete List and Index, pp. 197-232 (and for further details of the larger parent companies, Tables 2, 3 and 4, pp. 36-47. Country abbreviations are explained in footnote 3, p. 2.

and the Socialist countries appear to be reconciled now to such demands. Prices may be linked to a mutually acceptable index, such as that of export or import prices, or the cost of living. Similarly, interest rates may be tied to an agreed basic rate – for example 0.75 points above the London Inter-Bank Overdraft Rate ('LIBOR'). The Socialist ideological objection to paying more than 7 per cent may be overcome by incorporating the excess cost of financing into the price quoted to the Socialist purchaser.[14] More recently, cases were reported where some Socialist countries, anxious to obtain credits (such as Poland, Romania and Yugoslavia), reconsidered their previous attitudes and were prepared to pay up to 10 per cent (and even more in the case of Yugoslavia).[15] To provide for the lower quality of products supplied by Eastern partners, Western companies occasionally insist in industrial co-operation and joint venture contracts on a 10 per cent discount below the world market price.

(e) Taxes. As a hedge against the possibility of unexpected taxes and other charges, Western partners to licensing, industrial co-operation and joint venture agreements may include appropriate stipulations in the contract to protect their net earnings. Thus in 1974 Romania introduced a 20 per cent withholding tax payable by the Romanian purchasers of foreign licences, trade-marks and know-how; to ensure that the Western licensor receives the negotiated amount, 'net of tax' is now commonly stipulated in such contracts.

(f) Marketing. This is an important sphere of interest which is likely to be affected by the sale of a licence and by industrial co-operation or joint ventures. To prevent duplication and unfair

[14] Thus in 1974 a West German banking consortium – led by Commerzbank, the Dresdner Bank and the Westdeutsche Landesbank – agreed to extend nearly $600m. for 10 years to the Foreign Trade Bank of the USSR to finance the export of pipes to the USSR by Mannesmann-Export, and Thyssen Stahlunion. The interest rate payable by the Soviets is 7 per cent and the exporting firms agreed to compensate the banks up to the prevailing inter-bank lending rate (which at the time was just under 12 per cent. The interest 'subsidy' was included in the negotiated price, an arrangement which the Soviets preferred to accept not only for ideological considerations but also on practical grounds – not wanting to damage their credit relations with other Western countries by formally acknowledging higher market interest rates. *Handelsblatt* (Commercial News), Düsseldorf, 4/11/1974, p. 2.

[15] See, e.g., *Eastern Europe Report*, 10/1/1975, p. 7 and 24/1/1975 p. 22.

competition clauses may be inserted in agreement contracts specifying exclusive areas of marketing for each partner. If the Western partner undertakes marketing in agreed capitalist countries for the Eastern partner, a basis for the division of profits may also be specified in the contract.

(g) Risk. This is one of the most obvious aspects of concern to a Western firm. However, a variety of safeguards have been developed which, together with the well-known reputable adherence to contracts by the Socialist partners, have made dealings with the East in fact less risky than with capitalist firms. Guarantees to lenders against political risks are now provided in all leading Western countries, including the United States by state-owned (or state-controlled) entities (see Ch. 7C, pp. 133-4). The FR of Germany has extended this cover to private direct investment (joint ventures) in Yugoslavia since 1970, and Britain and France have done likewise since 1973. In the same year the USA also decided to provide such guarantees in application to Romania as well as Yugoslavia (through the Overseas Private Investment Corporation, established in 1969). Guarantees to capitalist investors in Yugoslavia can also be provided by the International Investment Corporation for Yugoslavia (based in London and Zagreb). The Soviet-owned insurance companies in the West – the Black Sea and Baltic General Insurance Co. (of London) and the Garant Verischerungs (of Vienna) – offer the insurance of credits extended by Western lenders on exports to all the European Socialist countries. In 1973 the Black Sea and Baltic, and Chubb Corporation (US) agreed to set up a joint insurance company to provide insurance for American firms conducting business in the USSR and Eastern Europe. In all three countries where joint ventures have been established (Hungary, Romania and Yugoslavia) the state provides guarantees as to the safety of the invested capital (against expropriation), the transfer of profits abroad as well as the repatriation of capital after the termination of the contract. Moreover in Hungary, the National Bank of Hungary provides a guarantee to the foreign partner in joint ventures against damages that may arise from actions of the Hungarian State or the Hungarian partner. Similarly in Yugoslavia, the joint venture legislation protects foreign partners against changes that may be enacted by the Yugoslav State, in effect allowing existing agree-

ments to operate under the original laws. To strengthen further confidence in East–West industrial co-operation, it has been proposed in some Western circles that 'guarantee funds' be established by each partner in the other country, from which damages could be paid with certainty and without bureaucratic delays.[16]

(h) The Settlement of Disputes. Contracts, of course, normally include provisions for the settlement of disputes, should they arise. Up to the early 1960s the Socialist countries insisted on the so-called 'domestication' of commercial litigation, i.e. before their own tribunals (and not in a capitalist country). But now most of them (viz. those in Europe) readily agree to possible disputes being referred to the International Chamber of Commerce (in Paris), or to a tribunal in a neutral country (such as Sweden or Switzerland), or some other country. These countries adhere to the New York Convention on the Recognition and Enforcement of Foreign Arbitral Awards of 1958 and to the European Convention on International Arbitration (put forward by the Economic Commission for Europe) of 1961, and they have never failed to pay the damages awarded by a foreign court or arbitrator to a Western plaintiff. Some Western firms have submitted their cases to Socialist arbitration tribunals and have found them fair and effective.

In addition to individual actions, the Western multinationals can also protect their interests by co-operating with other firms and by enlisting the support of their governments. Inter-firm co-operation has become quite common, in the form of permanent consortia and *ad hoc* syndicates. Such associations may not only enable the implementation of larger deals and minimize risk, but can also eliminate unnecessary competition and present a stronger stand to face the Socialist state. In view of the widening of joint action by the Comecon bodies in Western markets, more effective inter-governmental co-ordination of policies in the West (especially within the European Economic Community, or the North Atlantic Treaty Organization) has been advocated. Considering that there are more Socialist-owned enterprises in the West and they have more freedom than the other way round, if necessary Western governments can take retaliatory measures against the Socialist countries to greater effect.

[16] See, e.g., *Eastern Europe Report*, 13/12/1974, p. 379.

C. THE PROTECTION OF SOCIALIST INTERESTS

Although Socialist enterprises dealing with the Western multinationals are generally in a weaker position (in respect of size, hard currency resources, technology, the extent of markets), they have the advantage of state backing. And the power of the state in a Socialist country is, of course, much greater than is the case under capitalism – owing to the mono-party political system, the social ownership of the means of production, central economic planning and the solidarity of the Socialist states in general. As for the Western multinational firms, the contract is the principal instrument of the protection of Socialist interests, too. But in addition there is comprehensive legislation and a very well-developed state apparatus guarding against internal and external infringements. Following is a brief outline of procedures affecting Western multinational companies.

(a) Trade Deals. A Socialist country usually prefers to place large orders through one channel, in most cases through its monopolistic-monopsonistic foreign trade enterprises. This eliminates competitive bidding from individual domestic enterprises and may attract quantity discounts and other advantages associated with large contracts. In many cases Socialist negotiators also use the lever of purchases to facilitate the sale of Socialist goods ('counter-sales'). Multinational corporations are naturally the prime target for such deals, as they are more capable of filling large orders and have a greater capacity for absorbing or marketing Socialist products. The development of the Comecon multinational enterprises (see Ch. 8B, pp. 138-44) is likely to further strengthen the Socialist bargaining position in such deals.[17]

(b) Licences. In their quest for Western licences, the Socialist countries' effort has in recent years been directed towards the acquisition of the most modern technology and the strengthening of

[17] At the Polish–Soviet conference on 'International Socialist Property' held in Warsaw in 1974, the Polish delegate (W. Iskra), discussing the merits of Comecon multinational enterprises, said: 'All our countries maintain economic relations with capitalist countries. This should enable us to work together in buying equipment or whole plants. It would obviate a parallelism in buying new technology.' *World Marxist Review*, Prague, June 1974, p. 73.

their bargaining power to minimize payments to the Western multinationals. In tackling the first problem, a good deal of background investigation is now carried out not only by the interested enterprises but also by specialized state agencies, and in the actual contracts it is often stipulated that subsequent improvements in technology be supplied by the licensor to the licensee. To further induce the licensor to perfect continuously the technology in question and make it available to the Socialist licensee, royalties may be based on the *value* of the output *sold* (not on the volume of output produced, and certainly not consisting of a lump-sum payment). In an endeavour to strengthen their bargaining power, the authorities in each Socialist country do not permit competitive bidding by individual enterprises. Some of them have established exclusive state agencies specializing in the licence trade (and thus exercising a measure of monopsonistic-monopolistic power) to bargain on behalf of the interested entities,[18] and the technology acquired is then (as a rule) widely disseminated. In most Socialist countries, before a Western licence can be purchased, approval must be obtained at the ministerial level. More recently, the member countries of Comecon have begun to co-operate to avoid competition and duplication and to maximize the benefit to the grouping as a whole. There is evidence indicating that this co-operation now comprises three spheres – 'the planning of the acquisition of Western licences, negotiations and consultation on the maximum utilization of the acquired technology for the benefit of the member countries'.[19]

(c) Industrial Co-operation. In co-operation agreements the Socialist countries now generally insist on 'horizontal' association involving advanced technology, co-operation extending over long periods (at least five, and preferably, 10 or more years) and the Eastern partner contributing a substantial share to the complete product in question (in general 30 per cent or more). Co-operation agreements are usually negotiated on the Socialist side by a ministry or an industrial branch association (or they have to be approved by them), so that the national interest can be reasonably well safeguarded. The Socialist countries may very well develop an organi-

[18] In Bulgaria – *Tekhnika*, Czechoslovakia – *Polytechna*, the German DR – *Limex*, Poland – *Polservice*, the USSR – *Litsensintorg*.

[19] M. Guzek and S. Sołtysiński, ('The Technological Gap and the Principles Governing Industrial Co-operation in Comecon'), *Sprawy międzynarodowe*, 12/1973, pp. 127-8.

zation for negotiating their co-operation agreements with Western firms on a collective basis. This is precisely what was advocated at a Comecon Conference on East–West Economic Co-operation held in Moscow in October 1972.[20] The Western partner's vision of a sheltered, comfortable market in the Socialist country may be later shattered, owing to the Socialist drive to improve market supplies by competitive production and imports (especially from other Socialist countries).

(d) Joint Ventures. As joint ventures represent the closest form of collaboration with capitalist partners, the need for exhaustive safeguards is the most vital. Only three Socialist countries (so far) explicitly allow joint ventures within their boundaries and the main safeguards resorted to in these countries are as follows. First of all, in each country there is well-developed legislation specifying the general scope and limitations for joint ventures. However, to allow for flexibility in individual cases a good deal of freedom is left to the partners to negotiate an agreement to their best mutual advantage and protection, and the Socialist country may embody extra specific precautions in the joint venture contract. The state is usually represented or directly involved in negotiations, but in any case the final agreement must be approved at the top ministerial level to ensure the primacy of the national interest.[21] In Yugoslavia, although the Workers' Council may hand over some of its powers to the joint venture's Management Board, it has to ratify the final contract. A majority (i.e. at least 51 per cent) of the assets of the joint venture must be owned by the Socialist partner(s). A foreign partner is barred from acquiring assets beyond the permissible maximum share. Joint ventures are allowed only in those fields where they can make a substantial contribution to technological progress and efficiency, and to exports in particular. Their operations in the domestic market are carefully watched, and they are

[20] *Rynki zagraniczne*, 21/10/1972, p. 3.

[21] Thus, to illustrate by reference to Romania, proposals must be submitted to the specially created 'Advisory Committee on Proposals for Establishing Joint Ventures' (consisting of senior officials of vice-ministerial rank) and approvals must be obtained from the State Planning Commission, the Ministry of Finance, the Ministry of Labour, the Ministry of Foreign Trade and the Romanian Foreign Trade Bank. After it is ascertained that Romanian interests are adequately safeguarded, the Council of State issues a special decree whereby the joint venture is legally incorporated.

certainly not allowed to resort to restrictive practices. Certain sensitive branches of the economy are explicitly barred to foreign investors – in Hungary, in industry and most other material production, and in Yugoslavia in services (banking, insurance, transport, trade and public services). Although in Marxist theory land has no value (not being a product of labour), the Western partners are not allowed to turn this to their advantage. A joint venture has to either acquire the land (in which case it may constitute the Socialist partner's capital contribution) or pay rent; these values may be determined either by the market (in Yugoslavia, where 85 per cent of land is privately owned and is subject to market dealings) or arrived at calculationally. In Romania, to prevent the Western investor profiteering from 'cheap labour' and the socialization of the means of production, the joint venture legislation insists that all wages and other costs of the venture be calculated at 'world market levels'. All three Socialist countries insist on the long-term duration of joint ventures, exceeding five years (with implicit preference for 15 years or more), and termination before the date agreed upon in the contract is not generally allowed. Substantial incentives are offered for the reinvestment of profits to create a greater stake in a long association. In Yugoslavia, the minimum required investment by the foreign partner is 1.5m. dinars (about $100,000).

(e) Credits. The most obvious form of protection is the Socialist determination (with the qualified exception of Yugoslavia) not to borrow from Western nations unless it is absolutely necessary, and pay cash instead. This policy is dictated by the desire to minimize interest payments and dependence on capitalist countries, and avoid 'mortgaging the future' which otherwise might further complicate economic planning.[22] To this purpose recourse is made to counter-sales (tied to purchases from Western firms) and barter (see

[22] A recent illustration of the Socialist aversion to capitalist credits is provided by the Kursk metallurgical project. Negotiations between the USSR and a West German consortium (Korf, Krupp, and Salzgitter) began in November 1972 but repeatedly broke down during the following 16 months. The West Germans insisted on a 10 per cent interest on the $1,000m. credits demanded by the Soviets. Faced with the prospect of having to shoulder more than $400m. in total interest payments, the Soviets offered (after several increments) no more than 7 per cent, and finally in March 1974 decided to drop the credit issue and pay cash instead. *Die Welt* (The World), Hamburg, 10/1/1974, p. 9; *Handelsblatt*, 31/1/1974, p. 7 and 25/3/1974, p. 5.

Ch. 7A, pp. 116-17). When borrowing is resorted to, it is preceded by hard bargaining as to the terms. The lever of large orders is often used whereby Western multinational firms exert pressure on their banking affiliates and other financial institutions to accord favourable credit terms to their Socialist customers. To further keep interest rates down, the Socialist countries as a rule do not allow individual importing enterprises to borrow abroad. Instead, loans are usually negotiated by their foreign trade banks (or other state banks). Another measure taken in recent years in this direction is the use of the Comecon banks (the International Bank for Economic Co-operation and the International Investment Bank) to borrow on behalf of the member countries. The ideological escape from paying 'surplus' interest rates to capitalist lenders is implicitly to allow the Western exporter to include the extra cost of financing by capitalist standards into the quoted price of the order.

Thus it can be concluded that the Socialist countries have developed an impressive system of legislative, institutional and procedural frameworks for dealing with Western multinational companies. Whilst providing a range of inducements and guarantees, these countries have also evolved a variety of controls circumscribing the multinationals' power and freedom of manipulation. In contrast to their role in capitalist (especially less-developed) countries, multinational corporations can never critically dominate a Socialist economy, they cannot be as indispensable to investment and economic development, they cannot produce setbacks to employment, they cannot take over local enterprises and they cannot precipitate balance of payments upsets. Hinting a lesson to less-developed countries, a Soviet economist recently pointed out:

> ... social ownership of the means of production and the monopoly of foreign trade make it possible to reliably guarantee the national and social interests of states even under the widest contacts with the MNCs [multinational corporations], including large-scale economic co-operation on a long-term basis.[23]

[23] I. Ivanov, 'International Corporations and the "Third World"', *International Affairs*, Moscow, 8/1974, p. 42.

10 Ideology, Technology, Economic Common Sense

A. SOME INTRIGUING PARADOXES

THE very facts of the Western multinational corporations dealing with the Communist regimes and the development of Socialist multinational enterprises and their operations in the West provide a paradoxical theme. The preceding chapters, whilst preoccupied with specific fields, incidentally referred to some seemingly anomalous situations. In this section of the concluding chapter we shall highlight a number of cases of paradoxical attitudes, developments and practices, which may be taken as symbolizing the beginning of a new era in the evolution of the multinationals as well as of East–West relations in a rather striking manner.

(a) Concordant Features of the Multinational Corporation and the Socialist State. It is surprising that these two otherwise diametrically opposite institutions should have so many characteristics in common. Both are large organizations noted for centralized decision-making, hierarchical levels of authority and technocratic elements. Both are dominated by materialist (or materialistic) pursuits, both have an essentially international outlook with interests transcending national frontiers and both are accustomed to 'thinking big' in long-run cost-benefit terms. Both pursue short-term and long-term economic planning and engage in optimization studies with the aid of electronic computers. Thus IBM's long-term plans 'by objectives' (in terms of profitability, growth targets, manpower, etc.) consist of marketing, manufacturing, service, personnel and financial plans.[1]

[1] G. A. Steiner and W. M. Cannon, *Multinational Corporate Planning*, New York and London, Collier-Macmillan, 1966, pp. 81-90. Also see P. Lorange, 'Formal Planning in Multinational Corporations', *Columbia Journal of World Business*, Summer 1973, pp. 83-8; J. S. Schwendiman, *Strategic and Long-Range Planning for the Multinational Corporation*, New York, Praeger, 1973.

Business International in one of its publications recently concluded: 'Some Western companies seem to be even more fanatical about planning than the so-called planned economy countries.'[2] Both multinational corporations and the Socialist countries have a record of rapid economic expansion; over the period 1950-75, their industrial output grew at the average annual rate of 10 per cent – more than twice as fast as in the rest of the world.

(b) The Socialist Growing Predilection for Large Enterprises. Marx and other early founders of the Communist ideology yearned for small independent craftsmen and workshops as an ideal form of the industrial organization in their vision of the future perfect society. Nothing is further from that dream if we examine recent developments in the Socialist countries. Through mergers and absorption of workshops and smaller enterprises there has been some spectacular growth in the size of the largest enterprises in these countries, with a similar degree of concentration achieved as in the West. Thus in the German DR, as a result of amalgamations and the elimination of smaller enterprises, over four-fifths of the output of the metallurgical, shipbuilding and power-producing industries is contributed by entities employing more than 2,500 persons.[3] In Hungary in 1972, the 10 largest industrial enterprises (out of a total of 812) contributed 44 per cent of total industrial sales.[4] In the same year Yugoslavia had 1,386 foreign trade enterprises, but the 30 largest of them handled over 46 per cent of the total Yugoslav foreign trade; 'Jugometal', at the top of the list, transacted $378m. worth of business, compared with less than $4m. achieved by an average enterprise in the field.[5] The extreme form of this partiality is 'gigantomania', most noticeable in the USSR – the country claiming the right to the correct interpretation of Marxism. The Soviets in fact have the largest airline ('Aeroflot'), hydroelectric power station (at Krasnoyarsk), truck factory ('KAMAZ') and aluminium plant (under construction in the Southern Ukraine) in the world. The growing number and size of multinational enterprises in Comecon as well as those operated in capitalist countries (see Ch.

[2] *Eastern Europe Report*, Geneva, 31/5/1974, p. 162.

[3] See *Voprosy ekonomiki* (Problems of Economics), Moscow, 8/1971, pp. 99-100; *Economic Bulletin for Europe*, vol. 21, no. 1, 1970, pp. 70-72.

[4] *Figyelö* (Economic Observer), Budapest, 17/7/1974, p. 3.

[5] *Ekonomska politika* (Economic Policy), Belgrade, 27/8/1973, p. 26.

8B-D, pp. 138-59) further accentuate this trend. Moreover, in their choice of capitalist partners, Socialist countries show a definite preference not for small craftsmen and workshops 'exploited by national and international monopolies', but for large multinational corporations.

(c) Strange Partnerships. The Socialist countries have developed close links of collaboration with the international monopolies which Lenin once named and proscribed as arch-villains of exploitation and spearheads of imperialism (see Ch. 1B, p. 9). Ever since the Korean War, many Western multinationals have been in the forefront of pressurizing their governments to relax the strategic embargo on exports to the Socialist countries. The slowing down of the arms race in recent years has adversely affected many a Western concern, but in their disenchantment with Western governments they have found considerable consolation in their newly discovered Socialist saviours from financial difficulties. Some Socialist countries have established close bonds of co-operation with such pillars of the 'military-industrial complex' in the West as[6] AEG Telefunken (FRG, communications equipment), Bayer (FRG, chemicals), Boeing (US, aircraft), Creusot-Loire (Fr, heavy armaments), Dow Chemical (US, napalm and other chemicals), General Dynamics (US, aircraft), General Tire & Rubber (US, rubber products), Hawker-Siddeley, (UK aircraft), Hewlett-Packard (US, electronic equipment), Imperial Chemical Industries (UK, explosives), International Business Machines (US, electronic equipment), International Telephone & Telegraph (US, communications equipment), Lockheed Aircraft (US, aircraft, missiles), Radio Corporation of America (US, communications equipment), Rheinstahl (FRG, heavy armaments), Rockwell International (US, aircraft), Vickers (UK, naval vessels).[7] In 1973 the leading American aircraft manufacturers (including Boeing, General Electric, Lockheed Aircraft and McDonnel Douglas) invited a team of Soviet aeronautical experts,

[6] The extent of the multinational affiliations of the Western firms appearing in this book is indicated in the Complete List and Index, pp. 197-232, and further details of the larger parent companies – in Tables, 2, 3 and 4, pp. 36-47. For country abbreviations, see footnote 3, p. 2.

[7] For the extent of the military involvement of some of these multinationals, see J. F. Galloway, 'The Military-Industrial Linkages of U.S.-Based Multinational Corporations', *International Studies Quarterly*, London, Dec 1972, pp. 491-510.

headed by the First Deputy Premier (S. I. Kadishev) on a 'confidential tour' of their establishments; similarly a group of US experts was invited to inspect Soviet factories in 1974.[8] It was also recently reported that the US Secretary of State, Dr H. Kissinger, was approached by the Chinese on the possible purchase of armaments (including troop transport planes and tanks) from American corporations to protect China's border against the USSR.[9] In a recent issue of the top organ of the Communist Party of the Soviet Union the Communist Party leaders in the FR of Germany were praised for their militant books and programmes directed against West German monopolies and indicating what is in store for them once the Communists seize power;[10] at the same time, the USSR has been most anxious to forge bonds of collaboration with the same multinationals. The Communist regimes are apparently unaware or unmindful of the predictions made by a number of Socialist as well as Western economists that the share of the Western multinational corporations in the GNP of the non-Socialist world will rise from 20 per cent in 1970 to 50-80 per cent by the beginning of the next century – when the capitalist world will be dominated by less than 60 giant corporations, of which more than three-quarters will be American (see Ch. 10C, pp. 191-2).

(d) Ironical Alliances and Solidarities. Multinational corporations often prefer to sell their technology to the Socialist countries than to other competing companies in the capitalist world. It is known that they often hush up cases of industrial espionage by Socialist agents, even if the authorities in the Western countries are determined to uncover and prosecute the offenders.[11] On account of anti-monopoly legislation in the West, the multinationals often feel safer in expanding their operations in the East instead. Whilst IBM faced a stiff anti-monopoly action in the European Economic Community in 1974, it has been made welcome and given encouragement by Bulgarian, Czechoslovak, East German, Hungarian, Polish, Romanian, Soviet and Yugoslav authorities to expand its business

[8] *Eastern Europe Report*, 30/11/1973, p. 351.
[9] *China Trade Report*, Hong Kong, 1/1974, p. 13.
[10] N. Izvolenskaya, ('The Struggle of the West German Working Class against Monopoly Power'), *Kommunist*, Moscow, 4/1974, pp. 122-4; also see *International Affairs*, Moscow, 5/1974, p. 112.
[11] *Handelsblatt* (Commercial News), Düsseldorf, 4/2/1973, p. 22.

in their respective countries. In 1973 Westinghouse Electric (US) and its partner Energomashexport (USSR) supporting each other lodged a protest with the US General Accounting Office against the unfair competitive bids submitted by Allis-Chalmers (US) and Canadian General Electric (Ca) for generators and hydraulic turbines for the Grand Coulee Dam in the USA[12] Up to the early 1970s many American companies cultivated the good offices of the Japanese firms (by entering with them into industrial co-operation or joint ventures) with the primary purpose of using them as a façade for their operations in the Chinese market, and by this 'back-door' method beating the US version of the strategic embargo. As since the normalization of Sino-American relations they have been able to trade with China directly, some of those partnerships – to the surprise of some Japanese firms but not to others – have been discontinued (such as that of the Electric Furnace Co. with the Daido Steel Co.).[13] Ever since 1960 China has increasingly steered away from the Soviet and East European trade partners and has instead been embracing Western multinational corporations, and in 1973 it was publicly stated that she preferred economic and technical co-operation with the West than the USSR.[14] Yugoslavia prefers to deal with the capitalist multinationals than with the firms owned by Yugoslavs resident in capitalist countries – in fact carrying on business with such firms was made illegal in 1973.[15]

(e) The Multinational Corporations' Shares and the Socialist Countries. The large orders placed by the Socialist countries and impressive schemes for the joint development of resources (especially in the USSR) have on many occasions given support to the shares of such multinational corporations as British Leyland (UK), Citroën (Fr), Courtaulds (UK), Fiat (It), Gutehoffnungshütte (FRG), Occidental Petroleum (US), Olivetti (It), Pechiney-Ugine-Kuhlmann (Fr), Pepsi-Co (US), Pullman (US), Rank Organization (UK), Singer (US), Tokyo Shibaura Electric (Ja) and Volvo (Swe) – of which the Socialist countries appear to be well aware.[16] To this list we could add the beneficiary corporations otherwise 'suffering'

[12] *East–West*, Brussels, 10/9/1973, p. 2.
[13] *China Trade Report*, 3/1972, p. 10.
[14] Reported in *China Trade Report*, 5/1973, p. 4.
[15] *Eastern Europe Report*, 20/4/1973, p. 116.
[16] e.g., see *Sovetskaya Rossiya* (Soviet Russia), Moscow, 28/10/1974, p. 3.

from reduced Western military spending. Montedison is partly owned by the Vatican, and yet this chemical giant – obviously with the approval of its shareholders – has extended its operations to Hungary (Cardinal Midszenty notwithstanding), Bulgaria, the German DR, Poland, Romania and the USSR, and has even established a permanent office in Moscow. The Vatican also has substantial shareholdings in other multinationals widely involved in East–West dealings, such as General Electric (US), General Motors (US), Gulf Oil (US), IBM (US) and Royal Dutch-Shell (Ne–UK).

(f) Perverse Competition. Rivalry amongst Western multinationals vying for the Socialist market has become quite keen and common – to the amusement of the Socialist countries themselves. This may assume the form of competitive bids, concessional credit terms, discounts, free extras (spare parts, the training of staff, know-how) and the obliging acceptance of counter-purchases as part-payment. Thus for the Krsko nuclear power project in Yugoslavia, four Western multinational corporations had submitted competing bids – ASEA (Swe), General Electric (US), Kraftwerk Union (FRG; two bids) and Westinghouse Electric (US). The Soviets were also invited to bid, but in disgust they refused saying that they would do it only if the USSR were the only bidder. Westinghouse was finally awarded the contract. Tempted by such a huge potential market as China, Robert Bosch (FRG), Thomson-CSF (Fr) and Tokyo Shibaura Electric (Ja) have been falling over backwards in their efforts to persuade the Chinese to adopt their respective colour television systems. One of the stratagems resorted to by multinational corporations in their endeavour to beat their rivals and overcome anti-Western (or anti-multinational) feelings in less-developed countries is to enter into industrial co-operation or joint ventures with Socialist partners – as an indirect means of carrying on their operations in such countries. But chickens have a habit of coming home to roost. Some multinationals which have eagerly entered into licensing, industrial co-operation or joint venture agreements with Socialist partners have been confronted with stiff competition in their own backyard. This is best exemplified by passenger cars. The development or modernization of this industry in the Socialist countries has been aided with licences, know-how and equipment supplied by such companies as Citroën (to Poland, Yugoslavia),

Daimler-Benz (Yugoslavia), Fiat (Poland, the USSR, Yugoslavia), Renault (Romania, the USSR) and Volkswagenwerk (Romania, Yugoslavia). The Socialist exports of such cars as Daccia (by Romania), Lada (the USSR), Moskvich (the USSR), Polish Fiat (Poland) and Zastava (Yugoslavia) to capitalist countries have caused many headaches and second thoughts to the Western motor-car makers. Ironically, the Socialist export drive of cars was intensified during 1973-5 when the Western vehicle industry was already in difficulties.[17]

(g) Mutual Favoured Treatment. Western banks and financial companies usually charge lower interest on loans to the Socialist countries than is normal in the case of capitalist borrowers (see Ch. 7C, pp. 132-3) and find that their capital is safer – with a lesser chance of dishonesty, repudiation or insolvency. Similarly capitalist partners in many cases receive favoured treatment from the Socialist authorities, to the envy of local enterprises. In joint ventures in Hungary, Romania and Yugoslavia, the Western partner – in spite of his minority shareholding – usually enjoys an equal voice in management, and may even be allowed a larger share of profits than is warranted by his capital contribution. In Hungary, in contrast to local enterprises, the Western partner is exempt from capital charges, centralized depreciation deductions and wage-increase levies, and in Romania – from import duties. The Romanian legislation (of August 1974) also permits Western personnel to acquire private houses and villas from the state, or the state may undertake their construction for foreign partners residing or intending to reside in Romania – and not many Romanians can afford such luxuries. In Yugoslavia, the first real challenge to the near-absolute power of the Workers' Councils comes from capitalist partners in joint enterprises (see Ch. 9B, p. 166).

(h) Multinational Corporations, the Socialist Countries and Western Trade Unions. Western firms, by transferring their production of certain articles or parts (especially if they are labour-intensive) to

[17] The total export of passenger cars from the Socialist to capitalist countries rose from \$60m. in 1966 to \$100m. in 1970 and to about \$250m. in 1974 (these exports to the West in the respective years amounted to \$40m., \$70m. and \$200m.). Based on United Nations *Monthly Bulletin of Statistics*, 7/1972, p. xxxi and 7/1975, p. xxxv, and the author's estimates.

the Socialist countries under licensing, industrial co-operation or joint venture agreements, can reduce employment in their Western plants. Their ability to do this weakens the bargaining power of Western trade unions. Even Fiat, which of the Western vehicle producers (except Japan) enjoys the lowest labour costs, has found production co-operation with Poland and Yugoslavia most tempting, made even more necessary by the frequent industrial disputes in its domestic plants in recent years. Similarly whilst southern Italy suffers from neglect with regard to investment and employment opportunities, Montedison has recently signed large contracts with the Soviets to build a number of modern industrial plants in the USSR, worth $500m. – and all on credit. In a speech to the trade union congress in the USA in 1973, the President of the Plumbers' Union said:

> ... American Labour is increasingly concerned over some of the US multinationals becoming still more arrogant and dangerous through the love affair with the Soviet regime, now being pushed by Wall Street.[18]

Similar concern was expressed by Charles Levinson, Secretary-General of the International Federation of Chemical and General Workers' Unions.[19] Indeed, it is ironical that many trade unions which are endeavouring to evolve new protective measures to counter the growing power of multinational corporations, should find the Socialist countries – the professed champions of the working class – weakening such efforts by unwittingly providing escape havens for the multinationals. Evidently the West German trade unions did not put much trust in Yugoslavia's championship when in 1972 they protested against inferior conditions of employment accorded to Yugoslav workers in the branches of Yugoslav enterprises in the FR of Germany – compared with the conditions enjoyed by Yugoslav workers in the plants of the West German multinational companies.[20]

[18] Quoted from J. Nicholl, 'Bark v. Bite: The American Trade Union Movement and East–West Trade', *East–West Commercial Relations Series*, Institute of Soviet and East European Studies, Carleton University, Working Paper No. 5, Sep 1974, p. 15.

[19] C. Levinson, *International Trade Unionism*, London, Allen & Unwin, 1972, p. 150.

[20] *Vjesnik* (Herald), Zagreb, 22/6/1972, p. 5.

(i) Strikes. Multinational corporations also find that whilst they often suffer from strikes in their own and host capitalist countries, their production in the East (involving industrial co-operation or joint ventures) is virtually safe from industrial disputes, as strikes in the Socialist countries (with the qualified exception of Yugoslavia) are illegal. A Polish economist recently pointed out that South Korea prohibited strikes in foreign companies, a fact which is considered sinister by trade unions in capitalist countries.[21] She did not mention that the Western multinationals in effect enjoy the same protection in the Socialist countries. But there are also instances where strikers in Western countries played into the hands of the multinationals. Thus the Communist-inspired strikes in the British motor vehicle firm, Rootes, further aggravated its financial difficulties and led to its takeover by the American multinational company, Chrysler.[22]

(j) Socialist Participation in International Cartels. International cartels have traditionally been an object of Socialist attack as they are usually formed by large multinational companies in order to force prices up by restricting output or service. But in practice the Socialist countries themselves have formed similar organizations, and moreover have participated in restrictive agreements in collusion with multinational corporations. A number of cartel-like associations have been formed by the European Socialist countries under the auspices of the Council of Mutual Economic Assistance. One of them is the 'Bureau for the Co-ordination of the Chartering of Freight Ships', established in 1963, with its seat in Moscow, and another is the International Shipowners Association, established in 1970 in Gdynia (the latter being also open to shipowners from capitalist countries). Although they started in a rather innocent way, they soon learnt the facts of life. The Budapest Agreement of December 1971, under Article 3, provides for undertaking common action against capitalist shipowners in the case of discrimination against member countries; further, Article 5 clearly states that the member organizations will refrain from cutthroat competition

[21] Krystyna Dembińska, ('The Supra-National Might of Multinational Corporations'), *Życie gospodarcze* (Economic Life), Warsaw, 29/4/1973, p. 14.

[22] P. Hamilton, *Espionage and Subversion in an Industrial Society*, London, Hutchinson, 1967, p. 204.

amongst themselves.[23] The Soviets began to co-operate with Western international cartels in the early 1930s – when at least matches, phosphate, potash and platinum were subject to collusive agreements.[24] Since the late 1950s the USSR has on several occasions co-operated with Western multinationals in restricting the export of and maintaining agreed prices of aluminium and tin, not to mention oil. After an initial undercutting of freight charges (up to 33 per cent), the Soviet 'Baltic Steamship Line' forced its way into membership of the Australia-to-Europe Shipping Conference (comprising 23 Western European shipping lines) in 1969; it has since proved a co-operative and loyal member by raising its freights to the established level.[25] Shipping lines and brokers from Cuba, Hungary, Poland, Romania, the USSR and Yugoslavia are members (together with participants from 76 capitalist countries) of the Baltic and International Maritime Conference.[26]

(k) Socialist Investment in Capitalist Countries. In spite of the Socialist criticism of foreign investment by multinational corporations (especially in less developed countries) and the expropriation of their assets after the Communist takeover, most Socialist countries have embarked upon foreign investment in the capitalist world themselves. Many Socialist enterprises have established wholly or partly-owned subsidiaries not only in the West but also in less-developed countries (see Ch. 8C-D, pp. 144-59). By the mid-1970s the estimated value of these investments was about $1,000m. But there is a secondary paradox in this development. It appears that in some cases Socialist officials operating these ventures embark on

[23] *Technika i gospodarka morska* (Marine Technology and Management), Gdansk, 2/1974, pp. 68-70, 76-8.

[24] For details, see A. Gerschenkron, 'Soviet Policies Versus International Cartels: Four Historical Case Studies', *Slavic Studies*, Mar 1974, pp. 68-90.

[25] For details, see R. E. Athay, *The Economics of Soviet Merchant Shipping Policy*, Chapel Hill, U. of Carolina P., 1971, p. 121; W. Fox, *Tin*, London, Mining Journal Books, 1974, pp. 257, 296-300; L. Turner, *Politics and the Multinational Company*, London, Fabian Society, Dec 1969, p. 25.

[26] Several Socialist (especially European) countries are also participants to inter-governmental commodity agreements, such as the International Lead and Zinc Study Group (Bulgaria, Czechoslovakia, Hungary, Poland, the USSR and Yugoslavia, together with 24 capitalist countries), the International Sugar Organization (Cuba, Czechoslovakia, Hungary, Poland and the USSR, together with 44 capitalist countries) and the International Wheat Council (Cuba and the USSR, together with 45 capitalist countries).

their own free enterprise. Although such blossoming of private initiative is mostly hushed up as much as is possible, in the case of Yugoslavia it has become common enough to be taken up in official publications. According to reports published during 1972-3 many officials running Yugoslav enterprises abroad were exploiting their position by accepting bribes, engaging in black-market deals and establishing their own firms. It was concluded that local capitalist representatives or agencies would be more trustworthy.[27] In another report those operations were described as the 'privatization of Yugoslav social resources' and apparently they were most widespread in the subsidiaries located in Italy, Austria and the FR of Germany.[28] Of the 423 Yugoslav enterprises abroad at the beginning of 1973, only 308 were performing their functions honestly and efficiently.[29] In 1973 a law was passed to restrict the Yugoslav involvement in foreign investment – not because of the opposition of capitalist governments or the chicanery of the competing capitalist firms, but owing to the enterprising Yugoslav officials 'seizing business opportunities' in a more congenial environment.

B. THE ERA OF TRANSIDEOLOGICAL COLLABORATION?

The paradoxes outlined in the preceding section illustrate a new trend of our age – that in the face of the scientific and technical revolution which has been encompassing different countries irrespective of the social system, economic common sense (or expedience) can prevail over ideological prejudices. This development across the traditional East–West ideological, political and economic demarcation line can be described as 'transideological collaboration'.

The idea of 'transideological' relations in the East–West context can be traced back to at least the late 1940s, but the concept was first discussed more systematically by H. V. Perlmutter in 1969 when he applied it to joint East–West ventures.[30] In his analysis

[27] B. Vojvodic, ('Problems of the Yugoslav Enterprises Operating Abroad'), *Borba* (Struggle), Belgrade, 1/10/1972, p. 9.

[28] Steva Ivic, ('Regulation of Enterprises Operating Abroad'), *Kommunist*, Belgrade, 12/10/1972, p. 18.

[29] *Privredni pregled* (Economic Review), Belgrade, 26/4/1973, p. 2.

[30] H. V. Perlmutter, 'Emerging East–West Ventures: The Transideological Enterprise', *Columbia Journal of World Business*, Sep-Oct 1969, pp. 39-50.

of the theoretical explanations of the relations between capitalism and socialism propounded by different thinkers in the past, Perlmutter distinguished three conflicting theories – the 'submergence theory' (that one system must be overpowered by the other), the 'divergence theory' (that the two systems must increasingly become different) and the 'convergence theory' (that the two systems must ultimately coalesce into one organic whole by mutual assimilation). He rejects them all as invalid in the modern world being transformed by the scientific and technical revolution, because they 'all recognize that the world political-military system has identifiable boundaries between East and West' but 'they fail to recognize the character of the evolving world economy as it is understood by multinational corporations'.[31]

Instead Perlmutter put forward his 'emergence theory', which in his view better fits the emerging new world order characterized by ideological diversity (intra-Eastern and intra-Western included), economic interdependence based on the international division of labour (in accordance with the comparative cost advantage) and worldwide markets and geocentric science and technology.[32] The parallel coexistence of the two systems is assumed. Although convergence is not excluded as a long-run feasibility, the emergence theory realistically emphasizes pluralistic tendencies that are likely to continue with overlapping effects – so that the coalescence of the two systems as originally envisaged by the proponents of the convergence thesis may in fact become irrelevant. Developments since the publication of Perlmutter's article have given further support to his thesis and indeed as he pointed out in another contribution published in 1972, 'the forces in the direction of widening the *transideological industrial and commercial zone* seem irreversible'.[33] In his view it is not trade or states but rather the multinationals that 'will literally rise beyond the ideologies of capitalism or communism'.[34]

Although the term 'transideological' was at first applied in a

[31] Ibid., p. 46.
[32] Ibid., pp. 44-5, 48-50.
[33] H. V. Perlmutter, 'Towards Research on and Development of Nations, Unions and Firms as Worldwide Institutions', in H. Günter (ed.), *Transnational Industrial Relations*, London, Macmillan, 1972, p. 32 (emphasis in the original).
[34] Ibid., p. 29.

narrow sense referring to joint East–West ventures, the concept can be broadened to encompass other forms of East–West economic and technological collaboration, namely inter-governmental agreements on economic, industrial, scientific and technical co-operation, inter-firm licensing agreements and a variety of production, marketing and financial co-operative arrangements. In this transideological collaboration Western and Eastern multinationals (in the industrial, commercial and financial fields) are the main actors at the operational level, but capitalist and (more so) Socialist states are also participants in one way or another.

Transideological collaboration has been facilitated by the two traditionally opposing economic systems departing from their extreme features and practices and becoming increasingly similar. Capitalism is vastly different from the picture originally painted by Marx and – although to differing degrees – all Western countries have departed from *laissez-faire* capitalism and have adopted various forms of state intervention and social welfare programmes. Economic planning ('indicative', 'orientational', 'budgetary') is now common practice. The role of the private ownership of the means of production has been diminished by the nationalization of some key industries and some diffusion of property in favour of the working class (homes, bonds, shares in the firms of employment, paralleled by heavy inheritance taxes on large properties).

In large firms (including multinational corporations) ownership is largely divorced from control and profit is no longer such a dominant factor determining economic activity in the economy. The power of the employers over workers has been reduced by state legislation (safety regulations, minimum wages), the growing power of trade unions and in some cases by workers' participation in the management and even ownership of factories. Inequalities of income have been reduced by progressive taxation and the extension of social services. In several respects, multinational corporations are surprisingly similar to the Socialist states (see the preceding section, pp. 176-7).

At the same time, most Socialist countries (i.e. those in Europe, except Albania) have embarked on liberal economic reforms (Yugoslavia beginning in 1950 and the others since the early 1960s). As in the West the extent of these departures from the previous system has varied in different countries, in effect also producing pluralistic forms. In general, the centralized directive system of planning and management has been liberalized in favour of decentralization and greater independence of enterprises. There has been some decollectivization of farming land (in Poland and Yugoslavia) and some (limited) revival of private enterprise.

The market has been allowed to play a greater role in the determination of production and prices, and the role of the consumer in these processes has been enhanced. Profit has been adopted as the main criterion of enterprise performance, and differences in personal earnings are now quite surprising – even if comparisons are made with capitalist countries. The growing power of managers and technocrats and the substantial disparities in income are introducing new elements of social differentiation.

But in fact the obliteration of extremist East–West differences has advanced much further – into the ideological and political sphere as well. There has been a tendency for a decline of ideological fervour on each side. Some distinguished Western philosophers, political scientists and sociologists have described this trend as 'anti-ideologism', 'disideologization', or the 'end of the age of ideology'. Ever since the early 1950s they have argued that the ideological conflicts were merely outdated reflections of old grievances and prejudices and the traditional ideological systems are not only becoming pointless but in fact increasingly harmful. In progressive societies modern technology enables the solution of the basic economic problem – that of scarcity and poverty. This favours a decline in totalitarian ideas and practices, inducing ideological and political moderation. The decline of ideology began first in the more affluent West, but has also spread – to a lesser extent – to the East.[35]

The acceptance of the principle of peaceful coexistence (after 1956), the virtual end of the Cold War (with the signing of the

[35] For details, see R. Aron, *L'opium des intellectuels*, Paris, Calmann-Lévy, 1955 (also published in English translation: *The Opium of the Intellectuals*, Garden City, N.Y., Doubleday, 1957); D. Bell, *The End of Ideology*, Glencoe, Ill., Free Press, 1960 and *The Coming of Post-Industrial Society*, New York, Basic Books, 1973; Z. Brzezinski, *Between Two Ages: America's Role in the Technotronic Era*, New York, Viking Press, 1970; J. K. Galbraith, *The New Industrial State*, Boston, Houghton Mifflin, 1967; J. Tinbergen, *The Theory of the Optimum Regime*, Rotterdam, NEH, 1959; A. Toffler, *Der Zukunftsschock* (The Tumultuous Future), Berlin-Munich-Vienna, Scherz Verlag, 1971.

Anti-Test Ban Treaty in 1963), the retreat and disappearance of imperialism and colonialism in the capitalist world and polycentric tendencies weakening the cohesion and chauvinism of the power blocs on each side – all have provided a favourable background conducive to transideological collaboration. The moderating processes in East–West – as well as intra-Eastern and intra-Western – relations contrast with dogmatism, fanaticism and intolerance persisting in South-Western and intra-Southern relations. But the supporters of the conception of disideologization believe that this extremism is basically conditioned by backwardness and the multiplicity of formidable economic problems, which are not insoluble in the context of modern technology, and it is expected that even there ideology will eventually, like old soldiers, fade away.

Many Western thinkers believe that the processes bringing capitalism and socialism closer together will continue in the future. They maintain that the same scientific and technical developments produce similar patterns of organization and attitudes in all developed societies which will be most evident in the new emerging social order described as the 'industrial society' (by R. Aron), the 'new industrial state' (J. Galbraith), the 'post-industrial society' (D. Bell), the 'super-industrial society' (A. Toffler), the 'technotronic society' (Z. Brzezinski) and the 'optimum regime' (J. Tinbergen).

However, it must be pointed out that there are still powerful forces on each side with a vested interest in continued tension, militating against closer collaboration. Even if one accepts that East–West relations will not be broken by a major armed conflict, occasional setbacks in East–West collaboration are certain to occur periodically, as illustrated by the collapse of the much hoped-for American–Soviet trade agreement (of 1972) in early 1975. In the West there are right-wing political elements and influential military-industrial interests highly critical of the new trends – in particular of radicalism, the conciliatory 'building of bridges' and the transfer of technology to the East.

But the antagonism is more deeply entrenched in the East. The Communist Parties have by no means given up their Marxist objectives and Stalinist hardliners may regain the upper hand. Collaboration with Western multinational corporations is essentially looked upon by Communist leaders as an expedient for speeding up economic development in order to advance the Socialist countries to Full Communism sooner than might otherwise be possible. In their view, the commitment to peaceful coexistence does not amount to ideological reconciliation but only relentless peaceful competition bound to demonstrate the superiority of socialism and the victory of communism. Reflecting on the future of Soviet society, L. Brezhnev reassured the Party members in 1972:

> The CPSU [Communist Party of the Soviet Union] has always held, and now holds, that the class struggle between the two systems – the capitalist and the socialist – in the economic and political and also, of course, ideological domains, will continue. This is as it should be, because the world outlook and the class aims of socialism and capitalism are opposite and irreconcilable.[36]

C. PROSPECTIVE DEVELOPMENTS

There is little doubt that multinational corporations will continue expanding, in the near future at least, and their foreign operations are certain to grow even faster. This expectation is based on the fact that the corporations are predominantly involved in the technologically most dynamic industries, their capacity to reach the optimum scale of production and related operations (the size of which is likely to be rising in the future) and on the fact that continued progress in transport and communication will facilitate the expansion of their international operations. Whilst the size of these companies will continue to grow, their number is likely to decline.

Various estimates have been produced in the West as well as in the East on the future role of the multinational corporations. According to the well-known American futurologist, H. Kahn, during 1970-80 their total sales in real terms will be rising twice as fast as world output as a whole – 10 per cent, compared with 5 per cent, annually; they will rise from $500,000m. in 1970 to $1,200,000m. in 1980, or from 14.5 to 21.4 per cent of the Gross World Product.[37]

[36] Quoted from *International Affairs*, Moscow, 7/1974, p. 109.

[37] The White House Conference on the Industrial World Ahead, *A Look at Business in 1990*, Washington, GPO, 1972, pp. 14, 19.

The calculations carried out by a Soviet economist, J. V. Shishkov, suggest that the corporations' share in the Gross National Product of the capitalist world will be 32 per cent in 1980 and 82 per cent by the year 2000.[38] The figures produced by S. Hymer, an American economist, indicate that the multinationals' share in the total output of the non-Socialist world will rise (from 20 per cent in 1970) to nearly 50 per cent by the end of the century and to 80 per cent in the year 2040.[39] A French economist, R. Lattès, asserts that by the mid-1980s 60 giant corporations will dominate the capitalist world, of which no less than 50 will be American.[40] J. N. Behrman, a well-known American international lawyer, estimated that if recent trends continue in the future, by 1980 nearly 70 per cent of the capitalist world's GNP may be owned, controlled or financed by US-based multinationals alone.[41]

The author is convinced that the corporations' dealings with the Socialist countries will continue to grow in the sphere of trade, licensing, joint ventures and finance, but industrial co-operation provides the most promising field, with favourable spillovers to other dealings. The scope and size of production and marketing co-operation in manufacturing will be greatly expanded and individual agreements will cover longer periods than in the past. The joint construction of projects in the partner as well as third countries will become fairly common, and the casual *ad hoc* ties typical in the past will be increasingly replaced by more systematic and lasting associations. This co-operation is likely to be extended to projects necessitating complex and costly technologies, such as giant nuclear power stations (especially if involving fast-breeder reactors, and later thermonuclear fusion) super-airliners (à la Anglo–French *Concorde*), communication satellites and the like.

There will be more large-scale, long-term projects on the development of energy and mineral resources, in addition to the schemes

[38] Quoted from *Handel zagraniczny* (Foreign Trade), Warsaw, 2/1973, p. 50.

[39] Quoted from *Gospodarka planowa* (Planned Economy), Warsaw, 5/1973, p. 347.

[40] R. Lattès, *Mille milliards de dollars* (A Thousand Milliard Dollars), Paris, Editions et Publications Premières, 1970, p. 9.

[41] J. N. Behrman, 'New Orientation in International Trade and Investment', in P. Uri (ed.), *Trade and Investment Policies for the Seventies*, New York, Praeger, 1971, p. 13.

involving atomic power, coal, gas and timber in the USSR embarked upon by such multinationals as ENI (It), Kraftwerk Union (FRG), Krupp (FRG), Mitsui (Ja), Occidental Petroleum (US), Ruhrgas (FRG), Salzgitter (FRG) and VÖEST-Alpine (Au) for periods extending up to 1980-2005 (see Ch. 5C, pp. 90-6). Schemes of this type may also be ventured into in China, in particular the co-operative exploitation of the extensive gas and oil resources along her eastern and south-eastern coast. It is not impossible that such developments might lead to schemes dwarfing the Siberian projects, which might very well provide a solid basis for normalized and closer Sino–American relations. In fact, keen competition may develop between China and the USSR, courting multinational corporations. Whether the corporations become super-normal beneficiaries, will largely depend on the policies of the American and Japanese governments and multinationals.

Contrary to Lenin's arguments, multinational corporations may prove a vital factor in promoting peace. What partners – primarily interested in profit maximization on the one hand, and planned rapid development on the other – would want to go to war after having entered into 15-25 years' co-operation agreements, involving the commitment of investments running into thousands of millions of dollars? The expansion of business opportunities for the corporations is certain to continue. The rate of economic growth in the remaining part of this century is likely to be higher in the East than in the West – 6-7 against 4-6 annually, and industrial production will grow even faster owing to the continued emphasis on industrialization. The Socialist need of Western equipment and plants, technology and managerial skills can be assumed to be growing at least as fast as in recent years, and may be faster as the Socialist countries will pay greater attention to the principle of comparative advantage.

A larger Eastward flow of capital is a strong possibility and it will be enhanced further when other Socialist countries, in addition to Hungary, Romania and Yugoslavia, permit joint ventures. Poverty, lagging economic development and uncertainty in the countries of the Third World may make many corporations look more instead to the East – with its rapid and orderly industrial development, respectable fuel and mineral resources, rising standards of living and sound commercial and financial reputation.

In contrast to their past experience, the corporations may find a substantial and steadily expanding market in the East (especially the European Socialist countries) for industrial consumer goods. In fact the Western multinationals are likely to become an important factor in promoting 'consumerism' in these countries, not only by direct exports of such goods but also by playing a vital part in the development of the industries producing modern manufactured consumer goods – by supplying the required equipment, plants and licences and participating in industrial co-operation and joint ventures.

The Socialist-owned multinational enterprises, which are still in their infancy, will increase in number and size. This trend will be at first most pronounced within Comecon, but the capitalist world will also experience the growth of wholly or partly Socialist-owned subsidiaries. The object of their expansion in capitalist countries will be mainly marketing, but production may also receive considerable attention. In their operations, especially in less-developed countries, they may become targets for nationalistic reaction and may be accused of unfair competition and neo-colonialism. A possibility of the Comecon multinationally-owned enterprises entering into joint ventures with Western multinational corporations cannot be excluded. When such partnerships are established, East–West relations will advance to new, higher levels of transideological collaboration.

There will be an intensified drive, marked by occasional price undercutting, by the Socialist countries to expand the export of their manufactures to the capitalist world. Some Western multinational corporations are likely to be hit by competition from the very Socialist enterprises which they had supplied with equipment, licences and marketing expertise. But it may be assumed on the basis of experience in the recent past that once the Socialist enterprises establish their foothold in the market, they will want to co-operate and avoid market disruption. Economic common sense will dictate specialization in accordance with the principle of comparative advantage, and the sooner it prevails the better for the parties concerned.

To counter the growing bargaining power of the multinational corporations – by virtue of their increasing size and worldwide options – there will be greater efforts on the part of international trade unions in capitalist countries (such as the International Federation of Chemical and General Workers' Unions, the International Metalworkers' Federation, and the International Union of Food and Allied Workers' Association) to provide countervailing power. But although Communist regimes will naturally lend moral support, their initiative in, and influence on, such developments are likely to be limited. Most trade unions are opposed to Communist domination, and moreover the maintenance of close and delicate collaboration links with multinational corporations will tend to restrain the Communist regimes from direct involvement.

It is generally expected that some international code of conduct will be evolved in the future to control the practices of the capitalist as well as Socialist multinationals. The development of such a code will not be an easy task if it is to be reasonable to all the parties concerned. It should be based on inter-governmental agreements, preferably under the auspices of the United Nations and with the participation of the multinationals, to regulate central-local management, accounting procedures, transfer-pricing, taxation, the transmission of profits and the like. In this task, the Socialist approach and East–West experience may prove of great value.

A Complete List and Index of Multinational Corporations and their Affiliates Appearing in this Book

(a) For country abbreviations (given in brackets) see footnote 3, Ch. 1, p. 2.

(b) The number of foreign capitalist countries is followed (in brackets) by the number of foreign affiliates – branches (or divisions), subsidiaries, associates and sub-affiliates.

(c) *A* = Associate company (in which the parent company owns 15-50 per cent of the shares (as a rule).

S = Subsidiary company (in which the parent company holds 51-100 per cent of the shares; as such it may be a branch (or division).

AS = indicates that the firm is an Associate Company through a Subsidiary company of the independent parent company.

SSS = indicates that the firm is a Sub-Sub-Subsidiary of the independent parent company.

SA = indicates a firm being a Subsidiary company of an Associate company of the independent parent company.

(d) Where a firm's name is not followed by another, it indicates an independent parent company.

(e) Where no page references are given, it means that the firm has directly or indirectly been involved in dealings with Socialist countries but not specifically mentioned in this book.

Sources. Based on: *Who Owns Whom: Australasia and the Far East 1973; Who Owns Whom 1973/1974: Continental Edition; Who Owns Whom: North America 1973*; *Who Owns Whom 1974: U.K. Edition* – all published in London by Roskill. Daily and periodical literature published in Socialist and Western countries.

General Index

For Product Safety Concerns and Information please contact our EU representative GPSR@taylorandfrancis.com Taylor & Francis Verlag GmbH, Kaufingerstraße 24, 80331 München, Germany

Batch number: 10725981

Printed by Printforce, the Netherlands